GROWING UP ETHNIC

GROWING UP ETHNIC

Nationalism and the Bildungsroman in
African American and Jewish American Fiction

BY MARTIN JAPTOK

UNIVERSITY OF IOWA PRESS, IOWA CITY

University of Iowa Press, Iowa City 52242
Copyright © 2005 by the University of Iowa Press
All rights reserved
Printed in the United States of America
http://www.uiowa.edu/uiowapress

The University of Iowa Press is a member of Green
Press Initiative and is committed to preserving
natural resources.

Printed on acid-free paper

Library of Congress Cataloging-in-Publication Data
Japtok, Martin.
   Growing up ethnic: nationalism and the Bildungsroman in African American
and Jewish American ficton / by Martin Japtok.
      p.   cm.
   Includes bibliographical references and index.
   ISBN 0-87745-923-1 (cloth)
   1. American fiction—African American authors—History and criticism.
2. American fiction—Jewish authors—History and criticism.   3. Bildungsromans—
History and criticism.   4. Judaism and literature—United States.   5. Maturation
(Psychology) in literature.   6. African Americans in literature.   7. Ethnic groups
in literature.   8. Ethnicity in literature.   9. Youth in literature.   10. Jews in
literature.   I. Title.
PS374.N4J37 2005   2004058848

05 06 07 08 09 C 5 4 3 2 1

To my parents,

Horst and Margret Japtok,

and to my soulmate and partner in life,

Nagadya Mutawe

CONTENTS

ACKNOWLEDGMENTS

This book developed over time and has undergone extensive revisions and rewritings. Naturally, I owe a debt of gratitude to those who guided me through this process, especially Michael Kramer at the University of California, Davis, who gave me many helpful suggestions; Linda Morris, who read and commented on the manuscript in both its old and new versions; and Patricia Turner. Also many thanks to Clarence Major, Winfried Schleiner, and Peter Dale at Davis; to Rafia Zafar at Washington University, who also made many useful suggestions, and to Carol Taylor Johnson and Jim Natsis at West Virginia State College who, at various times, encouraged me to keep working on this book. Thank you to the readers of previously published material for helping me to refine my arguments. Thank you to Prasenjit Gupta, Charlotte Wright, and the staff of the University of Iowa Press for their support and to my copyeditor, Jennifer Usher of Mesa Verde Media Services, for many useful suggestions and improvements. Thanks also to librarians everywhere for enabling people like me to find books and materials, and to my students who are, after all, the main reason why I try to become an astute reader of literature, culture, and history.

Parts of chapter 1 and 3 have been published previously in somewhat different form, and I thank the publishers for allowing me to use my essays in this book. Chapter 1 includes altered and updated versions of "Between 'Race' as Construct and 'Race' as Essence: *The Autobiography of an Ex-Coloured Man*," which originally appeared in the *Southern Literary Journal* 28.2 (1996): 32–47, and "Socialism and Ethnic Solidarity: Samuel Ornitz's *Haunch, Paunch and Jowl*," which originally appeared in *MELUS* 24.3 (1999): 21–38. Chapter 3 contains modified and updated versions of "Paule Marshall's *Brown Girl, Brownstones*—Reconciling Individualism and Ethnicity," which was originally published in *African American Review* 38.2 (1998): 305–315 and is used here with the permission of *African American Review*, and of "Justifying Individualism: Anzia Yezierska's *Bread Givers*" in *The*

Immigrant Experience in North American Literature: Carving Out a Niche (Katherine B. Payant and Toby Rose, eds. Westport, CT: Greenwood Press, ©1999, 17–30; reproduced with permission of Greenwood Publishing Group, Inc., Westport, CT).

GROWING UP ETHNIC

INTRODUCTION

AFRICAN AMERICANS AND JEWISH AMERICANS

Starting in the early twentieth century with Jewish participation in Civil Rights organizations, but with much increased intensity from the 1960s on, a wealth of books, articles, and editorials has been published as part of an ongoing discussion about the nature of African American and Jewish American relations. By 1984, the volume of this debate as conducted in writing was such that Lenwood G. Davis could publish a book-length bibliography, *Black-Jewish Relations in the United States, 1752–1984*. The debate simply takes as its starting point that there *is* a relation between African Americans and Jewish Americans, and one might say that even if there had not been one, by now it would have been created by the very discussion itself.[1]

Much of that post-1960s debate acknowledges some historical similarities between the experience of Jews in the Old World and that of African Americans in the New, but then focuses on areas of friction between both groups in the U.S., especially in the wake of the Civil Rights Movement. The point of departure for this study, however, is the presence of *literary* similarities between African American and Jewish American coming-of-age stories in the early twentieth century which exceed what could be solely explained by direct sociohistorical correspondences and are instead the result of the way both African American and Jewish American authors have conceptualized the "ethnic situation" in which they have found themselves. (I will discuss my use of the term "ethnic" in the second part of the introduction.) "Similar" differs from "identical," of course, and more notably, the issue of "race" and its social repercussions defies any easy comparison. That the ethnic situations are far from identical in the case of these two groups, however, only highlights that there are striking thematic correspondences between a number of African American and Jewish American coming-of-age stories, particularly in the way they conceive of ethnicity.

I argue that the similarities between the three pairs of novels examined here—James Weldon Johnson's *The Autobiography of an Ex-Coloured Man* and Samuel Ornitz's *Haunch, Paunch and Jowl*, Jessie Fauset's *Plum Bun* and Edna Ferber's *Fanny Herself*, and Paule Marshall's *Brown Girl, Brownstones* and Anzia Yezierska's *Bread Givers*—can be explained mainly with reference to two factors which are ultimately intertwined: cultural nationalism and the Bildungsroman genre. To understand African American and Jewish American coming-of-age stories of the first half of the twentieth century, it is not enough to look either at ethnic nationalism or at literary form, but one needs to consider the intersections of both.

In exploring the relationship between African Americans and Jewish Americans, historians have often looked at African American/Jewish American relations in the early part of the twentieth century. Hasia Diner, for example, has studied interrelationships between Jews and African Americans in her 1977 book (republished in 1995) *In the Almost Promised Land: American Jews and Blacks, 1915–1935*, in which she focuses on the way Jewish Americans "used black people to construct their own identity in the United States" (xiii).

In contrast to Diner, I am not concerned with how each group perceived the other, but with how each perceived itself. Literary critics have mostly focused on texts produced after World War II, on the literary and intellectual debate between authors, and on how the two groups imagined each other. Adam Zachary Newton, for instance, in *Facing Black and Jew* (1999), juxtaposes mostly post–World War II African American and Jewish American texts so that they may illuminate each other as he explores the "allegorical story about culture and nation" they tell (16).

While I also am interested in culture and nation as reflected in texts, my method is more thematically oriented, more interested in direct similarities, and closer to the "invention of ethnicity" paradigm than is Newton's book. Emily Miller Budick's *Blacks and Jews in Literary Conversation* (1998) takes as its theme "how writers construct their separate, ethnic identities, textually, *in relation to each*" (1–2), and the texts she examines are all post–World War II as well, since as she says, "Jewish-black *Dialogue* as such does not commence in earnest until the 1960s" (10).

Though Jeffrey Melnick agrees, in his excellent 1999 study *A Right to Sing the Blues: African Americans, Jews, and American Popular Song*

(1999), "that some kind of special relationship" (12) does exist, he argues that it is more complicated than has been assumed and that "'Black-Jewish relations' needs to be approached—not exclusively but still significantly—as a story told *by* Jews *about* interracial relationships" (4). His book examines what uses Jewish musicians made of "Blackness" and black music to define their own role in the U.S., focusing, like the previously discussed studies, on "how Jews, African Americans, and others have discussed the relationship of the two groups" (12). His 2000 book *Black-Jewish Relations on Trial*, in examining the dynamics surrounding and following the 1915 lynching of Leo Frank in Atlanta, reiterates the point, if in a different context, "that 'Black-Jewish relations' is best understood as a Jewish story—a narrative of intergroup activity that speaks mainly to the desires of specific Jews" (11). Thus far, most studies have focused on how one group (usually Jewish Americans) has viewed the other (African Americans). *Growing Up Ethnic* will explore how each group views itself.

I want to return to the earlier "pre-debate" or "pre-conflict" period and examine not the interaction between African Americans and Jewish Americans but how authors of both groups conceive of their *own* ethnicities, how they construct them, and how they do so in strikingly similar ways; I intend to provide some answers as to why they do so. These similarities represent a kind of implicit dialogue in and of themselves.[2]

When one finds similarities in the ways stories proceed despite differing origins of their authors and protagonists, warning that those similarities might be conceived of in an ahistorical fashion and that they might serve different functions in their respective contexts is good cautionary advice. But overcaution that leads to a denial of similarities is just as much of an overreaction as if one overlooked glaring differences in the structures of the stories only to be able to pronounce sameness in a group of experiences or their literary mediations where dissimilarity abounds. The danger of ahistoricism lessens, however, in a comparison in which a rich source material studying relations between the two groups in question exists and continues to be published. In any case, I do not argue that literary similarities somehow grow out of supposed historical parallels (though those do play a role), however worthwhile it may be to explore them. Rather, they are the product of similar uses of ideology (ethnic nationalism) and literary form (Bildungsroman). These similar uses, though, also point to "Black-Jewish relations" of some sort—something, after all, prompts authors to make similar use of ideology and literary form. Though sociohistorical relations are not the focus of my study, they comprise an important background.

That there is a relationship is not self-evident. In fact, to "the casual observer [in the early decades of the twentieth century], there was little similarity between the status of Jews and blacks in America" (Diner 3). As Clayborne Carson explains,

> The anti-Jewish sentiments held by many Americans are quite different from antiblack ones. The former included stereotypes of group achievement and influence, the latter featured stereotypes of group inadequacy and impotence. The impact of anti-Jewish sentiment on American Jews has never been comparable to the institutionalized discrimination encountered by black Americans. (137)

African Americans had been marginalized primarily because of the color of their skin, even though color served merely as a "rationale for enslavement" (Jordan 52) or for later forms of economic oppression.

This study, being mainly literary in focus, cannot do justice to the complexity of the history of racism preceding the production of the novels considered here, but I presume that readers are familiar with its outlines. Racism is the driving force behind the meanings assigned to "blackness" in the context of colonialism. Unlike other ethnic groups, whose English name made no reference to color and whose arrival in North America was not involuntary, Africans and African Americans were referred to as "Negroes" (from Spanish 'negro') by the English colonists (Jordan 52).

Bell Hooks reminds us that not all Jews are white and that, in referring to Jews, one should not assume whiteness (Hooks 229–330). The Jews appearing as characters in the novels studied here, however, all come from European immigrant backgrounds, and I refer to them in this study as Jewish Americans. In contrast to the predominantly race-based and color-based oppression of African Americans, Jewish Americans have experienced discrimination primarily because of cultural differences, though those have often been conceptualized in terms of race, especially during the early twentieth century.

The history of anti-Semitism, even longer than that of institutionalized racism, exceeds the range of this study. Suffice it to say that justifications of anti-Semitism have often been cultural or religious in nature, at least in Europe, where Jews were regarded as the internal cultural Other and as supposed "'betrayers' of Christ" (Meltzer 57). Discrimination was often economically motivated as well, such as by "resentment over the disproportionate presence of Jews in certain commercial occupations" (West 72), occupations into which they had often been forced by Gentiles through exclusionary and segregationist laws.

For the U.S., Hasia Diner remarks that it "was not accidental that the years which saw the beginnings of real American anti-Semitism coincided with the slow but substantial movement of American Jews into the middle class and into positions of prominence" (15). Those years also coincided with substantial immigration of Eastern European Jews, so that economic competition and cultural difference affected Jewish immigrants as they did earlier immigrant groups, such as the Irish, who also faced significant hostility. The nature of anti-Semitism, however, remains a hotly debated topic, as can be seen in recent discussions about the "uses" of the holocaust and about the origins of Nazi and German anti-Semitism.[3]

There are more differences between the ethnic situations of African Americans and Jewish Americans, especially with regard to their position in U.S. society. As Julius Lester has said, ". . . in the broad context of Western history, Jewish and black histories have many similarities. However, in the specific context of American history, profound differences stand next to the historical similarities" (167). Addressing particularly the years 1890–1919, William M. Phillips Jr. identifies some of them:

> The stark and irreducible reality about the unlikeness of these two minority communities (without addressing here the nature of their relative size, settlement location, cultural and historical backgrounds, structural organization, racial identity or perception, and human capital characteristics) is their perceived, situational, status non-equivalence within American society. In other words, in terms of the hierarchical organization of racial and ethnic groups within the American social structure, the Jewish American minority community occupied, or was accorded, a superior status location, while the African American minority community occupied, or was accorded, an inferior status location. (28)

As a result of all of the differences mentioned above, African Americans and Jewish Americans found themselves in divergent social situations. Members of one group had a number of options open to them in responding to their position in American society, while members of the other found themselves more limited by external factors. Jewish Americans had, for example, the option of total assimilation for the high price of a renunciation of their religion and culture—Edna Ferber's *Fanny Herself* examines that option. For African Americans, the option of "blending in" typically did not exist, excepting the case of "passing," a choice scrutinized by both James Weldon Johnson's *The Autobiography of an Ex-Coloured Man* and Jessie Fauset's *Plum Bun*. The fact that passing is such a dominant theme in African American fiction of the late nineteenth and early twentieth century is not a coincidence. The depiction of an option only available to the few in many ways highlighted the situation of the many: living under an exclusionist and segregationist racism brought about the desire to pass.

Notwithstanding differences, African Americans and Jewish Americans "are conscious that the past plays a crucial role in shaping self-identity" (Diner x). Oppression, marginalization, and Diaspora play a significant role in the past of both groups. Both African Americans and Jewish Americans also share some of the ways in which the dominant group has thought about them. As Robert Philipson has said, "Blacks and Jews were forced to define themselves in opposition to and in conjunction with European ideas about who they were" (xiv). Kwame Anthony Appiah notes that "what blacks in the West, like secularized Jews, have mostly in common is the fact that they are perceived—both by themselves and by others—as belonging together in the same race, and this common race is used by others as the basis for discriminating against them" (17). This holds particularly true for the first decades of this century, the period under discussion in this study and a time of migration for African Americans and Jewish Americans.

The novels discussed in this study all depict the coming of age of their protagonists in the early decades of the twentieth century. I selected the pairs of novels due to their striking similarities to each other; more pairings would be possible, but the three presented here show a range of possibilities for negotiating the tensions between ethnic nationalism and the Bildungsroman paradigm. The selection of such novels requires some additional explanation, as the high point of the relationship between African Americans and Jewish Americans, according to most observers, occurs during and after mid-century, and most literary debate did not begin until the 1960s. Since this study explores similarities (and their causes) in African American and Jewish American coming-of-age stories, it is less concerned with debates and contentions than it is with conditions that may have served as enabling factors for those literary similarities. At the very period when the alliance is said to have been at its height (during the Civil Rights Movement), the Jewish American socioeconomic and political position was more secure than ever before, making even more pronounced the difference in status between the two groups. As Jules Chametzky has said,

> by the 1950s, the Jewish situation itself had changed in America. By then the Jews had moved well beyond the stage of cultural trauma familiar to all new immigrants, or of the aggressive defensiveness of the *arriviste* making his way in an essentially strange, if not actively hostile, society. By the 1950s a secure Americanism seems to have been won—a position, at least, of nonmarginality. (47)

In the early twentieth century, however, Jewish Americans were still closer to their immigrant roots and the direct, lived experiences of anti-Semitism and persecution in Eastern Europe. In addition, their social position was more fragile due to anti-Semitism in the United States as exemplified by the circulation of the writings of Houston Steward Chamberlain, the KKK, Henry Ford's publications, and—later on—Nazi ideology (Meltzer 239ff). Developments in Europe were also felt in the U.S.: "[I]n the last decades of the nineteenth century and the first half of the twentieth, the traditional legends which had swirled about the Jews in the past were revived as foils for racial mysticism and as instruments of political mobilization" (Mosse 59). Before and in the early twentieth century, Jews both saw themselves and were seen by others as a distinct "race," notwithstanding ethnic, "racial," geographical, and cultural differences. This notion of a "Jewish race" is reflected in Jewish American works of the time. As Gert Buelens says of Ludwig Lewisohn's works, his "fictional texts *The Island Within* (1928) and *Stephen Escott* (1930) testify to a conviction that Jewishness constitutes a pre-cultural essence, an inborn racial identity" (318). To a significant extent, the Jewish American works discussed here subscribe in part to similar convictions.

Immigration and migration patterns provide another reason why this study focuses on the early twentieth century. The period between 1880 and 1924 marks a peak of Jewish immigration—between 2.3 and 4 million people came during that time (Phillips 22; Meltzer 11). Since I am interested in stories about growing up in the U.S., as such stories best reflect formations of ethnic identity, the decades after the turn of the century seem suitable, because a generation of children has now been born and reared in the U.S. and can tell about it. Fictional accounts also focus on that period, presumably because 1924, with its new immigration laws, meant "the virtual cessation of Jewish immigration" (Hirshler 85).[4]

Through generational change, Jewish city culture, lacking "cultural renewal" which would come mostly from Eastern Europe, speeded up its process of "Americanization," and it is often that very process that both autobiographies and Bildungsromane describe. Jewish American works produced in the second half of the twentieth century do not offer themselves as readily to an exploration of the question of ethnicity because the "Americanization" process had advanced by then, so much so that Allen Guttmann, in 1965, wrote about the secularization and Americanization of Jews in "The Conversion of the Jews" and that by 1983, Bonnie Hoover Braendlin declared, quoting Sarah Blacher Cohen, that contemporary Bildungsromane written by Jewish American women "are largely 'devoid of ethnic accent'" (76).

In addition, the holocaust overshadows literature after the 1940s and is a subject of such horror it does not easily allow comparison, in literature or otherwise, to other experiences—though attempts have plausibly been made to compare the holocaust to the Middle Passage and slavery in the Americas.[5] But since that comparison would have to bridge hundreds of years, three continents, and vastly differing sociohistorical circumstances, it presents a host of methodological and ideological problems that cannot be dealt with in this study, which confines itself to the U.S. American (literary) context.

For African American coming-of-age stories, the first half of the twentieth century sees the emergence of works telling of growing up outside the context of institutionalized slavery. As Joanne M. Braxton says in her study of African American women's autobiography:

> Hurston and Thompson represent the first generation of black and female autobiographers who did not continually come into contact with former slaves; their works turn away from the restrictions and limitations of the slave narrative and extend the quest for a dignified and self-defining identity to include a search for personal fulfillment. (12)

Though neither Hurston nor Thompson is studied here, the argument holds: literary works dealing with coming of age under slavery, usually studied as "slave narratives," often served specific rhetorical and ideological purposes in the context of abolition. However, twentieth century African American autobiographies and Bildungsromane treat some of the same problematics (finding work, hostile reactions, poverty, etc.) as works of immigrant writers, especially if the setting is a big city. In many African American and Jewish American works, it is New York, because of its large concentrated Jewish and African American populations. The early twentieth century thus marks the first time African Americans and Jewish Americans encounter each other on a large scale in northern cities due to migration and immigration: "As black Americans moved to northern cities, especially from the 1920s through the 1960s, they found themselves having more direct contact with Jews" (Hacker 155).

Between 1890 and 1910, 200,000 African Americans left southern farms and moved to southern and northern cities (Giddings 79–80). Between 1910 and 1920, another 330,000 to 500,000 or more came to northern and western urban centers (John Hope Franklin 350; Giddings 141). The Great Migration of southern African Americans to northern and western cities took place in part because African Americans shared the economic hopes of the immigrant population—and struggled for some of the same jobs. In addition, both African Americans and Eastern European Jews were refugees from dire oppression and persecution.

After World War II, the social situation of African Americans began to change slowly, but socioeconomic advances for African Americans bore little resemblance to those of Jewish Americans. While the Civil Rights Movement of the 1950s led to important legal changes, the 1960s showed that progress was exceedingly gradual. Frustrations with mainstream recalcitrance led to an increasing radicalization of the movement, and urban riots testified to the fact that the frustration was also widespread in the African American urban population. The Black Power Movement and the Black Arts Movement signal that integration into the U.S. in ways sought previously was no longer a goal for increasing numbers of African Americans, especially among the intelligentsia. After World War II, then, the social, political, and economic situations of African Americans and Jewish Americans diverged so significantly that a literary comparison became increasingly unlikely against this historical background. Thus, Emily Miller Budick and Adam Zachary

Newton focus less on similarities or parallels between African American and Jewish American texts than on the terms of their debate and on arguments expressed in literary dialogue.

All of this is not to say that literature is a mere reflection of material reality. But since the imagination draws its materials both from what has been experienced—in an individual and in a collective sense—and from what is perceived as possible, sociohistorical circumstances are a significant factor in assessing literary parallels. Of primary interest for this study, however, is the way in which the imagination intervenes in sociohistorical realities and creates an understanding or a "reading" of them; in other words, I am concerned primarily with imaginative constructs, with how African American and Jewish American texts construct ethnicity. And in that context, it is important to note that the period also marks a flowering of both African American and Jewish American nationalism in various forms.

Paul Gilroy has identified several ideological concepts linking African Americans and Jews. He mentions the idea of a homeland, from which the group has at some point in time been separated and to which it might return; the involuntary separation from that homeland, or exile; and the "idea that the suffering of both blacks and Jews has a special redemptive power, not for themselves alone but for humanity as a whole" (208). We will see this idea formulated most distinctly in *Fanny Herself* and *Plum Bun*, pointing to the spiritual and communalist nature of nationalism. As Anthony Birch claims, "the dyed-in-the-wool nationalist is a romantic, not a rationalist. He is a communitarian, not an individualist. He thinks in terms of the spirit and culture of his people" (67).

Paraphrasing historian Martin J. Sklar, George Hutchinson has outlined some of the factors that contribute to the early twentieth century American preoccupation with questions of national identity. The decades around the turn of the century "witnessed the transformation of the American economy from the dominance of proprietary capitalism to the dominance of corporate capitalism" (Sklar quoted in Hutchinson *Harlem* 8). This was accompanied by a gradual change in the labor force composition. An increasing number of people did not work in "immediate production and reproduction of the material means of life" (Sklar quoted in Hutchinson *Harlem* 8) any more, and as a correlation, the number of college students increased fivefold from 1900 to 1930. These developments were accompanied by dramatically increased literary production and diversification of the literary market and its audience. In addition, the arrival of large corporations led to the creation of the Federal Reserve system and the implementation of a modern economic infrastructure. "In short, during the two or three decades leading up to the 1920s, the basic social relations and institutions of the United States were nationalized as never before," as George Hutchinson summarizes (*Harlem* 9).

Fueled by massive immigration and internal migration, and by nationalist fervor in European nations, debates about American national culture were the order of the day: "If all the vectors of social power were being organized increasingly along national lines, the cultural responses were bound to focus upon struggles for the 'national soul'" (Hutchinson *Harlem* 11). Since such debates were also punctuated by outbreaks of racism (the "race riots" after World War I), xenophobia (the anti-immigration of 1924), anti-Semitism (the lynching of Leo Frank in Atlanta in 1915), and nativism, it is little wonder that both African Americans and Jewish Americans asked themselves what their place was to be in the U.S., and that part of the response was the development of ethnic cultural nationalism.[6]

One literary consequence of this ethnic cultural nationalism is that a sense of chosen peoplehood is at work in the novels discussed in this study. The implicit call to reject mainstream materialism and embrace ethnic idealism of some sort—at the center of the work in *Fanny Herself*, *Plum Bun*, *The Autobiography of an Ex-Coloured Man*, and *Haunch, Paunch and Jowl*, and also present in *Bread Givers* and *Brown Girl, Brownstones*—and the call to adhere to what is seen as one's ethnic roots cannot be easily separated in the literary works of both groups in the early decades of the twentieth century.

One can thus see African American and Jewish American nationalism as one of the driving forces behind the literary similarities the novels exhibit. But ethnic nationalism is channeled and refracted through the Bildungsroman genre, and it is this combination that marks the novels discussed here. In order to establish this linkage more firmly, this study reads African American and Jewish American works side by side with close attention to their conceptualizations of ethnicity.

ETHNICITY OR RACE?

I have already used the word "ethnicity" in referring to both African Americans and Jewish Americans, but the choice of the term requires some explanation, especially because ethnicity theory is said to be based on an *"immigrant analogy"* (Omi and Winant 17) and one criticism of it has been that it can therefore not account for such a phenomenon as institutionalized racism: as Omi and Winant claim in *Racial Formation in the United States*, "Structural barriers continued to render the immigrant analogy inappropriate" (20). Typically, of course, race and ethnicity are not terms that are used interchangeably; though, as Steve Fenton has pointed out, the usage of these terms is often overlapping, and it is not necessary to establish a definite boundary between the two (3). Ethnicity, usually culturally defined, differs from race in that the latter tends to be defined by physical traits, color foremost among them. However, racial *categorization* and racial *identity* differ from one another in that "the term 'racial identity' actually refers to a sense of group or collective identity based on one's *perception* that he or she shares a common racial heritage with a particular racial group" (Helms 3), whereas racial categorization tends to be imposed from the outside. It is self-perception that this study focuses on, not racial categorization, though the latter impacts the former.

What do "Blackness" and "Jewishness" mean in the novels discussed here? What are the ideological implications of that meaning? What do authors have their characters do or not do depending on how they perceive their Blackness or Jewishness? Whether Blackness or Jewishness is defined as construct or as essence, as culture or as biology, as volition or as destiny are some of the questions that this study attempts to answer.[7]

Omi and Winant explain that "the ethnicity-based paradigm was an insurgent theory which suggested that race was a *social* category. Race was but one of a number of determinants of ethnic group identity or ethnicity. Ethnicity itself was understood as the result of a group formation process based on culture and descent" (Omi and Winant 15). Ethnicity theory does not overlook race as a factor in identity, nor does it claim that culture alone serves to form a group identity. Instead, race is seen as equivalent to other factors, such as language or cultural customs, a feature of ethnicity theory that has often rightly been seen as problematic. The overall intent of the ethnicity paradigm, however, is to study the

> *dynamics of incorporation* of minority groups into the dominant society. Ethnicity theory is therefore primarily concerned with questions of group identity; with the resolutions of tensions between the twin

pressures of assimilation (dissolution of group identity) and cultural pluralism (preservation of group identity); and with the prospects for political integration via normal political channels. (Omi and Winant 52)

Herein lies one of the attractions of ethnicity theory for this study: since the literary works under scrutiny in my study all have the tension between assimilative pressures and cultural nationalism at their core, and since ethnicity theory purports to study just such dynamics, ethnicity would appear to be the proper term to use in reference to African Americans and Jewish Americans in the framework of this study. As this study examines two African American passing novels (James Weldon Johnson's *The Autobiography of an Ex-Coloured Man* and Jessie Fauset's *Plum Bun*—and I would make a case for Edna Ferber's *Fanny Herself* as a kind of passing novel), the use of the term ethnicity is also justified by the fact that the passing paradigm frequently contests the notion of race. Passing novels show how some authors tentatively envisioned (though not usually condoned) the disappearance of race while embracing its cultural manifestations.[8]

Despite a mainstream public rhetoric of cultural pluralism, it is still "a widespread practice to define ethnicity as otherness," as an "opposition of ethnic and American" (Sollors *Beyond Ethnicity* 25). When an Anglo American mentions "ethnic food," it will almost always mean some type of Asian, African, or Latin American cuisine, maybe Southern or Eastern European cooking, but certainly not what is served in a steakhouse, a McDonald's, or even at a French or German restaurant.

Because "ethnicity" retains strong overtones of race as a social construct—"a way of conceptualizing and organizing social worlds composed of persons whose differences allow for arranging them into groups that come to be called 'races'" (Outlaw 61)—I differ here from Werner Sollors's use of the term "according to which ethnicity includes dominant groups" (*Beyond Ethnicity* 36). With the exclusion of "dominant groups," groups that have lost any appreciable sense of ethnic difference and become "American," "ethnic" can be defined as "minority"; nonetheless, ethnicity, as Werner Sollors says, is "superior to and more inclusive than any other existing term" since "'[m]inority' needlessly calls our attention to numbers" (*Beyond Ethnicity* 39).[9]

Ethnic groups often experience prejudicial or, at the very least, differential treatment, and, according to F. James Davis, "[d]ifferential treatment requires some kind of visibility" (4), meaning there have to be certain characteristics that set the ethnic group apart from "nonethnics." Differences "may be based either on physical or cultural traits. Culture becomes apparent in such traits as language, gestures, food customs, rituals, and religious symbols" (F. James Davis 4). Ethnicity thus becomes a relational term, a term that presupposes the existence of at least two groups, one of which is typically considered socioeconomically dominant and which therefore defines all other groups as "others." While my concern here is with novels and with the influence of word constructs, such as novels on the shaping of ethnicity, and while my study thus hopes to contribute to the discussion of the "invention of ethnicity," I do not want to imply that ethnicity is constructed through words alone, however powerful their impact may be.

When talking of the construction of ethnicity in novels by ethnic authors, one is in the land of self-perception (though, via "double-consciousness," the perception of outsiders is still likely to leave traces). For the novels discussed here, which conceptualize ethnicity often both in terms of culture *and* in terms of race as essence, ethnicity appears to me to be the more useful general term because it stresses the idea of culture without excluding other categories, such as color, ancestry, class, or nation. Race as an analytical tool focuses on color and its social, political, and economic consequences, and while it is useful to analyze those, such analysis depends upon the existence of racism. Race is only an important social fact because of racism—outside of it, all racial classification systems become meaningless. So it is in part also for ideological reasons that I prefer the term ethnicity here, because it allows for comparisons, for finding common ground across maliciously erected barriers. One may well say that there is no "outside" of racism, no realm into which it does not reach, and that ethnicity, founded as the concept is on the European immigrant experience, downplays the qualitatively different experiences of people of color. I strongly agree that at present no analysis of historical or present-day dynamics, whether in literature or life, can afford to ignore the fact of racism. However, ethnicity as an analytical category does not preclude taking the social fact of race into account.

However, my main reason for choosing ethnicity over race as the common denominator for a reading of African American and Jewish American novels is that the novels themselves, in their imaginings of what it is that makes for African Americanness and Jewish

Americanness, lean towards answers better understood in terms of ethnicity. They write against prejudice and discrimination at the very least vis-à-vis each author's racial or ethnic group. But in doing so, they also construct their characters' identities by falling back on notions more commonly associated with culture: music, art, and spirituality. Though at times these concepts, while usually situated in the realm of ethnicity, are constructed in essentialist ways, they still point to the realm of culture rather than to the realm of color. That is the case despite the influence cultural nationalism exerts on these novels, a seeming paradox, as the idea of the "nation" often leans towards "racial" conceptualizations of nationhood, as will be discussed in the final chapter.

It is just these kinds of paradoxes and ambiguities that are the subject of this study, and it is therefore befitting that the boundary between the terms "race" and "ethnicity" is often a thin one. Much of what can be said about the "invention of ethnicity" also applies to a group-based self-understanding of racial groups as reflected in the works discussed: race as something to be discovered, cherished, maintained, and expressed through cultural practices and inclinations. However, to come full circle, discussing race in these terms brings one close to ethnicity as a concept based more in culture than in ancestry.

Though sociological parallels between African Americans and Jewish Americans may serve as the basis for a literary comparison, such comparisons across ethnic boundaries have been controversial and the questions one faces in an undertaking of this kind need to be addressed.

TRANSETHNIC LITERARY COMPARISON AND ITS CRITICS

In *Beyond Ethnicity* (1986), Werner Sollors explores similarities among works of ethnic literature across ethnic boundaries. Focusing on rhetorical strategies and symbolic figurations, he discovers that much of ethnic literature makes use of similar rhetorical patterns. One of his primary examples deals with two narratives, one a novella by the immigrant Jewish writer Abraham Cahan (*Yekl: A Tale of the Ghetto*), the other a short story by African American author Charles Chesnutt ("The Wife of His Youth"). Their comparable figurations of old ethnic identity as older wife and of new identity as new wife, between whom the protagonists have to make a choice, led Sollors to introduce the category of "bluish writing," a term indicating the commonalities between African American and Jewish American texts.

Sollors's approach has been criticized for blurring the boundaries between ethnic groups. After all, his critics argue, African Americans and Jewish Americans did not have similar ethnic experiences. Sau-Ling Cynthia Wong, for example, believes that Sollors is "unaware that premature adoption of a transethnic approach, before the uniqueness of each group's historical situation and its manifestations are adequately understood, can be as static and ahistorical as any mechanically applied 'group-by-group approach'" (161).

Similarly, Curtis C. Smith, while acknowledging that Sollors, in "stressing 'bluish' literature and the universality of the ethnic experience . . . is onto an important truth," insists that "the *uniqueness* of Afro-American (and other ethnic) literature is also important" (69).

I am far from denying the historic specificity of individual ethnic experiences and have tried to outline some differences between Jewish American and African American ethnic situations. However, I maintain that the act of comparing not two literatures but a number of specific works does not, in and of itself, deny the uniqueness of the ethnic literatures they are part of. When one observes that one can find Gothic churches (with differences, but nonetheless identifiably Gothic) in, say, both France and Germany, does one thereby deny the particularity of French and German culture? Of course, the question takes on another dimension if one talks about oppression and real suffering. Here I agree with Alan Wald:

> [There is] a profound distinction—never to be forgotten—between the experience of people of color and the European ethnic immigrants [and their descendants] in the *mode and consequences* of their incorporation into the social formation, and their subsequent treatment. People of color were usually *forced* into the economy through an act of dramatic violence . . . [o]r else, people of color underwent other forms of *colonial-like* experiences. (23)

While I fully agree with Alan Wald, I maintain that an insistence on specificities is not at all incompatible with finding similarities, if they are really there. As it is, specificity in group experience and its literary mediation is what most scholars of ethnic literature *are* studying. The field of African American literary studies may serve as an example. Within the past two decades alone, a number of substantial studies have appeared, all focusing on the uniqueness of and the traditions within African American literature.[10] Is a comparison of works from different ethnic groups really "premature," as Wong says? She makes clear what her political objection to a transethnic approach is: "reading by ethnicity is a necessary act of tradition- and identity-building for those whose literatures have been rendered invisible by subsumption" (161). I agree. But since many scholars are already engaged in that undertaking, I choose to select a different focus, one that sees similarities. Postcolonial critics have successfully practiced such an approach for quite a while (with some of the same difficulties), and there is little reason to assume that the same cannot be done in a U.S. context. Indeed, Emily Miller Budick and Adam Zachary Newton explored the "literary conversations" between African American and Jewish American writers in their two book-length studies, presumably also partially motivated by the insight that seeking common ground is politically as important as identifying group-specific territory.[11]

One of Alan Wald's criticisms of a comparative approach to ethnicity focuses on color:

> Most damaging for the ethnicity school has been the charge that, in theorizing cultural difference, it privileges the category of ethnicity, relegating "race" to a mere feature of some ethnic groups. In contrast, the class, gender, race approach follows W. E. B. DuBois' view that the "color line" runs through our culture today in a central manner, and DuBois' later qualification that, among other things, the color line serves to support and rationalize real, material, social domination. (23)

Clearly, Du Bois is right. And "race" serves as the most important argument in explaining why, historically speaking, some immigrants have found it much easier to establish themselves socially and economically than others—and this is particularly true when comparing African Americans and Jewish Americans. Does one therefore have to deny similarities in the literary conceptualization of their ethnic situation by the authors who are in it? These conceptualizations are similar despite historical differences, and they constitute a kind of reality, too.

In light of this, Wald's dismissal of Sollors's "discussion of 'Bluish' writing, in which he purports to demonstrate a common methodology for the treatment of Black and Jewish writing" (28) seems overly harsh. According to Wald, Sollors's "method only focuses on the epiphenomenal conjunctures and parallels, missing the substantial differences in life experience and culture" (28). As I will attempt to show, the "parallels and conjunctures" are not as insignificant as Wald claims. And even if they were slight—given that there are "substantial differences," are not such parallels reason to stop and think, "What is going on here? Why are there any parallels?" instead of insisting only on the differences? My claim is not that experiences of African Americans and Jewish Americans are the same, or that some African American and Jewish American works are the same, but that some ethnic situations have been conceptualized in similar ways by some African American and Jewish American authors, judging by the thematic similarities of their literary responses.[12]

Patricia Hill Collins has noted, when comparing some Africanists' conceptualizations of what is "characteristically 'Black'" to some feminist scholars' claims of what is "characteristically 'female,'" that this "similarity suggests that the material conditions of oppression can vary dramatically and yet generate some uniformity in the epistemologies of subordinate groups" (662). While holding that the term "characteristic" is problematic when referring to groups, this study maintains that Hill Collins's assertion contains some significant truth.[13]

While comparisons of ethnic literatures have become a much more accepted practice in recent years (in part thanks to the growing institutionalization of postcolonial studies and due to such organizations as MELUS), with regard to African American and Jewish American literature comparisons usually focus on the period from the 1950s onward, when the volume of the debate about African American–Jewish American (literary) relations increased both in terms of decibel level and number of works written by writers from both groups with the other group in mind. At the same time, critics such as Anthony Appiah (*In My Father's House*), Paul Gilroy (*The Black Atlantic*), and Eric Sundquist (*To Wake the Nations*) have discussed the early twentieth century conjunction of Pan-Africanism and Zionism, noting the philosophical and historical affinities between these two ideologies, affinities that are important for this study as well. This study, then, can be seen as a combination of these two strands of inquiry into African American and Jewish American relations: it focuses on the *literature* of those two groups, but it does so in the context of the early, pre–Civil-Rights-Era phase of their association. My goal here is to assess the impact of ideological parallels and to look for their causes through delivering side-by-side analyses of literary texts by both ethnic groups.

Chapter 1 compares James Weldon Johnson's *The Autobiography of*

an Ex-Coloured Man and Samuel Ornitz's *Haunch, Paunch and Jowl.*
Both have protagonists who have a rather distanced relationship to
their ethnicity and who use crucial aspects of their respective ethnic
cultures for their personal advancement—music in the *Autobiography's*
case, Judaism in *Haunch's.* In effect, both protagonists enact a kind of
passing in that they exploit their ethnic group's culture without any
commitment to it, while appearing or purporting to work in their group's
best interest. Both novels exhibit their protagonists as negative role
models and imply that a commitment to ethnicity as the novels construct it is a morally higher choice than following a mainstream career.
In outlining both ethnicity and mainstream, the novels often rely on
essentialist constructions of what ethnicity means, even though the
protagonists themselves, in passing, trust in ethnicity's social construction. While both novels thus show tensions between essentialist and
constructionist conceptualizations of ethnicity, they are also equally clear
about the negative meaning of the mainstream and its destructive effect
on ethnicity. As the novels have it, the protagonists' individualism and
selfishness, though depicted as personal flaws, link them to the mainstream, while their more admirable qualities or strivings appear to be
derived from their ethnicity. In their tensions between individualism
and communalism, and connected with this, materialism and idealism,
these novels share much of the ideological configuration of nationalism.

Edna Ferber's *Fanny Herself* and Jessie Fauset's *Plum Bun* are the
subjects of chapter 2. These novels, too, concern themselves with the
notion of passing, their protagonists finding it necessary to resort to
that strategy to attempt to rise in the world. However, unlike the Ex-
Coloured Man and *Haunch's* Meyer Hirsch, both protagonists ultimately return to an affirmation of ethnicity, and both do so for similar
reasons: on the one hand, they experience ethnic life as richer and
mainstream life as shallow, so that their artistic inclinations, which the
novels clearly link to their ethnicity, can only flourish when they live
"ethnic lives"; on the other hand, the love for a member of their ethnic
group in part effects their return. Both novels circumscribe ethnicity
as a vague kind of essence having to do equally with artistic expression
and morality, and with ethnic solidarity as personal love writ large.
Both novels thus share in the individualism vs. communalism and
materialism vs. idealism configuration also present in the *Autobiography*
and *Haunch* and equally foreshadow and necessitate the discussion of
nationalism which is the subject of chapter 4.

Not all ethnic novels agree with the notion of ethnic solidarity or see the communal good as unequivocally more important than the individual good. Chapter 3 discusses two novels problematizing those issues: Paule Marshall's *Brown Girl, Brownstones* and Anzia Yezierska's *Bread Givers*. Both novels' protagonists rebel against a dominating parent figure who serves as a representative of the ethnic community. This rebellion leads them at first on a course away from what the novels present as the cultural norms of their ethnic groups. But the pressure of ethnic nationalism is still perceptible in these novels. Because their protagonists affirm their right to individualism and a life course different from that envisioned by the dominant parent, the novels must justify this course that appears to lead away from ethnic solidarity. In doing so, aspects of the ethnic community are depicted as repressive, while characters in rebellion against the community appear as idealists, thus seemingly inverting the oppositions which are part of the makeup of nationalism. Encounters with the mainstream and a maturation process, however, cause the main characters to reconsider their relationship both to the ethnic group in general and to the dominant parent figure in particular. Racism is acknowledged as a force pushing the ethnic group into a defensive posture, and both protagonists come to a kind of truce with ethnicity, affirming the importance, or inevitability, both of their ethnic heritage and of individualism. In effect, both novels may be regarded as a discussion involving both a cultural nationalist position and a position recognizing the hybrid nature of second-generation American ethnicity.

Informed by those readings, the study returns to the issue of cultural nationalism and develops its ideological parameters more fully. The role of chapter 4 is thus to consider the conceptualizations of ethnicity as they have emerged from the readings of six novels in a larger ideological and historical context and to understand how both the tensions at work in these novels and the ethnic revision of literary genres can be explained with reference to ethnic nationalism. Ethnic nationalism, however, is a revised version of mainstream nationalism, from which it has to differentiate itself if only because the latter has so often been put into the service of the oppression of ethnic groups. Ethnic nationalism thus not only reacts to but also revises mainstream discourse. As Richard Terdiman has said, "No discourse is ever a monologue . . . it always presupposes a horizon of competing, contrary utterances against which it asserts its own energies" (quoted in Ashcroft et al. 169). The parallels in African American and Jewish American novels may therefore be understood as the artistic expressions of similar "conversations" with the mainstream. The novels revise, react to, and shape both the Bildungsroman and ethnic nationalism, and these processes are complicated by the fact that Bildungsroman and ethnic nationalism represent differing ideological positions.

What follows here is a brief discussion concerning the choice of six "coming-of-age" stories, or Bildungsromane, and of the impact that ethnic authors have had on this eighteenth-century European genre, as well as of the impact the traditional genre may have had on works by ethnic authors. In chapter 4, the ethnic revisions of the Bildungsroman and of cultural nationalism will be seen as converging forces in the making of the novels under discussion. The following discussion of the Bildungsroman as genre establishes a basis for my claim that the interplay between individualism and communalism not only derives from the influence of ethnic nationalism but also from what has been a traditional concern of the Bildungsroman. Importantly, though, ethnic authors have shifted the outcome of that interplay.

THE BILDUNGSROMAN AS ETHNIC GENRE

How do the authors discussed here construct ethnicity? How do the protagonists conceive of their ethnicity? What characterizes being ethnic? What role does the ethnic community play in the formation of the protagonist? What is the relationship between ethnicity and mainstream in these works? These questions will help to explore the role ethnicity plays in the works to be discussed. I have selected texts that tell coming-of-age stories because in such texts, the protagonist's growing awareness of his/her ethnicity and its social significance, as reflected in the text, can reveal much about both the shape and importance a work gives ethnicity and its impact on the protagonist. The Bildungsroman as a genre is well suited for an exploration of the meaning of ethnicity because it focuses on the relations of a protagonist with the wider environment.[14] Because both autobiography and Bildungsroman, when in the hands of ethnic authors, often thematize ethnicity, they may also provide answers about how conceptualizations of ethnicity influence a genre, or vice versa. After all, the author's choice of genre must have some bearing on how s/he conceptualizes ethnicity. For this reason, it is worth looking into autobiography and Bildungsroman criticism, even though its concepts and generalizations have mostly European and Anglo American texts in mind. Those are often the models ethnic authors are acquainted with, however, and if one understands the confinements of the genre, one might be in a better position to judge how the authors' conceptualizations of ethnicity affect how they use and mold their genre of choice.

I have referred to both the main characters of Bildungsromane and the "I" of autobiography as "protagonist." In this study, the term "Bildungsroman" is used "as a heuristic tool which makes possible the comparison of a number of texts" (Swales 161) and as a term naming a genre which typically "traces its protagonist's growth into adolescence and young adulthood" (Sokoloff 26), but not as a historically specific term denoting a number of novels written in eighteenth-century Germany, as it is used by some scholars in German studies (Köhn 7–9; see also Beddow 1). The characteristics of that genre will be discussed later. Here it is enough to say that its similarity to autobiography—defined as a genre that "describes . . . the life of a human being not yet socialized, the history of that person's growing up and of his or her Bildung, of his or her growing into society" (Neumann 25 [my translation])—makes it possible to treat the two as if they were one.

One more factor that leads me to blend autobiography and Bildungsroman here is that the six works this study examines exhibit much ambiguity with regard to their genre. *The Autobiography of an Ex-Coloured Man*, though a novel, was published as a true-life account of its protagonist. Samuel Ornitz's *Haunch, Paunch and Jowl* pursues the same strategy and announces itself as *An Anonymous Autobiography* in the subtitle. Anzia Yezierska reverses that strategy and fictionalizes fact in *Bread Givers*, which, as Alice Kessler Harris maintains, is her most autobiographical novel (v).[15] Mary Helen Washington says of Paule Marshall's novel *Brown Girl, Brownstones* that it "explores her [Marshall's] own girlhood through the character of Selina Boyce" (322), and also Edna Ferber's novel *Fanny Herself* is at least "[f]aintly autobiographical" (Lichtenstein 132). And while *Plum Bun*'s "overarching frame" is "that of the *bildungsroman*," as Deborah McDowell notes in her introduction to the novel (xv), at least the setting is autobiographical: it is the Harlem of the Harlem Renaissance, and the novel's protagonist moves in circles Fauset herself moved in, with even W. E. B. Du Bois making a cameo appearance. The affinity between the two genres bears some further inquiry, especially because ethnic literature has been predominantly discussed in terms of autobiography but only occasionally in terms of Bildungsroman—with notable exceptions, such as Bonnie Hoover Braendlin or Sondra O'Neale—despite the fact that a substantial body of ethnic works seems to fall into the latter category.[16]

Like Robert B. Stepto, who has called African American literature "a prose literature dominated by autobiographical and Bildungsroman impulses" (147), many genre studies have talked about autobiography and Bildungsroman jointly, usually for the purpose of defining one of the two.[17] One explanation for this seems to lie in the fact that "Bildungsromane are highly autobiographical," as Jerome Hamilton Buckley notes (viii) for the English specimen of the genre. Another explanation hinges on the social instability of the modern period, according to Spengemann and Lundquist. Because of "the pressures and anxieties of social dislocation," the novel turned to the self, becoming more autobiographical, "searching for some surer experiential basis for reality and judgment," while the autobiographer, "[d]isenchanted with the conventional roles which society offered," turned to the "new novel . . . to examine personal experience without having to assume some ill-fitting social guise" (518). Lawrence Buell explains the confluence of autobiography and Bildungsroman with literary-historical developments:

> One source of pressure [in the antebellum period] that was changing literary fashion was slowly infiltrating America from abroad: the lyricization of poetry owing to the Romantic movement, and the development of the protagonist-centered novel (frequently told in the first person), from the eighteenth-century picaresque novel to the nineteenth-century bildungsroman. . . . On the one hand, writers were encouraged to push autobiography over into the domain of fiction . . . ; on the other hand, they were encouraged to autobiographicalize traditional fictional forms. (50)

A new focus on the "I" and a new conception of character are shared by the two genres and thus serve to bring them closer to each other. The result is an increasing blurring of boundaries between protagonist-focused fiction and autobiography.[18]

What, then, are the characteristics of both autobiography and Bildungsroman that have allowed for the frequent conflation of the two, and do these characteristics explain why both have been so popular with ethnic authors? Concerning the genesis of both genres, critics have noted that they prosper in an environment of crisis or instability and are indeed a response to those conditions.[19] Both autobiography and Bildungsroman strive for a sense of order in a world in crisis—and the world of ethnic communities tends to be subjected to constant change.[20]

All the works in this study follow the pattern of traditional Bildungsroman and autobiography to a significant degree; this pattern usually tells stories of socialization, of growing up and growing into society (Neumann 25) and focuses on the protagonist and his or her conflict with the environment (Köhn 21). So why is it that ethnic authors so often utilize two genres that talk about the formation, socialization, and Bildung of an individual?

As mentioned above, autobiography and Bildungsroman are forms that flourish in unstable times.[21] Particularly the period around the turn of the century marks wide-scale immigration and the aftershocks from the failure of Reconstruction, making it a highly unstable era for both African Americans and Jewish Americans. Not incidentally, the same circumstances that allow for a flourishing of autobiography and Bildungsroman also provide a fertile ground for nationalist tendencies, since nationalism, too, imposes a kind of order onto chaos by appearing to provide clear boundaries. The eighteenth century thus witnesses the birth both of the Bildungsroman and of nationalism as a political philosophy in Europe, and the late nineteenth and early twentieth century observed a flowering of both among Jewish Americans and African Americans. But while one can understand that the classic Bildungsroman with its bourgeois worldview would flourish at the same time as the bourgeoisie develops its ideal of a nation state, the twin flowering of both phenomena among ethnic Americans poses some problems. Why would a form with a largely individualist focus be attractive to authors who experience discrimination based on group affiliation?[22] The answer is that an assertion of individuality makes sense in the face of a denial of individuality, or even of humanity, because of one's group affiliation.[23]

As Edward Said has said of Third World narratives, "Local slave narratives, spiritual autobiographies, prison memoirs form a counterpoint to the Western powers' monumental histories, official discourses, and panoptic quasi-scientific viewpoint" (215). These forms serve as counterweights to the stereotypical views of ethnicity proliferated by the dominant culture. They offer the possibility of piecemeal, individual resistance, of a revision of mainstream views of ethnicity.

Protagonist-centered writing thus serves as a communication medium for ethnic writers: on the one hand, they share life experiences with other members of the writer's ethnic community; on the other hand, they communicate "authentic" views of ethnic life to mainstream readers. The works examined in this study mean to dispel ethnic stereotypes and are counter-narratives to a prevailing anti-Semitic and anti–African American reality. At the same time, they are, to a greater or lesser degree, beholden to essentialist conceptualizations of ethnicity, and thus they cannot avoid creating new stereotypes, which are sometimes old stereotypes with new valorizations; but that is "how counterhegemony functions—not on some other and unmarked terrain . . . but on the same terrain differently" (Layoun 253).[24]

In their focus on ethnicity, William Boelhower maintains, "The infinite variations of ethnic autobiography are always on a single theme—a hyphenated self's attempt to make it in America" ("The Making of Ethnic Autobiography" 133). Though this might be putting what ethnic texts are about in overly general terms, Boelhower is not alone in noting that both ethnic autobiography and Bildungsroman, despite their focus on the individual, ultimately also revolve around the relationship between ethnic group and mainstream society.[25] The interaction of ethnic and mainstream society is at the center of ethnic narratives. Because they explore the meaning of ethnicity in U.S. society, autobiographies and Bildungsromane offer ideal opportunities to analyze how ethnic writers configure ethnicity in their texts.

It must be emphasized, however, that when ethnic writers adopt these genres, they transform them. While both traditional Bildungsroman and autobiography heavily emphasize the protagonist and his/her development, and thus individualism, their ethnic equivalents seem to give more room to others.[26] While autobiography and Bildungsroman allow for an assertion of individuality, the very fact that the denial of one's individuality by the mainstream stems from the latter's view of one's ethnic group necessitates a dual strategy on the part of ethnic authors. The literary creation of the ethnic individual must go hand in hand with a vision of ethnicity which counters the mainstream's stereotypes, unless the work is to claim exceptionalism on the part of its protagonist while, partly or wholly, subscribing to the mainstream view of ethnicity. In other words, ideological pressures work on the ethnic autobiography and Bildungsroman, pushing them towards a more communal worldview.

The difference between the mainstream and ethnic versions of autobiography and Bildungsroman is, of course, not absolute, but one of degree. The traditional forms predominantly stress the individual but may also acknowledge a community; ethnic texts feature community involvement more prominently, but they also stress individual development, so that communalism and individualism exist side by side.[27] Group consciousness thus seems to be one characteristic that is more pronounced in ethnic texts than in the more protagonist-dominated traditional versions that provided models for ethnic authors.

The ethnic situation of the protagonist and the protagonist's group also accounts for another transformation wrought by ethnic authors. The traditional Bildungsroman has a tendency to see conflict as personal rather than societal (Buckley 22) and aims at a reconciliation of the protagonist with society.[28] Some ethnic protagonists, of course, reach that point of harmony with the environment through engaging themselves in the process of assimilation (Holte "The Representative Voice" 34).

Ostensibly, the protagonists of the *Autobiography*, *Plum Bun*, and *Fanny Herself*, blend in with a mainstream environment—but only at the price of renouncing their ethnicity. Maybe more typically, "[s]ome writers . . . observe the opposite lesson; it is the dominant culture that keeps them out for reasons of class, ethnicity or race" (Holte "The Representative Voice" 35). The same novels which depict a problematic "blending in" if ethnicity is rejected also show that the desire to "pass" stems from discriminatory treatment by the mainstream. Accordingly, some critics have rightfully questioned the possibility of a protagonist reaching harmony in a system that is hostile to him/her.[29]

But whether harmony with the environment is ultimately reached or not (and I will show that some passing narratives have their protagonists arrive at a mock harmony), the texts also show the liabilities of being ethnic in the United States. This feature of the ethnic Bildungsroman did not solely come into being as a literary choice but because of the status of ethnicity in society at large. This reality, which usually consists of open or subtle economic, political, and social inequalities and their psychological consequences, must be dealt with by the ethnic protagonist not as a matter of choice, but because she or he has been put into that reality through the sociopolitical arrangement of society. What David L. Dudley has said of African American men's autobiographies applies to both ethnic Bildungsroman and autobiography.

They can be called a "literature of reaction" because they, to some degree, have to confront the "cultural standards and traditions of white America" (192); they explore what ethnicity means for the protagonist who had no choice but to be in an ethnic situation (unless s/he is a first generation immigrant who came to the U.S. without evading tremendous pressures or dangers in his/her home country).

Because ethnic autobiographies and Bildungsromane react to an ethnic situation, critique of both the ethnic and the general environment becomes one of their important functions.[30] As Esther Kleinbord Labovitz has noted, "the heroines of the female *Bildungsroman* challenge the very structure of society, raising questions of equality, not only of class, but of sexes, as well" (25).[31] Ethnic women protagonists negotiate both ethnicity and gender (Braendlin 78), but, by analogy, Labovitz's statement can be applied to the ethnic Bildungsroman in general, whether it focuses on a female or a male protagonist, since that protagonist, too, challenges the "structure of society" by "raising questions of equality" with regard to ethnicity.[32]

What may be called the ethnic transformation of the Bildungsroman consists, then, of a development away from the more exclusively personality-oriented plot of the traditional Bildungsroman and towards a more political and social vision. Jeffrey L. Sammons's more open definition of the Bildungsroman genre as including works focusing on Bildung "whether the process of *Bildung* succeeds or fails, whether the protagonist achieves an accommodation with life and society or not" (41) gives room for this expanded vision of the genre, because a failed or problematic Bildung might serve to indict the circumstances that make it problematic.

Bonnie Hoover Braendlin thus defines the ethnic Bildungsroman as follows:

> The *Bildungsroman* of . . . disenfranchised Americans . . . portrays the particular identity and adjustment problems of people whose sex or color renders them unacceptable to the dominant society; it expresses their struggle for individuation and a part in the American dream, which society simultaneously proffers and denies to them. This new *Bildungsroman* asserts an identity defined by the outsiders themselves or by their own cultures, not by the patriarchal Anglo-American power structure; it evinces a revaluation, a transvaluation, of traditional *Bildung* by new standards and perspectives. (75)

However, Jeffrey Sammons emphasizes that the Bildungsroman continues to have "something to do with *Bildung*, that is, with the early bourgeois, humanistic concept of the shaping of the individual self from its innate potentialities through acculturation and social experience to the threshold of maturity" (41). So one might ask whether twentieth-century ethnic authors adhere to an old-fashioned vision. Roger Rosenblatt asserts that, to some extent, they do: "The ideals of black autobiography are the preposterously traditional ideals of reason and consistency" ("Black Autobiography" 523).[33] These ideals, just as the concept of Bildung, predominated in eighteenth-century Western ideology.

Ethnic Bildungsroman and autobiography attest to the fact that Western societies, should they ever have meant to make Bildung, reason, and consistency possible for all its members, have not succeeded. The protagonists of ethnic coming-of-age stories strive for their Bildung, they work on shaping their personalities, and often their social environment offers more hindrance than support, so that reaching harmony within a more or less hostile social order might be a tenuous proposition at best. Not to adjust to that order but to embrace ethnicity as the text outlines it and choose a more "ethnically-oriented" life rather than a career in the mainstream offers itself as one other alternative for the protagonist of the ethnic Bildungsroman. *Fanny Herself* and *Plum Bun* explore this alternative after their protagonists have become disenchanted with mainstream life. To seek some combination of mainstream and ethnicity is the chosen life course for the protagonists of *Brown Girl, Brownstones* and *Bread Givers*. Ethnic Bildungsromane thus complicate the vision of what it may mean to adjust to an environment simply because the potential options have multiplied. Given that the authors discussed in this study have all chosen to write within what might be called the parameters of the Bildungsroman, however, one may say that the Bildungsroman, by the early decades of the twentieth century, had been firmly established as an ethnic genre.

CHAPTER ONE

The Autobiography of an Ex-Coloured Man and
Haunch, Paunch and Jowl: Two Versions of Passing

T*he Autobiography of an Ex-Coloured Man* and *Haunch, Paunch and Jowl* serve here as the first two examples of ethnic literary revisions of the Bildungsroman. Both are also parodies of the autobiographical genre, particularly the autobiographical success story, a genre known in the U.S. since Benjamin Franklin. They adopt the individualist focus of the traditional Bildungsroman and autobiography only to make their protagonists failures because of their exaggerated individualism. Thus, both novels argue that, for their ethnic protagonists, a more (ethnic) communalist orientation would have led to a more fulfilling and, as the plots strongly imply, more ethical life. In effect, the genre revisions performed by the two works are the result of their preoccupation with ethnic identity and of the influence ethnic nationalism exerts on them, and it is this preoccupation and its similar manifestations in both novels which this chapter will explore.

James Weldon Johnson's *The Autobiography of an Ex-Coloured Man* was published anonymously in 1912, purporting to withhold its author's name so as to avoid compromising him. In this way, the protagonist is able to reveal "the great secret of [his] life" (3) without having to give up his cover—he is passing. In fact, the anonymity was also a sales trick as "Johnson . . . felt that curiosity about the author" (Levy 126) would increase public interest. In addition, few African American novels had been published, while African American autobiography was a well-established genre, reaching from Frederick Douglass to Booker T. Washington (Goellnicht 18). However, the trick did not work: the novel initially received little attention. The novel's publishing company, Sherman, French & Co., closed its doors soon after publication, and even the black press offered few, though positive, comments (Levy 127, Collier "Endless Journey" 365). The book was republished in 1927 and has not been forgotten since.

The history of Samuel Ornitz's *Haunch, Paunch and Jowl* reverses that of the *Autobiography*. Though, at the time of its publication, it seemed to have touched a nerve and was a "commercial success, selling in excess of one hundred thousand copies" (Miller "Samuel Ornitz" 210), the book has now been virtually relegated to the dusty back shelves of literary history and little has been published on it. Pocket Books published a paperback edition in 1968, and the book is currently in print again, after Markus Wiener Publishers brought it back on the market in 1985. Like the *Autobiography*, *Haunch, Paunch and Jowl* appeared anonymously in hopes that "the book would sell better if the public thought it the actual memoir of a judge who had died five years earlier" (Miller "Samuel Ornitz" 209). Similar to Johnson, Ornitz had few predecessors when it came to Jewish American novelists. According to Gabriel Miller, "There was then no 'American Jewish novel' as it has come to be known, no sense of tradition. . . . Only a few American Jewish novels had appeared" ("Introduction" xi). The novel's reception in the Jewish community was mixed: "The book attracted much attention. Contemporary newspaper accounts chronicle sermons by rabbis who damned it as 'lecherous and degrading.' . . . On the other hand, many Jews and Jewish organizations praised the novel. It was serialized in two working class papers, the *Morning Freiheit* in America and, years later, in the *Rote Fahne* in Germany" (Miller "Samuel Ornitz" 210). Given the plot of the novel, the responses were predictable: Ornitz (as a narrative presence) does not openly reject Judaism— though the protagonist does—but the novel seems to suggest that socialism of a kind ought to be the new Jewish (and American) religion.

Like Johnson's novel, it is about a kind of passing: the protagonist lives in a Jewish American community, poses (or passes) as a dedicated Jew, but suppresses all emotional ties to his community, rising to success on the backs of his fellow Lower East Siders. While there are differences in the kinds of passing that the protagonists enact, both novels imply, through the careers of their main characters, that the success they gain comes at a high price: their ethnic heritage. This heritage appears as intrinsically connected to everything that may serve as the opposite of materialism, be it idealism, spirituality, or artistic ability. It is this conceptualization of ethnicity that reveals both novels' debt to ethnic nationalism. Accordingly, both the *Autobiography* and *Haunch* show that following the path of materialism is not only a betrayal of the "ethnic nation" but also of traits the novels construct as inherently ethnic.[1]

The Autobiography of an Ex-Coloured Man is the coming-of-age story of a light-skinned African American who is raised by his black mother and meets his white father on only a few occasions in his early childhood. Nonetheless, he grows up believing he is "white," learns in school that he is "coloured," and repeatedly switches from "white" to "black" identity in the years to follow, retaining throughout a heightened awareness of his "colour." After traveling and experiencing, or rather observing, various facets of African American life in the U.S. and of European American life both in the U.S. and in Europe, the Ex-Coloured Man decides ultimately to pass for white, being jolted into that decision by witnessing a lynching. He becomes a businessman, marries, has children, but then looks back at his life with feelings of regret.

Even this brief plot summary makes clear that one of the central problems of the novel is the question of identity. Indeed, Henry Louis Gates Jr. sees the Ex-Coloured Man as an incarnation of Du Boisian double-consciousness ("Introduction" xvii)—aptly so, as the protagonist himself refers admiringly to *The Souls of Black Folk* (169). Once he knows he is coloured, according to U.S. racial logic, he cannot be white again the same way, regardless of the fact that he is both white and black. In other words, he accepts that logic, internalizes it, and acquires double-consciousness; he cannot simply be but is always conscious of being, seeing himself, through a Du Boisian "veil," as whites might see him. To quote from the *Autobiography*: "He [the African American] is forced to take his outlook on all things . . . from the point of view of a coloured man" (21). What does that mean, though? Does Johnson imply that societal forces alone constrain the Ex-Coloured Man to be a coloured man or does the novel imply that there is such a thing as a coloured point of view regardless of social constraints? Does the *Autobiography* posit race as something socially constructed or as something natural?

Answers to these questions have ranged over the entire spectrum of ethnic critical theory from essentialism (race as natural fact) to constructionism ("the position that differences are constructed, not innate" [Fuss xii]). Eugenia Collier sees the Ex-Coloured Man "on the verge of surrendering the part of him which is white and letting the black self emerge victorious"; the black self fails to win, however, so that the protagonist ends up being "white on the outside as well as on the inside" ("Endless Journey" 371). Collier thus emphasizes essential blackness and whiteness, in both psychological and physical terms. Houston Baker Jr.

describes the protagonist as unquestionably black: "the narrator . . . *is a black man of culture* recording the situations and attitudes that have succeeded in driving him underground" (*Singers* 22 [emphasis mine]). Baker thus accepts as fact what I claim the *Autobiography* is calling into question. Henry Louis Gates Jr., however, has no doubt that Johnson critiques essential racial identity: "Johnson's decision to chart his mulatto pilgrim's progress back and forth, . . . between black and white racial identities, is intended to establish the fact that such identities are entirely socially constructed" ("Introduction" xvi).

According to Eric J. Sundquist's *The Hammers of Creation*, it is the hybrid forms of blackness and whiteness, especially the musical ones, that the *Autobiography* delineates. However, while the Ex-Coloured Man may have "chosen an art [ragtime] emblematic of his racial hybridity" his lack of cultural connectedness does not allow his hybridity to "[produce] fruitful symbiosis" (16). Instead, the protagonist chooses "literal marriage and physiological incorporation into white culture" (22), a step that "enacts both the *physical* and *semiotic* destruction of a world in which color and language bear the meaning of ancestry" (39 [emphasis mine]). While Sundquist sees the possibility of cultural amalgamation, hinted at and symbolized through biological hybridity, he describes how, instead, the *Autobiography* illustrates the obliteration of black culture through cultural and biological assimilation, as Johnson might have feared it. Sundquist's analysis thus shows the *Autobiography* to adopt a position between essentialism and constructionism, linking culture to color; what is more, it shows the significance of "race" while also subscribing to constructionism. John Sheehy, in turn, argues that the passing trope intends to show the impossibility of establishing stable categories: "Since both categories [black and white] are to a certain extent *imposed* from the outside and to a certain extent *constructed* from the inside, the dividing line between the imposition and the construction . . . is difficult to fix" (405). But this very difficulty may provide an opening, as passing signifies "the possibility of a discourse of racial identity which moves beyond the terms of both our racial antipathies and our racial sympathies" (414). Samira Kawash, however, argues that "the narrative . . . works against the simple black-passing-for-white logic of passing and its attendant model of race as the expression of a prior, proper identity" (146). If there is no such thing as "race," then there can be no such thing as "passing."

While a variety of rhetorical positions on ethnicity in the novel have been convincingly explored, the duality in Johnson's approach to the question of identity bears further emphasis. I believe that rather than adopting one specific position on race, the *Autobiography* goes both further and not as far as that: while Johnson shows racial identity as socially constructed, he also insists that certain traits are inherent to whiteness or blackness, thus employing seemingly incompatible strategies. While the novel destabilized race, it also uses rhetoric steeped in essentialism as well as constructionism. The novel improves upon the intent of much of the "passing" literature preceding it to point out the absurdity of the color scheme through enacting a kind of reverse passing in that its protagonist pretends to be black more than he pretends to be white.[2] This strategy doubles complications by depicting not merely a character who, knowing he is black, attempts to pass for white, but a character who thinks he is white, learns he is seen as black by whites, attempts to be black, does not succeed, decides to be white and now thinks of himself as somebody black passing for white.

However, while highlighting the social construction of race, the protagonist's life also serves as an indictment of the value system of the novel's European American middle class through relying on the notion of inherent "racial" traits. In other words, the protagonist's ethnicity is outlined both as something "made up" and arbitrary *and* as something "real." The *Autobiography* thus partakes in a rhetoric of constructionism *and* in a rhetoric of essentialism. While the novel embraces some aspects of white society and critiques others of its black counterpart, the deployment of this double rhetoric serves to establish as the overall tenor of the book a double critique of white middle-class society while at the same time allowing Johnson to show African America's moral (and artistic) superiority. Johnson himself tells us that he set out to do nothing less than that. He records, in his autobiography *Along This Way*, a conversation he had with H. L. Mencken on "Negro literature" and "Negro writers":

> "What they should do," he said, "is to single out the strong points of the race and emphasize them over and over and over; asserting, at least on these points, that they are better than anybody else." I called to his attention that I had attempted something of that sort in *The Autobiography of an Ex-Coloured Man*. (305)

Thus, to rephrase Diana Fuss's assessment of a conscious use of essentialism, essentialism and constructionism used side by side also prove to have "strategic or interventionary value" (20).

To understand how this happens, it is necessary to show how the novel delineates whiteness and blackness, how each of these comes to be seen as characterized by distinct qualities through the life-path the protagonist takes, and how, as a result, the Ex-Coloured Man is indeed passing for black more than he is passing for white in the terms of the novel. How, then, does the Ex-Coloured Man acquire his whiteness and his middle-class values? Usually, the blame has been put on his father, who is aptly remembered by the narrator by "the material objects associated with him" (Fleming *JWJ* 31), such as a gold chain and a gold watch. His mother has been accused of being "an adorer of white values" (Kinnamon 173) and has generally received little sympathy from critics. However, she is not only complicit in teaching her son materialism but is herself a victim of double-consciousness and is instrumental in bequeathing it to her son. She spanks him memorably for uprooting glass bottles stuck in the ground, which marks a violation of African (American) cultural customs and as Robert Stepto has explained makes her a "custodian of those aspects of black culture" (101). Yet she also—in the very same paragraph—scrubs the narrator "until [his] skin ached" (4) in an apparent (symbolic) attempt to make him more white (Fleming "Irony" 86).

It is his father who gives the narrator coins, but it is his mother who teaches him "to promptly drop [them] in a little tin bank" (5), showing him the value of deferred gratification which will come in handy in his investment schemes. While she is more comfortable—"freer" (8)— when playing "old Southern songs" (5), she is not assertive about her ethnicity when directly confronted by her son: "No, I am not white, but you—your father is one of the greatest men in the country" (18). Eugenia Collier has noted that she denies "his [and thus her] blackness but not his whiteness" by only commenting on her "lack" of whiteness while emphasizing her son's white descent ("Endless Journey" 367). Through her contradictory behavior, which foreshadows the narrator's own ambiguity, the narrator's mother reveals her own unresolved psychological tensions, her ambiguous acceptance and simultaneous rejection of her own ethnicity.

The way she initially rears the narrator seems to be geared towards avoiding the development of double-consciousness in him—at the expense of his African American cultural heritage. As the narrator says, "She was careful about my associates" (7), and one can assume that they are white: his mother surrounds herself exclusively with white women and the narrator, throughout the novel, "gives no racial designation to white characters but labels instead the black ones" (Collier "Endless Journey" 366). She sews for "a great many ladies" (7) and, in a punning transposition of color from the givers of money to the object given, makes a "fair income from her work" (7).

Not surprisingly, "the protagonist assumes that he is white" and, as a consequence, he "[absorbs] the racism of his schoolmates" (Kinnamon 173). His experience of racism as a racist turns out to be the ideal breeding ground for double-consciousness: "I had first learned what their status was, and now I learned that theirs was mine" (23). He understands only too well how European Americans see him—better than any of the other African American children in his class—because he himself evidently looked at African Americans pejoratively. In one of the few instances in which the narrator uses "we" with an ethnic association,[3] he is chasing after African American classmates: "We ran after them pelting them with stones until they separated in several directions" (15). This persecution is the result of one African American boy striking back after having been taunted in a racist fashion by a European American crowd of children. What this demonstrates is that double-consciousness results from a racist construction of whiteness itself, which is defined in contradistinction to blackness: the narrator experiences a feeling of ethnic identity (of "we"ness) only when he can see himself as part of a clearly defined group with an equally well-defined "enemy." The former self-definition then turns itself against the narrator. In a bitterly sarcastic turn, his certainty as a citizen of his nation expresses itself here through disdain against those excluded from the national "norm." Ironically, the mother's attempt to protect the narrator from acquiring double-consciousness only ensures that his will be even more pronounced than hers. Through this strategy then, and paradoxically, through the portrayal of the narrator's essentializing of race (us vs. them), the novel emphasizes the constructedness of both race and racism.[4]

Given his white upbringing, it is befitting that it is by the pen of a European American author that he is initiated to the social significance of being coloured: "[*Uncle Tom's Cabin*] opened my eyes as to who and what I was and what my country considered me; in fact, it gave me my bearing" (42). This kind of initiation, of course, is only likely to deepen his tendency to see blackness through white eyes. His initiation to his race through a book, of course, further highlights the constructedness of blackness. As Samira Kawash has said, "In a sharp contrast to the supposed naturalness of racial feeling, the narrator presents his becoming colored as an autodidactic course of deliberate self-transformation" (142). At the same time, his having read the book opens up the possibility of instruction by his mother on matters of ethnicity: "As a result, she was entirely freed from reserve, and often herself brought up the subject, talking of things directly touching her life and mine and of things which had come down to her through the 'old folks'" (42). Although we never learn what those things from the old folks are, they do inspire him to become interested in the South, which marks the first time that he takes an affirmative attitude towards his newfound ethnicity.

Uncle Tom's Cabin does leave its traces, though. For example, it strengthens his tendency towards middle-class gentility, what he himself calls, in reference to his childhood days, being a "perfect little aristocrat" (7). This prejudice appears in Stowe's novel in the form of condescension for those characters speaking vernacular (who are usually dark-skinned) and a more equitable treatment, even admiration, for those characters—such as Eliza and George—who are closest to Anglo-Saxon norms in their speech patterns, values, education, and looks. The Ex-Coloured Man adopts both the class and color prejudices easily, having been predisposed at least to the former since his childhood. As a result, he becomes a class snob (Faulkner 150), alienated from the "darker, poorer members of his ethnic community" through "color and class prejudice" (Bell 90–91).

Roger Rosenblatt has ascribed the narrator's stance on class matters to his sense of audience: "The hero . . . shows contempt for dialect . . . [and] notes class distinctions among other blacks to demonstrate to the middle class white reader . . . that he fully shares his reader's notion of what constitutes class superiority" (*Black Fiction* 177). But the narrator goes even further than that: he does not condemn dialect per se but only its occurrence among African Americans, particularly those of a "better class." This becomes apparent when he comments on Southern and Northern middle-class African Americans, clearly preferring the latter:

> I could not help being struck by the great difference between them
> [Bostonian African Americans] and the same class of coloured peo-
> ple in the South. In speech and thought they were genuine Yankees.
> The difference was especially noticeable in their speech. There was
> none of that heavy-tongued enunciation which characterizes even
> the best-educated coloured people of the South. (152–153)

The narrator does not object to a white Texan's speech pattern when
he overhears a conversation in a railroad car, even though one may
assume that the Texan spoke with a type of southern accent as well.
The protagonist's behavior and judgment is that of someone who is
not merely appealing to a specific audience but who identifies with it
to the point that dialect in middle- or upper-class African Americans
is something to be noted and censured while dialect in middle-class
European Americans escapes judgment because it is natural and therefore invisible—to someone who is white. This sense of identification
explains why he does not "take greater issue [in his discussion of *Uncle
Tom's Cabin*] with his opponents' charge that there never was a slave-
holder as bad as Legree than with their claim that there never was a
Negro as good as Tom" (Stepto 110), and it also foreshadows his "total
absence of [an] emotional response to the Texan's slurs [as] another
indication of the fact that the main character does not feel like a member of the insulted race" (Fleming "Irony" 94).[5] Much of the narrator's
foray into the South confirms that he is passing for black more than
he is passing for white and establishes a strong link between the protagonist's classism and racism.

Even before he departs for the South, signals for his reverse passing are loud and clear. When listening to one of his black classmate's
(whom he nicknames "Shiny") graduation oration, he speculates on
what his friend's feelings might be:

> What were his thoughts when he stepped forward and looked into
> the crowd of faces, all white with the exception of a score or so that
> were lost to view? *I do not know, but I fancy* he felt his loneliness.
> *I think* there must have rushed over him a feeling akin to that of a
> gladiator. . . . (44 [emphasis mine])

The narrator empathizes with Shiny, but he also makes clear that he
is making imaginative leaps. In the interpretation of the audience's

enthusiastic reaction, he does not take similar caution: "The sight of that boy gallantly waging with puny, black arms so unequal a battle touched the deep springs in the hearts of his audience, and they were swept by a wave of sympathy and admiration" (45). He can be more affirmative about the audience's reaction because he seems to know the audience better than he does Shiny, and he admires their "love of fair play" (45). When the narrator departs for the South, then, he has already chosen sides and can therefore "strike out into the interior" as if he were "a European explorer in colonial Africa"(Sundquist *Hammers* 12).

Once in the South, it becomes clear that even though "the protagonist has apparently accepted his membership in the race he is describing, his attitude toward black people is curiously aloof" (Fleming "Irony" 89). As a matter of fact his "first sight of black people en masse unnerves him" (Collier "Endless Journey" 367) and can be called racist as a function of his middle-class sensitivities: "The unkempt appearance, the shambling, slouching gait and loud talk and laughter of these people aroused in me a feeling of almost repulsion" (55–56). His stance is essentialist in that he makes no distinction between "race" and "class" in this encounter which, significantly, has no counterpart in his sojourn in the white world.[6] In this context, his eventual choice of lodging proves to be symbolically significant. His landlady is a "rather fine-looking, stout, brown-skin woman" (67), but it is her interior decorating that appeals to him, as he describes at length the "cane-bottomed chairs, each of which was adorned with a white crocheted tidy . . . a white crocheted cover . . . and several trinkets, each of which was set upon a white crocheted mat" (67). Though the narrator conveys a sense of irony about such middle-class tidiness, he does decide to settle in where he can be surrounded by so much whiteness.

Even his subsequent stay in New York and his enthusiastic participation in African American nightlife do not significantly diminish his cultural and emotional distance from African Americans. His reaction to a number of photographs on the wall of a nightclub reveals this distance:

> the walls were literally covered with photographs or lithographs of *every colored man in America who had ever 'done anything.'* There were pictures of Frederick Douglass and of Peter Jackson. . . . The most of these photographs were autographed and, *in a sense*, made a really valuable collection. (104 [emphasis mine])

The use of relativizing or slightly ironic phrases betrays his unwilling-
ness to commit himself fully to the cultural scene he describes. Significantly, he merely comments on the photographs' collectability, "the
value imputed to them more monetary than cultural" (Kinnamon 174).
Even when he comments on ragtime music and its artistic value, his
yardstick for assessing the music's artistry is not the application of any
African American intra-cultural standards but—in a parallel to his
interest in the white audience's reception of Shiny's speech—the
appreciation of a European (American) audience:

> One thing cannot be denied; it is music which possesses at least
> one strong element of greatness: it appeals universally; not only the
> American, but the English, the French, and even [sic] the German
> people find delight in it. (101)

Though on the one hand, the narrator uses ragtime as proof of African
Americans' "originality and artistic conception" (87), he seems eager
to pull the music out of its ethnic orbit and give it a universal, i.e., a
"non-ethnic" and non-essentialist, cast. For the narrator, a true sign
of ragtime's success is that in "Paris they call it American music" (87).
The same is true for every item on the narrator's list of African American accomplishments: it has to pass the test of a white American or
European audience (with the exception of the camp meeting, which
I will discuss later)—so that essentialism in its Eurocentric variety is
introduced through the backdoor, because white acceptance assumes
the place of an absolute standard here. He relates with pride that "[t]he
newspapers have already told how the practice of intricate cakewalk
steps has taken up the time of European royalty and nobility" (87), or
that "the Fisk singers made the public and the skilled musicians of both
America and Europe listen" (87).

While it is understandable that popularity abroad is taken as a sign
of success and artistic greatness, the narrator's tendency to enlist exclusively European (American) reception as the measure of that success
is telling. Ethnicity, for him, carries the mark of inferiority (though,
ultimately, the novel embraces the opposite view, as I will show), and
African American art, according to that logic, can only disprove inferiority if it appeals to a white audience. Once ragtime has lost some of
its ethnic flavor through universal acceptance or through being clas-
sicized, its greatness is assured. Clearly, the narrator's wish to give ragtime a "higher form" (87) tends to the same end. However, this wish,

as well as his perception of Douglass's portrait as valuable in the material sense, not only demonstrates his "[alienation] from the deepest bonds of his race" (Stepto 125) but also indicates two of his character flaws as the novel establishes them, which are inextricably connected with his alienation—and essentially connected to whiteness. And those very character flaws also play a crucial role in Johnson's revision of the Bildungsroman.

Character flaw number one is the Ex-Coloured Man's materialism; flaw number two is his selfishness. Both are related and intertwined. Both also call into question the traditionally individualist orientation of the Bildungsroman. While, in the traditional genre, the protagonist is (usually) expected to rebel against his society in order to establish his own place in it eventually, the *Autobiography* enacts a warped form of that rebellion. The protagonist alienates himself from his ethnic community and eventually integrates into the hostile mainstream (more on that later), an unsuitable ending for an ethnic Bildungsroman. Even the individualism which might have helped him in the formation of his character appears here in an exaggerated form as selfishness accompanied by materialism.

It has now been shown that the narrator acquires his materialism from his father and mother in early childhood. Here I will attempt to trace what this materialism means in his life. Eric Sundquist has aptly noted that the father's gift, the "gold coin he hangs around his neck," is "the chain of neoslavery" (*Hammers* 18). This proves to be true in two ways: on the one hand, the coin is symbolic of "the property of whiteness" (Sundquist *Hammers* 18); on the other hand, it foreshadows the narrator's enslavement to materialism (though the novel shows whiteness and materialism as closely related, as I will show later).

The Ex-Coloured Man will stay true to this inheritance from his father for the rest of his life. One way in which this becomes apparent is through his "[equation of] respectability with affluence" (Collier "Endless Journey" 369). Illustrations of this are manifold during his stay in the South, but the attitude remains the same when he sojourns in New York, where he regrets not having become acquainted with a single respectable family:

> I knew that there were several coloured men worth a hundred or so thousand dollars each, and some families who proudly dated their free ancestry back a half-dozen generations. I also learned that in

Brooklyn there lived quite a large colony in comfortable homes which they owned; but at no point did my life come into contact with theirs. (114)

Apparently, the narrator's notion of respectability even has a price tag.

But his materialism—and his selfishness—may be demonstrated most clearly through his relationship to music. In the following the narrator enumerates the advantages garnered by his ragtime playing:

By mastering ragtime I gained several things: first of all, I gained the title of professor. . . . Then, too, I gained the means of earning a rather fair livelihood. . . . And, finally, I secured a wedge which has opened to me more doors and made me a welcome guest than my playing of Beethoven and Chopin could ever have done. (115)

All of his gains relate either to fame, money, connections, or all three of them. This bears out Robert Stepto's observation that "for him, the modulation and occasional exploitation of America's race rituals [such as music] are persistently more important than true and honest contact with his race" (127), particularly if one remembers that the doors that open for the narrator through his ragtime playing are the doors of his millionaire friend and of European high society. Ironically, then, his choice of ethnic music (ragtime) over Beethoven and Chopin distances him further from the African American community, at least initially. Music is a "mine" for him, as he will say later when revisiting the South, and his relation to music is expressive both of his materialism and of the absence of any desire for connection with an ethnic community (Stepto 119). While the way he relates to (African American) music emphasizes the traits that the novel connects with his white heritage, the music of his choice, ragtime, is itself, as Eric Sundquist has shown, "emblematic of his racial hybridity" (*Hammers* 16) and points to the possibility of "fusion . . . in the process of aesthetic creation" (Sollors *Beyond Ethnicity* 172). His pragmatic and self-oriented, rather than artistic, relationship to that music preempts that possibility, however, for his interest in material gain overshadows his artistic exploration of African American and European culture.

The novel's focus on ethnic identity thus occasions a revision of the Bildungsroman: the connection between whiteness and exaggerated individualism parodies the traditionally white protagonist's quest for individuality and puts this quest into the context of white-black relations.

In this context, striving for individuation appears suddenly as suspicious. Once the Ex-Coloured Man's exaggerated individualism has been established, even his attempts at ethnic communion do not seem trustworthy.

Accordingly, when the narrator seems to connect with African Americans, the reasons are dubious. On board a ship bound for the South, the Ex-Coloured Man befriends an African American doctor whom he clearly admires: "He was the broadest-minded coloured man I have ever talked with on the Negro question" (151). The continuation of the passage reveals one of the reasons for his admiration: "He even went so far as to sympathize with and offer excuses for some white Southern points of view" (151). The doctor's stance resembles the narrator's own apologetic discussion of *Uncle Tom's Cabin* or of the Texan's racist opinions. "Like the protagonist, the doctor can discuss the 'Negro question' in objective, detached terms" (Fleming "Irony" 93). This passage marks another instance in which the Ex-Coloured Man uses "we" with an ethnic connotation; significantly, though, he only refers to having used the pronoun in the past rather than actively using it in the present, indicating his distanced stance at the time of his narration: "In referring to the race I used the personal pronoun 'we'" (150). The doctor's detachment seems to have the same foundation as the narrator's: egocentrism. He objects to racism only when he himself is affected by it (Fleming "Irony" 93): "I don't object to anyone's having prejudices so long as those prejudices don't interfere with my personal liberty" (150).[7]

The narrator thus constructs a self without allegiance to any group. As a result, his literal allusions to African American traditions serve only to highlight his egocentrism. When he refuses to give his name or details about his childhood in the opening pages of the novel, one remembers Frederick Douglass's elision of geographical and personal specifics. But while Douglass protects others still in slavery, the Ex-Coloured Man protects only himself (Stepto 105–106). Even when he invokes a larger societal context and seems to speak for a group of people rather than for himself alone, one does not trust him because his statements serve to clear him of any responsibility for his decision to become white. When he explains that passing or "marrying lighter" is "in accordance with what might be called economic necessity" (154), one recognizes this as "part of his ongoing self-serving argument about color and class relations" which is an attempt "to justify the choice the protagonist will make" (Sundquist *Hammers* 7). By invoking a rhetoric of parenthood, the narrator seeks to hide his selfish motives and enlist the reader's sympathy, making us believe that the choice of passing is really a selfless choice made with the future of one's children in mind:

> Nor is it any more a sacrifice of self-respect that a black man should give to his children every advantage he can which complexion of the skin carries than that the new or vulgar rich should purchase for their children the advantages which ancestry, aristocracy, and social position carry. (155)

The argument sounds hollow if one considers that it is precisely his self-respect that he jeopardizes, as the end of the novel reveals. The parallel he draws between skin color and money/caste is telling in that it reveals his materialist obsession as well as his belief that whiteness equals material success, spelled out as "Have a white skin, and all else may be added unto you" (155). What is really at stake is his own success, not that of his children, and the general "tendency toward lighter complexion, especially in the more active elements in the race" (154), in which he enlists himself here, serves merely as support and justification of his decision to be white.[8]

Despite his self-constructedness between ethnic and racial groups, his very character flaws highlight how the novel implies links between ethnicity and behavior. While "the conflict in the narrator can easily be seen as not only one of racial identity but also as one between materialism and spirituality" (Dickson 256), racial identity has a lot to do with whether one chooses to be materialistic or spiritual in *The Autobiography of an Ex-Coloured Man*, whether one resides in the Du Boisian "sole oasis of simple faith and reverence" or "in a dusty desert of dollars and smartness" (Du Bois 8). In one of the few moments of discarding his distance—at the camp meeting—the narrator explains the importance of the role of the congregation's lead singer, "Singing Johnson":

> It is indispensable to the success of the singing, when the congregation is a large one made up of people from different communities, to have someone with a strong voice who knows just what hymn to sing and when to sing it, who can pitch it in the right key, and who has all the leading lines committed to memory. (178)

Lucinda MacKethan explains that here, "James Weldon Johnson gives us his own ideal of selfhood through a voice that is freed from the circle of white oppression by its ability to sing and to express its own heritage" (146). Indeed, the narrator seems to overcome his class prejudice for a moment, focusing on the integrative and communal power of the singing leader, whose "one-eyedness" might well be symbolic of having only one consciousness: an African American one. It is through music that African American spirituality and communalism are enacted here, and it seems that the narrator implies that "Black people . . . find their real spirituality only among themselves, outside the purview of whites" (Dickson 257). At this moment, the novel reveals its bias towards a communalist model of self-development, quite opposed to the individualist model of the traditional Bildungsroman. However, the Ex-Coloured Man's intense double-consciousness makes it impossible for him ever to be outside Dickson's "purview of whites," which explains why for him music is more interesting for what it can get him than for its tradition or potential communal value.

Nonetheless, his internal conflict is highlighted by the fact that "his gifts and powers and promise are all as a black man" (Cooke *Afro-American Literature* 52)—at least the novel outlines them in this essentialist manner. The reader is to understand that, in his youth, he is naturally drawn to music and particularly to the blue notes on the piano keyboard. To underscore the biologism of that inclination, the narrator, when talking about the African American originators of ragtime, affirms that they "were guided by natural musical instinct and talent" (99) while not stressing the naturalness of such an instinct in a German musician later in the novel. The narrator does develop his musical talent but, in a "self-protecting disengagement from black rural culture," he rejects the "cultural demands" (Sundquist *Hammers* 12–13) of music in the African American context, a context which, through its call-and-response pattern, is communalism, as the camp meeting shows. Ethnic communalism is set aside for its implicit opposite, whiteness. This rejection becomes utterly clear when, in courting his future wife, he ends "Chopin's Thirteenth Nocturne on a major triad—not the minor it requires" as if he meant to "outwhite" Chopin, "thus silencing the minor key of his black life for good" (Sundquist *Hammers* 45).

What, then, leads to this rejection? Materialism, selfishness, and middle-class values—all of which are shown to be inextricably connected with whiteness. "In the *Autobiography*, Johnson pairs racial pride and the virtues of the middle class, though reconciling their sometimes conflicting implications occasionally proved difficult" (Levy 139) as the narrator's attitude towards African Americans who are not middle class amply demonstrates. Except for his lapse during the camp meeting, the Ex-Coloured Man admires those African Americans most who have most successfully erased every sign of their ethnicity but their skin color, such as the doctor he meets on his ship passage to the South or Bostonian African Americans who "[i]n speech and thought . . . were genuine Yankees" (153). To become middle class, in terms of the novel, is to become whiter, and nothing illustrates this better than the narrator's wish to classicize African American folk music "to insure [its] recognition" (Baker *Singers* 24). Recognition by whom? For the narrator, "black art is a pawn in the larger struggle for recognition from whites. . . . To aid in this endeavor the protagonist wishes to . . . merge the black and white cultural idiom into one" (Gayle 94), an endeavor of which the narrator's ragging of the Wedding March is an apt expression.

It is the ragging of Mendelssohn's music that makes the narrator's fame and allows him to meet the millionaire who proves to be instrumental in the furthering of the protagonist's materialism and selfishness, the former through exposing him to a lifestyle of leisure and wealth, the latter through attempting to convince him not to go back to the South "since evil is a force that cannot be annihilated [and] the best one can do is to seek such personal happiness as one can find" (Payne 34). Though the narrator rejects the millionaire's advice at first, maybe "recognizing the selfishness in the proposal that he remain in Europe to study music" (Skerret 224), he follows it after having witnessed a lynching. The choice of studying music in Europe, not an irrational one if he wants to study classical music, can only be seen as selfish against the implied background of ideas of racial solidarity. Solidarity as an ideal thus comes to be associated with blackness. And again, one can see how the novel's genre revision connects with its focus on ethnic identity. By implying that a quasi-nationalist solidarity is a higher value than individualism, the novel not only subtly revises the traditional Bildungsroman but also stands on its head the traditional Western hierarchy of colors. The symbolic meanings of blackness and whiteness as the novel assigns them are key in understanding the implicit ethnic nationalism of the novel's overall argument.

The millionaire's suicide later on, "as an ironic commentary on his own attempt to escape both personal misery and time" (Payne 34), is of significance for the novel's revision of the color hierarchy, because one comes to understand that the wages of exaggerated individualism are physical death (for the millionaire) or a kind of spiritual death (for the narrator, as I will show). That such selfishness is symbolically linked to whiteness is not only shown through the millionaire but also through the narrator's choice to become white after he sees a lynching, "to ally himself with the persecutors rather than the persecuted" (Fleming "Irony" 95). The lynching, as Gayle Wald argues, does not only "literally interrupt the ex-coloured man's travels, but it disrupts his fantasy of recuperating a stable 'black' self through a self-conscious immersion in black musical traditions" (38), which had been the goal of his travels. It is bitterly ironic that it is a lynching that effects his ultimate decision to pass, since, in much of African American literature, such moments cement group membership and fire a determination to work in defense of African Americans.[9] But this very antiheroism and antinationalism underlines the narrator's selfishness. Just when a communalist commitment, associated with blackness, is most needed, when the ethnic Bildungsroman form would call for a turn to the ethnic community, he turns to whiteness. When deciding to become white, the narrator feels "as weak as a man who had lost blood" (190). In a way, he has left the realm of the living. And it is through rhetoric of this kind that the novel repeatedly connects blackness to humaneness and forms of spirituality while whiteness represents materialism and a Faustian pact resulting in loss of humanity and spirituality.

At least two passages are of interest in this context. One describes the narrator's thoughts after the lynching he witnesses in the South:

> I could understand why Negroes are led to sympathize with even their worst criminals and to protect them whenever possible. By all the impulses of normal human nature they can and should do nothing less. (188)

On the one hand, the passage strongly suggests that the narrator does not consider himself African American. On the other hand, his own inaction and flight appear to be not quite human, at least by implication, even if one applies a segregational logic, which would bind only members of the same ethnic group in sympathy. But he does not subscribe to that logic, as his denouncement of southern whites, immediately following the quotation above, shows:

> I do not see how a people that can find in its conscience any excuse whatever for slowly burning to death a human being, or for tolerating such an act, can be entrusted with the salvation of a race. (188)

The narrator thus indirectly presents himself as having lost his humanity by joining such "a people" instead of acting on behalf of African Americans in some way.

The second passage of interest is more of a suggestive coincidence. When the narrator encounters his father and half sister at a Paris opera house, the performance they attend is *Faust* (Payne 33). There is something strangely befitting in this moment: the encounter of the father who is strongly associated with materialism in the narrator's youth with the son who will give up his African American heritage for economic advantage against the background of the Faustian legend about selling one's soul to the devil for worldly advantage. In the juxtaposition of those two passages, the symbolic meaning of being white or black is outlined.

The point is driven home in the much-quoted ending of the novel—"I cannot repress the thought that, after all, I have chosen the lesser part, that I have sold my birthright for a mess of pottage" (211)—which makes clear that the narrator's "externally upward [journey] . . . to material success . . . was really a fall; [his] very success was [his] failure" (Sollors *Beyond Ethnicity* 170–171). As Michael G. Cooke has pointed out, this allusion to the story of Esau "is most appropriate" since it highlights the narrator's "materialism and fear of suffering" (*Afro-American Literature* 50); however, keeping the birthright hinges "on the acceptance of blackness" (Faulkner 151). If one remembers that this birthright is both a dynastic and a spiritual one which entitles Jacob to be the continuance of a line of Jewish leaders and prophets, the opposition of blackness/birthright/spirituality to whiteness/pottage/materialism assumes its full symbolic range. Since the narrator has predominantly displayed white characteristics throughout the novel, one might say with some justification that he enacts a reverse passing which allows Johnson to critique simultaneously both his white traits and his desertion of his race—and both of these critiques are anchored in essentialist conceptualizations of ethnicity. "In explicitly critiquing their protagonists' individualized choices," Gayle Wald has said, "literary passing narratives build a critique of passing based on a theoretical and political cognizance of the collectivizing dimensions of racial discourse" (35). As America as a nation does not extend its protections to African Americans because of their race, African Americans are forced to respond as a group, as an ethnic nation. The protagonist, however, uneasily resolves the tensions brought about in his search for self by integrating into the mainstream and seeking shelter in whiteness, and the novel's polarized meanings of whiteness and blackness are anchored in nationalist conceptions of community and identity.

It is the narrator's own recognition of his reverse passing which leads him to say, "Sometimes it seems to me that I have never really been a Negro" (210). But his problematic and ambiguous stance on the question of ethnicity also makes him "feel that I have been a coward, a deserter, and I am possessed by a strange longing for my mother's people" (210). The "strange longing" hints at an essentialist conceptualization of ethnicity, the feeling that, in the tautological fashion of nationalist ideology, he should belong to his ethnic group because he is a member of it. Ethnic nationalism beckons here as the haven the protagonist never reaches. Pride in ethnic accomplishment points him there, but he prefers the tacit national identity of whiteness for his own safety.

The dualism in his feelings not only reflects his racism-induced double-consciousness but also the unresolved tensions in the novel. The narrator deplores racism and resolves to "[bring] glory and honour to the Negro race" (46), if for selfish reasons. At the same time, he tries very hard to erase the ethnic qualities of ragtime and plans to do the same for black folk music, but he also affirms ethnic essences by commenting on "natural musical instinct." His life, with its fluctuations regarding which ethnicity he belongs, illustrates the absurdity of racial categorizations, yet he faults himself for having chosen the wrong identity. Through these tensions, the novel attacks racism on the grounds of having demonstrated that it is nonsensical while at the same time arguing the corruptness of white middle-class values in implicitly opposing them to artistic achievement, spirituality, and solidarity, which are associated with a black identity.

Johnson achieves this double effect by combining the tried-and-true strategy of social constructionism inherent in the passing theme with the overall essentialism of *The Souls of Black Folk*, reflected in Du Bois's insistence on the "message" that "Negro blood has . . . for the world" (3). In concentrating either on Johnson's usage of the passing theme (the constructionist argument) or on his implicit criticism of the Ex-Coloured Man for making the wrong decision when choosing a race (the essentialist argument), one risks missing his double-pronged attack. While the novel's protagonist is both "psychologically" (as Eugenia Collier says) and (mostly) physically white and usually accepted as such by whites, the mere fact of a black ancestor suffices for that acceptance to be revoked, to be turned into exclusion and an implicit charge of inferiority even after equality, under the guise of whiteness, has been demonstrated—thus the argument of the first attack. White society is exposed as hypocritical, as applying absurd, invisible standards of admission.[10] But is admission so desirable?

The passing theme also addresses this question, as it allows the protagonist insights into two societies. Here, the second argument, essentialist in nature, comes to bear, and it does so most effectively because it plays itself out against the background of the first argument. While the protagonist's fate faults white society for its injustice, the protagonist's decision to pass exposes the materialism and selfishness that come to be seen as inherently white, while his artistic and spiritual potential is expressed through his blackness. Through this strategy, then, constructionist and essentialist argument become merged in the character of the protagonist. Because the Ex-Coloured Man enacts a reverse passing, his white characteristics are highlighted even more than his black ones and his stance towards the black community becomes, as it were, self-condemning. His final regret, then, emphasizes what the plot's delineation of whiteness and blackness have already shown: the novel inverts the hierarchy of color, particularly when it comes to the question of moral value. And while doing so, the *Autobiography* also stresses ethnic solidarity over individualism, revising the Bildungsroman genre in the process through focusing on the meaning of ethnic identity.

As Johnson would say twenty-one years later, in his autobiography: "the truth flashed over me that in large measure the race question involves the saving of black America's body and white America's soul" (318). Johnson shows his protagonist as materialistic and as artistic, as white and black, and leaves little doubt which side he should have chosen. But even as the Ex-Coloured Man's fusing of European- and African-derived musical idioms highlights his questionable motives for doing so, it also symbolically opens up the possibility that such a thing might be done. Even ethnic literature heavily invested in essentialism might accomplish more than "the establishment of a 'reverse discourse'" to racism, to use Anthony Appiah's words (59), if it critiques the notion of essence while deploying it.

The tensions created by this side-by-side use of essentialism and constructionism recur in differing form in all of the works discussed here and will prove to be endemic to the fusion of Bildungsroman and ethnic nationalism.

Haunch, Paunch and Jowl: An Anonymous Autobiography is the cynical coming-of-age story of Meyer Hirsch, son of Russian Jewish immigrants to New York's Lower East Side. His story delineates his early years in cheder and street gangs, his rise as a lawyer and politician, and his final success as a judge. As Gabriel Miller has said, "Individualism pervades the world of *Haunch, Paunch and Jowl*; Meyer absorbs it very early. The notion of communal values has all but disappeared" ("Introduction" xv). Meyer Hirsch appears as the ultimate opportunist: despite his rejection of Judaism and his highly developed egocentrism, he succeeds in gaining a reputation as a pious and zealous defender of Jews, thus gaining the political support of the Lower East Side population while having his own enrichment in mind. Regrets come through, mostly in his reflections on an unfulfilled love affair, sometimes in begrudging admiration of his idealist friends. Nonetheless, he remains the opportunist to the end, deliberately missing all chances for personal change.

An overview of the plots makes clear that there is a significant resemblance between Ornitz's and Johnson's novels. Like the *Autobiography*, *Haunch* implicitly deplores its protagonist's exaggerated individualism, juxtaposing it to a communalism and idealism that is associated with ethnicity. Like the Ex-Coloured Man, Meyer Hirsch adopts materialistic and self-serving values that the novel depicts as mainstream; the successful individuation of the classic Bildungsroman is caricatured as the protagonists exploit and distance themselves from ethnicity.

There are some obvious differences between the *Autobiography* and *Haunch*, not the least of which is that while the Ex-Coloured Man experiences his ethnicity largely as a function of the tension between black and white communities, Meyer Hirsch lives largely in a Jewish world. To that extent, the novel fulfills Gershon Shaked's observation that "American Jewish writers place less emphasis on pressure from the outside and emphasize the positive-negative bond between the characters and their identity" (78). However, while the outside world does not often exert explicit pressure in *Haunch*, its influence is both implicit and ubiquitous.

In contrast to the Ex-Coloured Man's wide traveling range, Meyer Hirsch's world is confined geographically, as he does not leave New

York, and only at times leaves the Jewish districts of New York. As a result of their differing settings for the development of their protagonists' identities, the degree of "ethnic self-consciousness" varies greatly in the two novels with regard to the psychological profiles of their protagonists: while the Ex-Coloured Man constantly contemplates questions of ethnic identity, Meyer Hirsch reflects on his Jewishness much less often, and it does not seem to pose a problem in his development, despite his early rebellion against Judaism in cheder. Nonetheless, both novels quite self-consciously thematize ethnicity, the *Autobiography* in terms of Du Boisian double-consciousness, *Haunch* in terms of "the Jewish Problem" (192), the question of how Jews as a group were to conduct their relationship with the "mainstream": through minimizing cultural differences and assimilation (and *Haunch* probes the effects of that course) or through retention of old cultural practices (an effort the novel seems to regard as doomed).

The partial difference in both protagonists' motivation for passing is important as well, as it highlights one of the discrepancies in their respective ethnic situations: Meyer rejects ethnic solidarity out of a disbelief in Judaism and a lack of emotional connection to his community and its way of life. He merely seeks his personal advancement and gratification—individualism is more important to him than ethnic solidarity or a sense of community. The Ex-Coloured Man, though, while also pursuing personal gain first and foremost and equally lacking in any commitment to the African American community, also has to face the threat of potential violence against him as an African American. As a result, the Ex-Coloured Man decides to pass completely and conceal his societally ascribed ethnic identity, while Meyer Hirsch only "passes" vis-à-vis the religiously committed Jewish community, pretending to adhere to Judaism and ethnic solidarity.

Notwithstanding these notable differences, the two novels show interesting parallels in structure, in character delineation, and—related to these two—in their rhetorical and ideological stances on ethnicity. Hand in hand with this goes a revision of the Bildungsroman. Like the *Autobiography*, *Haunch* parades the exaggerated individualism of its protagonist while censoring it at the same time, exposing it as moral flaw and as the source of Meyer Hirsch's gnawing dissatisfaction. *Haunch, Paunch and Jowl* and the *Autobiography* suggest that a renunciation of commitment to one's ethnic group in exchange for material success is both a Faustian pact and a denial of antimaterialistic traits inherent in ethnicity as the novels construct it. In outlining ethnicity in this fashion, both novels betray their debts to ethnic nationalism.

Samuel Ornitz does not seem a likely candidate for authorship of a novel indebted to Zionism. He himself favored the transethnic ideology socialism, as his novel indicates, and claimed not to have had Zionist intentions when writing the novel; instead he found "most gratifying . . . the spontaneous testimony of non-Jewish men and women . . . expressing surprise that the Jews, themselves, were reading race-consciousness into the book, while they, the non-Jews, read it as a book of general or universal significance" (Miller "Samuel Ornitz" 210).

One finds a similar dualism between ethnic consciousness and universalism (or transethnic "Americanism") in the history of American Zionism in the early decades of the twentieth century. Should American Zionists insist on a national territory in Palestine and thus risk "potential accusations of dual loyalty" (Karp 248) or should Zionism be a cultural religious movement bringing about greater cohesiveness among American Jews, serving "as a cultural force that could infuse new spirit and could create new Jews proud of their heritage" (Karp 249) while stressing their "Americanness"? Ornitz's novel stands as testimony to the fact, noted by Hasia Diner, that "both left-wing radicalism and Zionism shaped the political and ideological lives of many Jews who emigrated to the United States beginning in the 1880s" (7) and that many of the "socialist leaders were deeply committed to Jewish culture" (9). When a novel devoted to advocating a transethnic ideal shows strong nationalist traces, one can begin to understand the ideological strength of Zionism in particular and the nationalist paradigm in general in the early decades of the twentieth century.

In order to show the reader what ethnicity means, Ornitz paints a broad canvas of Jewish life in the Lower East Side. What has been said of the *Autobiography*—that it is "panoramic" in intent—holds for *Haunch* as well (Sollors *Beyond Ethnicity* 169). In the *Autobiography*, the protagonist experiences African American life in the South and in New York, in rural and in urban settings, and among people of varied class backgrounds and varied stances on ethnicity. In *Haunch, Paunch and Jowl*, one finds a variety of positions on ethnicity as well, and, as in the *Autobiography*, they are represented both by a number of characters and by the depiction of several ethnic scenarios. As Louis Harap notes, "many facets of life on the East Side in the second generation—vocational, artistic, and political—are exemplified in the lives of the book's characters" (50). In both novels, the protagonists' reaction and relation to these various facets of ethnic life play a crucial role in delineating their respective characters and in highlighting how exaggerated individualism leads to their moral doom, thus parodying both traditional Bildungsroman plots and the genre of the success autobiography.

It is worthwhile to consider the differing class affiliations or affinities of the protagonists in some of these reactions. The *Autobiography*'s protagonist has a pronounced tendency to look down on the African American working class, but Meyer Hirsch looks with disdain and envy at upper-middle-class Jews, particularly German Jews, who around the turn of the century constituted much of that class within Jewry; to that extent, the struggle with middle-class values is much more open in *Haunch* than in the *Autobiography*, where the protagonist accepts them unquestioningly.

Two minor characters who embrace assimilationist strategies illustrate this point. We have seen how the Ex-Coloured Man admires an African American doctor and his friends who in "speech and thought . . . were genuine Yankees" (153)—an admiration which may be reflective of Johnson's own "Talented Tenth" affiliations, as a number of "Talented Tenth" leaders did embrace assimilation as a strategy (see Levering Lewis "Parallels"). Meyer Hirsch, however, takes a decided dislike to Lionel Crane, an apparently passing Jewish psychologist who proposes assimilation as the solution to "the Jewish problem." His dislike, however, is not caused by Crane's ideological position but by the very fact that the latter acts like a "genuine Yankee." His first reaction on meeting Crane shows this:

> Where did he get the bang-up snobbish name—doesn't go with his face. . . . On the spot I disliked him, this Lionel Crane, né (Harvard matriculation) plain, vulgar Lazarus Cohen. Like velvet rubbed the wrong way, sickeningly soft, creepily irritating, was his meticulous, modulated speech with its heavy Harvard accent. It cloyed. Inconsonant in him, not by his right, therefore an affectation, I felt, as were his distinguished manners. (191)

Though Meyer admits that jealousy might play a role in his assessment, since Esther, a woman he admires, seems to like Crane, his criticism immediately focuses on those features which seem to betray upper- or upper-middle-class affiliation, such as manners and speech. Given Meyer's own earlier constructionist assertion that "you are nothing but what people think you are" (74), his sudden conversion to a more essentialist position comes as a surprise: Crane, according to Meyer, does not have a right to behave like a New Englander, to adopt ways not native to his ethnic culture. Since he detects a dissonance in Crane's "Harvard affectation," Meyer suggests that Crane finds himself unable to hide his Jewishness, and that Jewishness somehow would be more natural to him, just as he, presumably, would not experience a Harvard accent as "creepily irritating" on a New Englander.

The contradiction in Meyer's stance—while also related to jealousy and the narrator's unreliability, which will be the subject of further elaborations—indicates the wariness with which one has to regard Meyer's view of Crane, though there are moments in which Crane appears as if he were meant to be taken as a stand-in for the author. A representative passage from Crane's pronouncements may illustrate this point:

> here, in America, shall we condone usury, faginism, receiving stolen goods, corrupting officials, procuring, brothel-keeping, sharp-dealing, legitimatising the cheating and overcharging of Gentiles, labor-sweating? . . . And they are but a handful comparatively, this riffraff, this scum of the wretched, cynical Continental civilization. Because the Professional Jews won't permit criticism and house-cleaning this handful of riffraff is made representative of the great population of poverty-stricken, hard-working, clean-living, simple, law-abiding Jews . . . So they stifle criticism, these Professional Jews who are doing nothing but working on their lucrative jobs of appealing to the racial vanity of their people. . . . What if the criticism pierces like the probing, cleansing lancet, and burns and pains like antiseptic poured on festering sores? (199)

Crane's litany of the "Professional Jews'" misdeeds reads very much like a description of Meyer's career, and since Meyer is the antihero of the novel, one who opposes the likes of him would seem to voice the author's viewpoint. In addition, the passage compares well to what Ornitz told an interviewer about his motivations for writing the novel: "I kept thinking the East Side leaders were a rotten example. The boys and girls I knew, brought up between two cultures, had caught with racial idealism the spirit of the New World. Then they grew older and saw the successful of their people playing a mean and sordid game" (Miller "Samuel Ornitz" 209). The juxtaposition of ruthless materialism and "probing, cleansing" criticism implicit in Ornitz's comment appears to be the juxtaposition of Meyer Hirsch and Lionel Crane.

However, several factors undermine Crane as a character and therefore make his pronouncements subject to suspicion: for one, his description of Jews has marked anti-Semitic overtones that are steeped in middle-class notions of respectability. When one hears him berating a "Jewish way" of dressing, one cannot help but remember "his English cut clothes, his simple cane, pince-nez with its little black streamer" (192) and is forced to read his descriptions of "bizarre Jewishness" against the background of his own outfit:

> The Jews will create a Jewish Question in America as long as they cling to their bizarre Jewishness . . . What calls immediate, curious attention to the Jews . . . his outlandish ways and attire—his beards and ear-locks. . . . He is always the repellent foreigner awakening unpleasant associations of the historically misrepresented Jew . . . his slovenly, baggy clothes, or his overdressed, bejeweled, flashy appearance; his blatancy and vulgarity. (198)

Ultimately, this sounds a lot more like the Ex-Coloured Man in a bout of extreme, even self-destructive, double-consciousness than like the socialist Samuel Badisch Ornitz. Though the novel embraces socialism, a transethnic ideology that might also encourage the shedding of ethnic specificity, much of Crane's criticism expresses his character's limitations and cannot be taken as the author's position.

What finally makes Crane—to whom I devote so much time because his speeches appear as the longest uninterrupted sermon on Jewishness in the novel—suspect is that he, too, succumbs, like Meyer, to mammon's lure, fulfilling Meyer's cynical expectations:

> I had a sneaking feeling that giving Crane a good job and a chance to mix with the higher-ups, he would play the game, and forget his crusade against the Professional Jew and his theory of intermarriage as the saving tonic for the Jewish race. And I wasn't far from right, for Crane sought eagerly the job of establishing a social settlement under the patronage of the exclusive Fifth Avenue Temple. (260)

By discrediting Crane in this way, the novel also distances itself from an extreme assimilationist position.

David Martin Fine explains that "Ornitz sets Hirsch off against ancillary characters, each offering a gloss on his career" (27), and arguably, no character plays a more important role in the delineation of Meyer's character than Esther, a neighborhood girl he befriends. She has been variously described as the principle of pure innocence (Dittmar 166) or as "the romantic symbol of peoplehood" (Guttmann *Jewish Writer* 37), making clear that she serves a symbolic function. She is beyond the factionism of the East Side youngsters, whether atheist, socialist, pious, or materialist; she "is a girl . . . whom we all respect. She is natural" (75), Meyer says of her. Possessing an unearthly beauty, she enraptures the entire neighborhood, or at least its young male component: "Esther is their deity, before whose altar they offer their ideals for consecration. She exalts them into high resolve" (122). Her kindness and purity even subdues Meyer: "Her beauty was too much for me. I fell to my knees . . . I was worshipful, too" (123).

Through religious diction, the novel establishes Esther as a kind of Muse, an embodiment of goodness, purity, and altruism. That she is liked by everyone in her ethnic neighborhood, is kind to everyone, and devotes herself to social causes suggests that she is indeed a Lower East Side angel, a personification of an idealized Lower East Side. In that context, it is significant that she later marries a Gentile millionaire, also devoted to social causes, as that reveals a seemingly problematic element in the novel's ideology. Though having the most spiritualized Jewish character marry a Gentile millionaire might call into question the novel's stance against acquisitiveness, his devotion to social causes mitigates this potential contradiction and points to the importance the novel gives to causes, the devotion to which has the potential of overcoming boundaries of class, ethnicity, and religion.

At the same time, Esther also functions as a kind of consciousness of the Jewish community. To illustrate: when some of Meyer's former gang friends are indicted for murder, she feels "that under other conditions these condemned murderers might have been of some good to themselves and their community" (236), and the book shows her working towards such improved conditions. Seeing her as a symbol of Lower East Side Jewry and ethnicity is also useful in understanding Meyer Hirsch's reaction to her and ultimately points to the content which *Haunch* gives ethnicity.

When one sees Meyer as incapable of understanding Esther's altruism, one understands how out of touch he is with high moral ideals that, since Esther personifies them, arguably represent idealized ethnicity as the novel constructs it:

Esther was heartbroken over Davie [a common friend who has just died], and she was looking for forgetfulness and consolation in giving her life to the children of the East Side. Esther looked out on the water, and my spirits sank as I saw the calm repose of her face and her eyes alight with joy at the beauty of the sky and sea. And she was more baffling than ever to me. (162)

Meyer appears to be incapable of comprehending altruism to the extent that he has to ascribe Esther's devoting her life to children to a broken heart. Even so, he also sees that her actions come out of an inner restfulness. The passage aestheticizes altruism, establishing links between selflessness, spirituality, aesthetics, and ethnicity that we have already seen similarly in the *Autobiography* in its treatment of African American music, particularly at the camp meeting. (We will see a similar view of ethnicity at work in *Plum Bun* and *Fanny Herself.*) Here, Meyer's inability to understand Esther, whom everyone else in the novel seems to have no trouble understanding, marks him as an outcast; in Bernard Sherman's words, "Meyer's evil character is not simply the stereotype of the Jew of English literature brought to these shores. . . . [T]his is a tale of the deviating Jew" (57).

Esther's symbolic meaning emerges perhaps most clearly when Meyer almost gives in to some part of himself that wants to marry her. Just before he virtually proposes to her, he realizes the gulf between them: "She seems to live in a world wholly apart from mine. She teaches school and directs girls' clubs in the little social settlement Barney Finn started with his aunt's money" (186). A life committed to social service for one's ethnic group contrasts so greatly with his own that he expresses the difference in terms of differing universes. Yet, there is an attraction:

Her sentient charm takes me away from Meyer Hirsch, ever present before my eyes in a Narcissus reflection. I quail before her clear, broad understanding. . . . And yet I do not for a second think of marrying her. Ambition is my undying desire. Marriage must socially and financially further my ambition. . . . Career. Ambition. Greatness. Honor. Wealth. High Places. Look out! A dream-stupefied girl. Nowhere: that's where you will get with her. Nowhere. Nowhere . . . But I do not heed the warning din. I shut my eyes to the conjuring high places . . . I put out my hand. All that I held precious—those jewels I had crystallized from life—lay in my hand, held out to her. What if Esther had taken it? . . . would I now be writing a different history of Meyer Hirsch? Ignoring my appeal, disdainful of what I had to proffer, she drew herself away. (187–188)

Embodying selflessness, Esther is able to rupture Meyer's self-focus. But in the choice between a selfless life committed to social work in the Lower East Side and a career devoted to acquiring power and material wealth, he firmly subscribes to the latter—until a moment of weakness. Because the novel takes great pains to establish Meyer as a ruthless and cynical materialist, and because of his "account of his rise" as "self-justifying" (Fine 27), his repeated yearnings for what Esther symbolizes seem almost out of character and might be seen as suggesting a drive towards altruism also manifested, successfully, in a number of his childhood friends. Here is the "racial idealism" Ornitz mentioned. Meyer follows materialism and power hunger, with which ethnic idealism is incompatible, and Esther, given that she personifies the ethnic idealism, rejects "all that [Meyer holds] precious." Materialism and ethnic idealism are irreconcilable, as the Ex-Coloured Man's career also shows.

And just like the *Autobiography*'s protagonist, Meyer wonders wistfully how his life would have turned out had he followed Esther's route: "there is a muted regret about abandoning the spiritual values of an earlier generation. Hirsch never succeeds in winning the love of Esther, a girl who eventually devotes her life to serving the poor, and this loss is a recurring source of regret to him" (Miller "Samuel Ornitz" 209–210). Doubts about his life course follow him until the very end of the novel. He sits at home, in a somewhat melancholic mood, hearing his wife Gretel sing a song that one of his childhood friends had composed and that his mistress "Margot had made its refrain famous, something about . . . 'tell me, life, tell me, what's it all about'" (300). At that moment, Gretel calls him:

> "Come, Meyer, come and eat. I got something you like. Gedampfte brust und patate lahtkes" [potted breast and potato pancakes] . . . I heave my great bulk and waddle towards the dining room . . . Again Gretel sings . . . "Tell me, life, tell me, what's it all about; tell me, life, what's it all about?" . . .
> What—
> It smells good.
> Gedampfte brust und patate lahtkes— (300)

Here we have another case of "mess of pottage," one might say. Meyer is called to the meal as he attempts to ponder the meaning of his life; the meal, however, dispels such thoughts, and again he chooses the immediate and materialist over the long-term and idealist, the irony being, of course, that the pottage is an ethnic one.

Both Johnson and Ornitz respond to the autobiographical success story as a well-known genre of the time by questioning the price of that success (Rideout 119, Vauthier 174). By juxtaposing Esther to Meyer, Ornitz also provides an alternative model of identity formation or Bildung. Rather than extolling individualism, this model promotes idealism and ethnic solidarity, in keeping both with the ethnic revision of the Bildungsroman and ethnic nationalism. But not only the late-in-life regrets are common to Meyer and the Ex-Coloured Man; the journey to that place bears some similarities as well.

Their dominant character trait—selfishness—plays a crucial role in that journey and reveals itself early in group interaction. A childhood scene is paradigmatic in both novels. Early in the *Autobiography*, the protagonist tries to find a place for himself on his first day of class:

> The teacher had strung the class promiscuously round the walls of the room for a sort of trial heat for places of rank; when the line was straightened out, I found that by skilful maneuvering I had placed myself third and had piloted "Red Head" to the place next to me. (11)

This passage can be read against a crucial scene in *Haunch* in which the protagonist attempts to become part of a street gang in his neighborhood:

> The gang is huddled about the wood fire in a grocer's milk can with large holes cut out for vents. It is a compact circle seated shoulder to shoulder on assorted boxes. I long, passionately, to be part of it. . . . [A] daring idea is born . . . I pull Hymie, the twelfth leader, from his place. . . . The surprise attack gives me an edge on him, and soon Hymie is persuaded to relinquish his place at the fire and the twelfth leadership. And the thirteenth leader by inaction and silence abdicates his right. (18)

Both of these passages are from the early parts of the novels and help to delineate the characters of the respective protagonists. Both of them struggle for a place in a hierarchical order, and they both achieve their goals by a mixture of scheming and action. This strategy, enacted here in childhood play, also propels them to material success in their adult years and, to that extent, these early scenes foreshadow the later plot and hint at the protagonists' main character flaw: selfishness.

Even what appears to be motivated by altruism in the *Autobiography*, the protagonist's placing of "Red Head" next to him in line, is a calculated move to ensure Red Head's friendship, since, as the protagonist informs us, he "had been quick enough to see that a big, strong boy was a friend to be desired at a public school" (11). The protagonist of *Haunch*, too, develops a friendship with the strongest boy in the neighborhood, the leader of the gang: "I take my place next to Boolkie, as self-appointed adviser, strategist—anything—except fighter" (35). Both protagonists pursue their goals through manipulation of people and circumstances rather than through reliance on their own strength, and in this, one may see the seed of what the novels develop as a full-fledged lack of commitment to the protagonists' ethnic group when faced with danger or with the choice of personal success versus ethnic solidarity.

This lack of commitment is rooted in selfishness, a trait the two passages above illustrate. Rather than being concerned with the group as a whole, the protagonists vie for a prominent place in the group, a place that will bring *them* advantages, not the group. The group thus becomes a vehicle of advancement, not something the protagonists see themselves as an integral part of. The plots of the novels confirm what these microcosmic episodes predict: both main characters will use aspects of their ethnic groups for personal gain but will not take part in their group's struggle for social justice.

Accordingly, both protagonists often adopt a constructionist view of ethnicity because that turns out to be the most pragmatic stance. The Ex-Coloured Man's decision to "let the world take me for what it would" (190) is mirrored by a crucial passage in *Haunch*—crucial because it marks his decision to pass as a pious Jew:

> I feel keenly responsive to all the flow and activity about me. I am thinking hard of how I am going to fit into it all. I try to be as impressive as I know how with the greenhorns . . . How I thrill to it—what people think. I am convinced that is the big thing in life, there is nothing else; *you are nothing but what people think you are.* . . . The pious say, that's the clever lad who harangued the congregation in Hebrew so eloquently . . . The worldly say, he's got a practical head, is a school graduate. (73–74 [emphasis mine])

Meyer Hirsch's chameleon-like intention "to fit" people's expectations—in fact, "The Chameleon" was one of the titles Johnson considered for *his* novel—emphasizes social constructedness. However, unlike the protagonist of the *Autobiography*, Meyer Hirsch's decision to be all things for all people is made deliberately, without pressure, and without an ill-concealed desire to justify his actions. What he says about his fellow gang members applies to his perception of his congregation as well: "I looked upon every one of these boastful fools as rich meat and drink for me" (74); all of them are potential customers since he intends to become a lawyer.

Detachment of the protagonist from his ethnic group is a prominent feature in both novels, though it finds expression in different ways. While the Ex-Coloured Man breaks away from African American surroundings throughout the narrative and ultimately so at the end of the novel, Meyer Hirsch stays closely connected physically with Jews, as he lives in the Lower East Side and serves as an elected representative of his community. Even after achieving material success, he merely moves to a part of town populated by wealthy escapees from the Lower East Side, so that his detachment never leads to the same outright rejection of the ethnic group as the Ex-Coloured Man enacts it. Nevertheless, the emotional distance of the protagonists from African Americans and Jewish Americans respectively is equally severe. The detachment in and of itself speaks for the constructedness of ethnicity, as it shows that affinity for one's ethnic group is not inherent. Their emotional distance from their ethnic groups also makes identification with the protagonists exceedingly difficult—and in this, the novels differ from the traditional Bildungsroman—as the reader is repeatedly surprised by an obvious lack of emotion on their part.

At the same time, *Haunch*, like the *Autobiography*, ultimately condemns the lack of attachment of its protagonist. Their stories serve as warnings and as implicit calls for ethnic commitment. Meyer Hirsch, though living among Jews, disdains and rejects Judaism. As he says, "on my confirmation day I simply felt,—I can't swallow that bunk: I puke it right back" (63). However, he keeps practicing its outward forms for personal gain, while he uses and abuses other Jews to attain wealth and prominence. For both protagonists, however, there is ambiguity in this detachment. The Ex-Coloured Man is moved by spirituals and by "Singing Johnson"; Meyer Hirsch is attracted to Esther, who personifies Jewish altruism. When crisis situations demand commitment (a lynching in the *Autobiography*, unionism and possible revenge for the execution of Meyer's friends in *Haunch*), selfishness and materialism prove to be the stronger motivations for both protagonists. But the ambiguity in their detachment implicitly seems to point the way to how the novels would have the protagonists behave and feel, and thus they suggest ethnic solidarity as the better course while they give detachment from the ethnic community a taint of the unnatural.

I have already tried to show this for the Ex-Coloured Man, who does not show "all the impulses of normal human nature" after he sees a lynching (188). Meyer Hirsch's reaction to finding himself in the position of having the murderer of his friends at his mercy has similar unnatural overtones. The Governor has refused to transform his three gang friends' death sentences for a robbery in which Dope Ikie Schneider, a mentally disabled gang member, kills a ticket agent.

> When the Governor and I met again I had one of his personal friends in a black pocket. I had him cornered. This friend of the Governor's, a prominent society man, member of an old aristocratic American family, was found out as an unspeakable criminal, a corrupter of children, a poisoner of the spring of womanhood. And this same Governor bought me off, bought me off to suppress the evidence. (237–238)

What he receives for suppressing evidence is a judgeship. We thus see him as eager to join the ranks of those who have created the system that has led many of his Lower East Side friends into a life of crime, emulating the ruthless materialism they see. By accepting the judgeship in return for eschewing the possibility of avenging his friends' deaths, he aligns himself with the forces the above passage mockingly denounces, becoming a criminal, corrupter, and poisoner himself, leaving his ethnic friends' memories behind for the rewards of the mainstream. The classic Bildungsroman's (re)integration into the mainstream thus functions here as a kind of betrayal of ethnicity.[11]

The critique of materialism that both novels present is thus embedded in their protagonists' personalities. While this would seem to point to genetic predisposition and essentialism, the development of both characters is shown as a response to their environments. Both protagonists are shown to emulate materialism and, as products of materialism, their character flaws imply a connection between the socioeconomic system and individual behavior that calls into question the notion of individual formation usually implicit in the European Bildungsroman.

Meyer Hirsch's Uncle Philip functions as an important influence in this respect. When Meyer is still young, his uncle decides to become a capitalist and voices what may be regarded as his new creed:

> There's nothing self-sustaining. Everything lives off something else. The stronger element absorbs the weaker. The weak lives only to nourish the strong . . . [W]e capitalists, . . . we who see life, the earth, its forces and elements, just for what they are, are going to organize and control the world. We will be kings of a new order: the empire of efficiency. We will be a driving force as merciless as nature for results. (100–101)

A strong element of Social Darwinism imbues his beliefs; interestingly, he links his views of the world specifically to living in the U.S., or rather, living in the U.S. enables him to put them into practice. Accordingly, Bernard Sherman notes that it is "a result of their Americanization [that] both men [Philip and Meyer] are untouched by the moral strictures of Judaism" (56–57). When challenged by his sister to have mercy on his future employees, whom he expects to exploit ruthlessly, or at least to open up a union shop, Uncle Philip cynically replies: "It's a good thing," he says, "this is a free country and I can exploit whom I like" (104). Materialism thus appears to oppose ethnic (and class) solidarity—or group cohesiveness can be made to serve exploitive ends, since the workers whom Philip will exploit are all Jewish. More than that, according to the novel, materialism in some cases erases ethnicity; Philip announces to his nephew: "Meyer, we've got nothing to look back to. It's up to us to be ancestors" (105). Unaware of how he is shaped by his environment, Philip regards himself as the ultimate individualist: he does not even have ancestors. As the novel has it, the ethnic past must be renounced for a capitalist future, in accordance with the maxim that both novels establish: the apparent incompatibility of ethnicity and materialism.

Meyer Hirsch absorbs these lessons well. Later in the novel, he contemplates the path some second-generation Lower East Siders have taken. While the frankness of his assessment befits his character, the cynicism bespeaks Ornitz's intention to expose "a mean and sordid game":

> They didn't want to become needle workers; they saw the hell of a life their fathers led. And what of the ambitious fellows who looked

for economic salvation in business and professional life? A few rubs
of the rough-grained world wore away the idealistic tenderness and
left them with a protective skin of callousness. It did not take them
long to see that the straight and narrow path was long and tortuous
and ended in a blind alley. There was nothing in the conspicuous
examples of American life to inspire anything else. Politics stank of
corruption and chicanery. Big business set even a worse example.
Daily the people were treated to scandal after scandal in commerce,
industry and government . . . The order of the day was—PLAY
THE GAME AS YOU SEE IT PLAYED. (226–227)

The religious overtones of the passage highlight the incompatibility of
idealized ethnicity as the novel constructs it and materialism. What some
of Meyer's former companions and he himself are seeking is "economic
salvation," not the spiritual one their parents sought with a determination which allowed them to stay on the "straight and narrow path."
The passage strongly emphasizes the negative and corrupting impact
of the dominant social environment on the ethnic individual. In a self-
justifying move, Meyer shows that "America" corrodes ethnicity and
replaces it with Social Darwinism.

The novel illustrates the negative impact of that order by providing alternative models of behavior. Singing Johnson makes for such a
model in the *Autobiography*, Esther and Avrum Toledo play this role
in *Haunch*. They are depicted with a certain reverence even by Meyer.
Particularly in his eulogy on Avrum Toledo, however, in which the
latter is quoted in his own words, silencing the novel's cynicism for
a moment, we see a good example of the novel's transethnic (or,
one might even say, assimilationist) ideology which seems at odds with
the ideal of ethnic idealism as it is implied in other passages of the
novel:

In the little office of the settlement Avrum told Esther, "I find that
there is no such thing, as yet, as an American workman. . . . They
look down upon each other from the heights of their nationalism.
. . . But it will be different when the workers of America become
a racial identity. . . . When we break down the class lines, the snob-
bery of nationalism, replace it with a commonality of spirit, then
labor in its dignity and knowledge will share equally with capital
the good things of the earth." (224–225)

Avrum, socialism personified, and an important element in Ornitz's "destructive foray against capitalist society" (Rideout 118), talks to Esther, embodiment of spiritual and altruistic ethnicity, about long-term amalgamation which Esther herself seems to perform in her marriage to Barney Finn. He sees the aggressive potential of nationalism and wishes to replace it with class-based solidarity. Yet, though he speaks to Esther, who personifies the positive potential of ethnic solidarity, Avrum appears not to differentiate between ethnic and American nationalism ("heights of their nationalism"). Thus, the novel exhibits some tensions here between transethnic and ethnic idealism.

David Levering Lewis has pointed out common strategies of African American and Jewish elites in the first decades of the twentieth century. He sees their efforts as largely transethnic or assimilationist. Some of the same personages who figure in my narrative on nationalism serve, paradoxically, his on acculturation: Louis Brandeis, James Weldon Johnson, and W. E. B. Du Bois. This may be explained, however, through the varying positions each of these have held during their careers as public figures and through Levering Lewis's caveat that "the same spokesperson could and, frequently enough, did endorse opposite convictions" ("Parallels" 18). Nonetheless, he comes to the conclusion that "Du Boisian Pan-Africanism was strikingly similar to the intellectual Zionism of Brandeis" ("Parallels" 26). This apparent contradiction seems to have been something of a cultural phenomenon: George Hutchinson maintains that in the pages of the *Messenger*, next to the *Crisis* and *Opportunity*, one of the important Harlem Renaissance magazines, "Race pride did not conflict with a militant integrationism or even assimilationism; it seems, overall, to have been considered essential to achievement of true integration. Thus J. A. Rogers, one of the most persevering historians of global black achievement, was at the same time an avowed proponent of American 'amalgamation'" ("Mediating" 533).

The tension between assimilation or acceptance as full citizens and ethnic distinctiveness—maybe best explained through a "transitional essentialism"—underlies some of the novels as well. As I will show, Yezierska's novel might be the most explicit example of it, but the spiritual ideal of ethnicity suggested in *Haunch* and the *Autobiography* (as well as in *Plum Bun* and *Fanny Herself*) partakes in this tension through its essentialist/universalist duality. But even in assimilationist circles, the appeal to a common and distinctive legacy of suffering was made.

Levering Lewis quotes the prominent Jewish American jurist Louis Marshall speaking to an NAACP convention in 1926: "I belong to an ancient race which has had even longer experience of oppression than you have" ("Parallels" 19).

The coexistence of ethnic solidarity with transethnic ideals is not unique to Ornitz's novel, though its aggressive promulgation of the latter might be, explaining some of the negative reaction the novel caused in parts of the Jewish community. Even conservatives such as banker Jacob H. Schiff did not see ethnicity and transethnic Americanism as antithetical. According to David Levering Lewis, "Jacob Schiff would never have considered personal religious conversion," yet he believed that "[e]thnic pride . . . could be sublimated in the dogma of unexceptionable public conformity to the best ideals and behavior of white Anglo-Saxon Protestant (WASP) America—the better to guarantee private space for retention of what was most precious in minority culture" ("Parallels" 18). But what is "most precious in minority culture"? Avrum and Esther and a variety of socially committed Jews who all receive sympathetic depiction make one wonder whether commitment to social causes and altruism in itself might not be the sign of ethnicity in the novel, even if it is meant to lead to transethnic goals. Since deciding on their selfish course leads to negative results for both protagonists (unhappiness for the Ex-Coloured Man, an almost unmanageable body and melancholy for Meyer—as Walter Rideout notes, "the grotesqueness of capitalism appears concentrated in a Meyer grown . . . monstrously fat" [119])—one might say that while the protagonists' deviation shows that there is no *essential* ethnic behavior, the novels suggest that there is a *correct* one.

A second strategy through which this is accomplished is the depiction of the protagonists as self-serving users of important traits of their respective communities' ethnic cultures—indeed those traits that often serve to help define those cultures: music and religion. The Ex-Coloured Man sees music as his ticket to fame. While he purports to wish to gain acceptance for African Americans through making their music known to a white audience, the strategy which he means to employ (to classicize spirituals and ragtime) entails emptying the music of its ethnic form, if not its content. Similarly, Meyer Hirsch intends to use Judaism to his worldly advantage, though he does not hide his intent from the reader, while the Ex-Coloured Man never admits to selfish motives. In his youth, Meyer finds that pious behavior serves as a successful cover for stealing—"My ways are modest, my talk quiet, respectful, aye, pious, and thus I beguile the storekeeper whilst my accomplice lifts and loads" (30)—a lesson he never forgets. As a politician, he visits the synagogue to appear religious, knowing this will gain him the goodwill and the votes of his district. Particularly on Jewish holidays, he makes sure to put in an appearance in front of his potential clients (Dittmar 166). Indeed, on those occasions, he might be said to be passing for Jewish. Like the musical education the Ex-Coloured Man receives from his mother, a Talmudic education helps Meyer and particularly his law partner Maxie to further their position in the world. The latter "finds law a cinch after the heart-breaking intricacies of the Talmud" (120). Talmudic reasoning skills and a cover of piousness gain them entrance into circles of customers otherwise closed to them.

In both novels, the use for gain of these signs of ethnicity is implicitly condemned. As it is the *use* of ethnicity to monetary advantage that leads to a kind of assimilation (in behavior) into the dominant economic structure in *Haunch* and in the *Autobiography*, a spiritualized ethnicity becomes a sign of resistance against the mainstream. In *Haunch*, the fate of both Rabbi Zucker and the idealists shows this. Rabbi Zucker attempts to shut down Allen Street, the red light district of the Lower East Side, which is seen as an outgrowth of a market-oriented, materialist society. The diction of the sentence summing up its description makes that clear: "A busy, noisy *mart* . . . highly *profitable* to cadets, landlords, politicians and policemen" (54 [emphasis mine]). In his attempt, he is struck down: "Just one blow, well placed, and Rov Zucker toppled to the gutter. A wounded cry went up, not from the Rabbi, but from the onlooking people, as blood gushed from the old man's forehead" (58). In *Haunch*, his fate symbolizes the fate of Judaism under capitalism, but also shows that the Jewish community, while apparently unable to help, deplores that fate.

The idealists reject Judaism but not their Jewish neighbors, and they do not abuse Judaism to further personal goals. They personify the transformation of Judaism into worldly philosophies. While socialism or trade unionism, their avowed creeds, are transethnic or universalist goals, they also aim for reform of a vaguely spiritual kind (as does the Rabbi). Even Meyer recognizes that: "In the East Side the radicals were making headway. Were they bringing spiritual fare for the spiritually hungry?" (296–297).

The religious spirituality of Judaism, however, has now been changed to a striving for secular intellectual and artistic culture, or as Meyer calls it, a "fanatic cult of intellectualism . . . a fine-frenzied idealism . . . art, literature, music, social science and politics in the pure meaning of the word" (297). The work these idealists do, though, is predominantly in and for their ethnic community. As Werner Sollors has shown for the *Autobiography* and Abraham Cahan's *The Rise of David Levinsky,* "It is the visionary, artistic and socially engaged quality somehow associated with descent which [the protagonists] . . . have surrendered to selfishness and practical success" (*Beyond Ethnicity* 171).[12] The novel, then, appears to reject (Meyer's) assimilation into the existing social order, which it depicts as corrupt; shows as praiseworthy those characters who work for their ethnic community (and beyond); and embraces transethnic ideologies.

In effect, however, *Haunch* calls for an assimilation into a society which does not yet exist, a socialist society in which ethnicity has ceased to matter and transforms itself into a universal culture. The *Autobiography* also expresses support for a kind of communalism in the "Singing Johnson" scene, in which matters of class or color seem suspended in a communal ritual. However, the explicit emphasis is on ethnicity here, since the camp meeting is an African American one, and the form it takes—its songs and its interactions between the audience and the preacher or singer—is specifically African American. The communalism depicted here is thus an ethnic one, not aiming at transethnic goals politically. However, since the ritual is a Christian one, one could say that the final goal of this communalism is transethnic as well.

But as already mentioned, the advocacy of transethnic goals does not necessarily preclude pride in ethnic culture, even though both stances tend to be aligned with the opposing stances of universalism and essentialism, respectively. *Haunch,* like the *Autobiography,* shows an awareness of the African American origin of ragtime music and also of its commercial uses: "The negroes had given America its music. Soon the white man started stealing the negro's music and making it his own. There was money in the negro's music" (146).

Unlike the *Autobiography,* Ornitz's novel emphasizes the Jewish role in the development of ragtime and claims certain inventions as Jewish in origin, clearly distinguishing Jewish from white. James Weldon Johnson accedes in his autobiography that, "This lighter music has been fused and then developed, chiefly by Jewish musicians, until it has become our national medium for expressing ourselves in popular form"

(*Along This Way* 328). However, since ragtime is part of his argument for an essential nonmaterialistic African American culture in the *Autobiography*, that novel does not emphasize Jewish participation in ragtime's development. That task falls to Ornitz; in *Haunch*, not only music but also dance become expressive of Jewish cultural accomplishments. When Meyer and his friends need money for school, they form a singing quartet under the management of Al Wolff, a cantor's son who has "deserted the synagogue for the theatre" (125) and is thus one more of the many characters symbolic of the novel's focus on worldliness and the transformation of Jewish cultural values. "Al introduced the Bowery Wiggle. . . . It was the father and forerunner of the Turkey Trot and modern dancing" (147).

Al also claims counterpoint as a Jewish invention. When the piano player the quartet works with, O'Brien, compares Al's method to that of sixteenth-century composer Palestrina, Al responds, "Palestrina, me eye . . . that's my old man's method. He is a chazan. You know what that is, a cantor. He got the method from his father, and his father from his father, and so on. Say, Palestrina must be some four-flusher. The method is as old as the Jews" (149). As Jeffrey Melnick notes, Ornitz "introduces the idea that Jews—through a paternal legacy of cantorial music—not only are qualified to produce ragtime and jazz, but are actually previous to it: musical ancestors" (*A Right* 90).

But counterpoint is not the only arena expressive of Jewish creativity: "Al tells him, 'Well, kid, jazz her up.' It was the beginning of their use of the word 'jazz.' Whenever they appropriated a melody or strain they simply jazzed it up into one of their syncopated hodgepodges" (160). Even syncopation is claimed as Jewish. In the relative absence of religion in both the *Autobiography* and *Haunch*, music and dance come to partly fill the gap left by religion. Though both books also recognize that culture may become mammon's servant, their open admiration of creative energy and their eagerness to claim cultural phenomena as originating with their respective ethnic groups makes clear that art in its various forms signifies ethnicity. Indeed, Melnick argues that music, and especially Black music, played an important part in Jewish cultural identity:

> music industry figures such as Irving Berlin, George Gershwin [and others] established Jewish agility at expressing and disseminating Black sounds and themes as a product of Jewish suffering and as a

variant of Jewish cultural nationalism. In direct competition with the
Black cultural nationalism of Harlem in the 1920s and 1930s, these
Jews . . . organized Broadway and Tin Pan Alley as central sites of
Jewish cultural productions. (*A Right* 12–13).

The very pride about dance and music displayed in *Haunch* indicates
that Ornitz, despite his universalist aspirations, is not willing to let go
of expressions that can be firmly tied to a particular ethnicity. And this
pride in ethnic accomplishment points to ethnic solidarity as one of the
novel's ideals, which is juxtaposed to an (exaggerated and parodied) individualism, which, in turn, is the mark of traditional Bildungsroman.[13]

Moreover, in both novels, the critique of the dominant culture is
expressed through both an essentialist and a constructionist rhetoric.
Haunch, Paunch and Jowl achieves this double strategy by showing, on
the one hand, a panoramic view of Lower East Side life, both as far as
Jewish fates and Jewish opinions are concerned, and by pointedly titling
a subchapter "Jews Are Not Jews: They Are American Jews, German
Jews, English, Galician, Lithuanian, and so on, Geographically, Jews"
(92). In that respect, Ornitz sounds remarkably like Johnson when the
latter has the Ex-Coloured Man commenting on the adaptability of
people of African descent: "I have seen the black West Indian gen-
tleman in London, and he is in speech and manners a perfect English-
man. I have seen natives of Haiti and Martinique in Paris, and they
are more Frenchy than a Frenchman. I have no doubt that the Negro
would make a good Chinaman" (153). On the other hand, both Meyer's
pride in ethnic inventions and his almost lifelong struggle with his
infatuation for Esther, personification of all that is noble in the Lower
East Side, suggest that there are certain essences in being Jewish which
appear to have a natural attraction for Meyer and which he must overcome to be the ruthless careerist that he is.

The novels link artistry and spirituality to ethnicity and implicitly
advocate kinds of ethnic communalisms that are vaguely nationalist,
though their protagonists fail to live up to these ideals. Like the *Autobiography, Haunch, Paunch and Jowl* shows that there is no such thing
as essential ethnicity, but exposes the protagonist as a "deviating ethnic." It will be left to the last chapter to more fully explore the origins
of this apparent contradiction.

CHAPTER TWO

Fanny Herself and *Plum Bun*:
Art and Ethnic Solidarity

essie Fauset's *Plum Bun* was published in 1929 by Frederick E. Stokes in the U.S. and by Elkin, Mathews and Marrot in London, receiving mostly positive reviews upon appearance. Criticism of it, however, focused on its gentility and middle-class values, a charge leveled against Fauset's work in general. As Carolyn Wedin Sylvander says, "Her work has been said to reflect the respectable, proper, educated, imitation-white values and goals of the elite Black American, divorced from the Black masses and from the wealth of folk art which is nourished by and nourishes those masses" (1). While Fauset herself, as a Cornell-educated scholar, as literary editor of the *Crisis*, and as one of the central personalities of the Harlem Renaissance, was one of the "Talented Tenth," it would be reductive to read her work as elitist, and Jacquelyn McLendon rightly claims that "[c]ritical discomfort with the so-called bourgeois ethos of Fauset's . . . novels" (2) has been caused by focusing too much on Fauset's own class affiliation.

Of course, Jessie Fauset's own life story does enter the novel in a number of ways: Angela Murray's early school experience, for example, mirrors Fauset's. As she revealed in an interview in 1929: "I happened to be the only colored girl in my classes at high school, and I'll never forget the agony I endured on entrance day when the white girls with whom I had played and studied through the graded schools, refused to acknowledge my greeting" (Sylvander 27).

At the same time, Fauset's ideology may have been more Pan-Africanist and nationalist than she is usually given credit for. In an article on "Impressions of the Second Pan-African Congress" in the *Crisis* of November 1921, Fauset wrote, "All the possibilities of all black men are needed to weld together the black men of the world against the day when black and white meet to do battle" (Sylvander 112). It is this ideology that ultimately informs *Plum Bun*, even if in decidedly less militaristic terms. One answer to Carol Allen's question "How then does an intellectual who devotes a great deal of her time to nations and pan-cooperative organizations come to write four novels that concentrate so intensely on the home?" (53), a question asked in reference to Fauset's journalistic work, is that in *Plum Bun*, Fauset examines nationalist dynamics in regard to their application at home, and that "home" is, indeed, the ethnic nation.[1]

Edna Ferber's *Fanny Herself* was published serially in the *American Magazine* before appearing as a book. Frederick A. Stokes Company published the novel in late 1917, but it "sold only mildly," according to Ferber herself (*Treasure* 233). As the author says about her novel, "A good deal of it was imaginary, a good deal of it was real. Certainly my mother, idealized, went to make up Molly Brandeis. Bits and pieces of myself crept into the character of Fanny Brandeis" (*Treasure* 223).

Ferber, like Fauset, moved in the literary and journalistic elite of her day, and her novel reflects middle-class values as well, manifested in ideas about lifestyle, money, amenities, proper comportment, and marriage. More interesting for the purposes of this study is how Ferber thinks about ethnicity in this novel, though that issue is not separate from middle-class notions. Both *Fanny Herself* and *Plum Bun* advocate ethnic solidarity—and both in novels about passing. Barbara Christian has noted that there is something paradoxical about that strategy, and her remark holds for both novels:

> Ironically, passing is a major theme in the 1920s when race pride was supposedly at a peak [the time also marked a high interest in Zionism, following the Balfour Declaration]. One might first think that this theme fed into the American belief system that it is better to be white than black. In actuality, the theme, as it was presented in the twenties, heightened the white audience's awareness of the restrictions imposed upon talented blacks who then found it necessary to become white to fulfill themselves. (*Black Women* 44)

How ethnic solidarity and the rejection of passing manifest themselves, however, has a lot to do with the class standing of the protagonists and with Victorian notions of proper activities for women. Art is the medium of ethnicity in both novels, and artistic ability an ethnic domain. The ethnic artist, in *Fanny Herself* and *Plum Bun*, thus appears as the embodiment of ethnic solidarity.

Because of this focus on ethnic solidarity, both novels follow the pattern of the ethnic Bildungsroman in that they propose a more communalist-oriented model of development. Like the *Autobiography* and *Haunch*, they do so by probing the consequences of an extreme individualism (though not one as exploitative of ethnicity) for their protagonists and come to the conclusion that isolation from the ethnic community results in self-denial and unhappiness. This ends once the protagonists rejoin their respective ethnic groups; thus, the Bildungsroman revisions of *Plum Bun* and *Fanny Herself* are more explicit than those of the previous two novels, since the latter merely implied (if strongly) that their protagonists should have followed a more communalist-oriented course. *Plum Bun* and *Fanny* leave nothing implicit about their calls to ethnic solidarity.

As a consequence, they rely more on essentialist definitions of ethnicity than Johnson's and Ornitz's novels, despite the fact that they are also novels about passing, a theme that challenges biological definitions of ethnicity. To trace how both novels develop their conceptualizations of ethnicity and how they arrive at a communalist vision of identity beholden to ethnic nationalism is the task of this chapter.

At the outset of *Fanny Herself*, it seems that Ferber intends to let Fanny Brandeis appear as not particularly ethnic and even as somewhat distanced from ethnic customs. Her family background suggests this. Molly Brandeis, her mother, is introduced as strongly individualistic, and though we see that she is part of an ethnic community in Winnebago, as "every member of the little Jewish congregation" (7) comes to her husband's funeral, she is also set apart to the extent that she runs a shop and thus seems to be, in her town, the only middle-class Jewish woman who works in a business. Also, she does not adhere to the rules of Jewish orthodoxy. Not only does she not keep kosher, she also joins a debating society that meets on Friday nights. Fanny's mother, being of German Jewish descent, follows Reform Judaism, which did not adopt many of the Orthodox practices regarding religious observances. Reform Judaism sought to minimize the differences between the Gentile and the Jewish worlds to enable the assimilation of Jews into nation states. But even given her Reform background, Molly Brandeis's adherence to religious practices is slight at best. Her pragmatic stance towards religion is epitomized by her greatest business success—the purchase and successful sale of Catholic religious figurines.

Mrs. Brandeis also does not encourage her daughter Fanny in the keeping of Judaic rites. Fanny, too, is depicted as different, but what initially sets "her apart in the little Middle Western Town" is the "real difference," which is described as "temperamental, or emotional, or dramatic, or historic, or all four" (24). The novel thus alludes to "Jewishness" as a trait the nature of which is left vague at this point—the adjectives evenly split between ascribing some quasi-inherent essence ("temperamental, or emotional") or tending towards social construction.

However, though Fanny shows a certain fascination for Judaism, Ferber makes clear that this grows out of a purely aesthetic interest (29), foreshadowing Fanny's later sublimation of ethnicity into art. Even her attempt to keep a fast is depicted more in terms of character strength than in terms of religious fervor, and Talmudic wisdom interests her for its practical application rather than for any spiritual value. In what may or may not be a play on words, Fanny's interest in literature is described as "catholic" (42), indicating that she does not favor any specific philosophic, religious, or aesthetic tradition while, at the same time, alluding to her mother's and her friendship with a Catholic priest who will play a crucial role in the rediscovery of her ethnicity. In fact, it seems that she has more respect for him than for the rabbi of her congregation. If ethnicity in *Fanny Herself* is defined by anything, then, it is not by an adherence to Judaism.

Despite the fact that Fanny comes across, paradoxically, as both a pragmatist and an aestheticist when it comes to Judaism, Ferber leaves no doubt that Fanny is Jewish, though she "had never formally taken the vows of her creed" (126) and though she does not "look Jewish": "She was not what is known as the Jewish type, in spite of her coloring" (91). The novel conceives of her Jewishness as manifesting itself through essential character traits or abilities. An early sign of this strategy, used throughout the novel, is Fanny's imagination, which the novel explicitly ascribes to her ethnicity rather than to her individuality:

> Little Oriental that she was, she was able to combine the dry text of her history book with the green of the trees, the gray of the church, and the brown of the monk's robes, and evolve a thrilling mental picture therefrom. (25)

Her vivid fantasy results from her "Orientalness," or at least her ethnicity provides the background that allows her to let history come to life. Implicitly, then, her mental life is more active than that of the other students, who do not have her advantage. To that extent, ethnicity figures as a positive trait, putting her above others.

Another way in which Fanny experiences her ethnicity, however, is through the anti-Semitic taunts of Gentiles (44–45, 72). Indeed, as Lawrence R. Rodgers has said,

> Coming to terms with anti-Semitism proved more crucial to forming the basis of both the author's and her character's Jewish identities than any abiding sense of religious devotion. In this way, Ferber foregrounds her and Fanny's Jewish affiliations less through a rich heritage of Jewish "assets" than through representations negatively imposed by non-Jews. (xv)

And despite the very different ethnic situations of African Americans and Jewish Americans, one can talk of Fanny's later strategy as "passing" in this context.

Gayle Wald says that passing has been generally assumed to be "a historically and socially constructed practice shaped by the exigencies of Jim Crow and by the binary organization of racial discourse" (15). Jewish passing can be understood against the background of anti-Semitic discriminatory practices and a Jew/Gentile binarism with racialist overtones. In the early twentieth century in the U.S., the threat of violence against Jews was largely absent, while it was an intrinsic element of anti-Black racism. But both novels, with their middle-class settings, focus on the economic potential inherent in passing and, at least implicitly, on socioeconomic discriminatory practices (though Ferber does so far less than Fauset).

Fanny's reaction to those discriminatory practices is fury. Because of this strongly emotional reaction, one might expect an equally strong attachment to her ethnic group. Instead, though, she shows an early interest in historically prominent Jewish figures such as "Disraeli, Spinoza, Mendelssohn, Mozart—distinguished Jews who had found their religion a handicap" (74), manifesting her latent intention to pass. She comes to see her gender, her class, and her ethnicity as handicaps quite explicitly, commenting to a friend of her mother that moving up on the social ladder is quite impossible to her because she is "a working woman, and a Jew, and we haven't any money or social position" (85–86).

Nonetheless, the de facto rejection of her ethnicity does not come to pass until her mother dies (100). Thus, although her mother did not strengthen any ethnic in-group feeling nor fully embrace Judaism, she appears to be the strongest tie that Fanny has to her ethnic group at that point. Since the rejection of her mother's way of life, which stressed duty and self-sacrifice, goes hand in hand with the rejection of ethnicity, Fanny perceives her mother's way of life as connected to Jewishness. This can be deduced from her resolve not to act like her mother: "I'm through being sentimental and unselfish," she says to herself; "What did it bring her? Nothing!" (106). Her exclamation implicitly foreshadows the choice to be made between ethnicity and materialism. Therefore she immediately resolves to shed "[r]ace, religion, training, natural impulses—she would discard them all if they stood in her way" (107). This enumeration again emphasizes the novel's wavering with regard to what defines Jewishness; the social and the biological are used side by side and are seen as equally disposable.

Fanny's rejection of ethnicity is underlined by a number of symbolic acts, one of which is her decision to move away from Winnebago so as to literally leave behind her heritage, not only ideologically but also spatially (109). To that extent, her rebellion resembles that of the classic Bildungsroman hero/ine who often, in search of a wider sphere of development, leaves his/her place of origin and goes to the city. Here, however, the focal point of rebellion is ethnicity, as Fanny's second symbolic act makes clear.

This act is the burning of her mother's apron in the furnace—almost a sacrificial offering up of her ethnicity. But to which god? It turns out that that deity is materialism. Apparently, she must decide to be either ethnic or materialist, and since she has just rejected her heritage, the choice is clear. (106, 120). Interestingly, then, one finds a similar constellation at work as in the *Autobiography* and in *Haunch*. In those two novels, being materialist was associated with being mainstream or white. In *Fanny*, this never becomes quite as clear, but is always implied. And, as in the other two novels, materialism and individualism seem to be inextricably intertwined. Like the Ex-Coloured Man and Meyer Hirsch, Fanny intends to use her ethnicity in her quest for success:

> Thousands of years of persecution behind her made her quick to appreciate suffering in others, and gave her an innate sense of fellowship with the downtrodden. She resolved to use that sense as a searchlight aiding her to see and overcome obstacles. She told herself that she was done with maudlin sentimentality. (108)

A sense for fellowship—for ethnic solidarity—is bent to individualist ends here, though it is unclear how that transformation is to be accomplished. It entails, though, the rejection of her ethnicity, so that she will now appear to the world as nonethnic, and it is in this role that she intends to realize her materialism. As will be seen, her rejection of materialism toward the end of the novel also means taking a lower paying job. Implicitly, then, the nonethnic world is equated with materialism and individualism, the ethnic world with other qualities.

What those qualities are remains to be defined. Paradoxically, it is the outsider, the Gentile, who first attempts a listing of those characteristics that define Jewishness. This occurs at an interesting moment in the novel. Fanny explains her future plans to the Catholic priest who is a friend of the family, and it becomes apparent that she, in her planning to pass, relies on the social construction of race. She insists that she is "just like any other ambitious woman with brains" and that "Ethnologists have proved that there is no such thing as a Jewish race" (121). The priest, however, responds by listing essential ethnic characteristics which, according to him, not only will Fanny be unable to deny but she should make the most of. It is worth quoting this long passage, which comes in response to Fanny's above assertion:

> H'm. Maybe. I don't know what you'd call it, then. You can't take a people and persecute them for thousands of years, hounding them from place to place, herding them in dark and filthy streets, without having some sort of brand on them—a mark that differentiates. Sometimes it doesn't show outwardly. But it's there, inside. You know, Fanny, how it's always been said that no artist can become a genius until he has suffered. You've suffered, you Jews, for centuries and centuries, until you're all artists—quick to see drama because you've lived in it, emotional, oversensitive, cringing, or swaggering, high-strung, demonstrative, affectionate, generous. (121–122)

Here we have the novel's conceptualization of ethnicity in a nutshell. Earlier, Ferber had suggested that Fanny's talents and abilities are related to her ethnicity. Now one hears the assertion directly—and by a member of an institution that has often provided the very circumstances which, so the priest claims, have created the traits that differentiate Jews.

Despite the negatively charged terms with which this differentiation is characterized (a "brand," no less), Father Fitzpatrick regards them as an "asset" (121). One may assume that the negative connotations of "brand" reflect the centuries of persecution while Fitzpatrick's positive assessment of the ethnic potential relates to the ethnic transformation of that persecution into a specific Jewish differentiation—but the journey from "brand" to "asset" is the very one Fanny will travel in the course of the novel.

The list of Jewish characteristics leaves out from whom it differentiates Jews, presumably because it doesn't need to be said: from some invisible norm represented by the mainstream, into which Fanny intends to delve. As Father Fitzpatrick sees it, passing is not only undesirable but also impossible. The plot will prove his assessment right, and Ferber's insertion of the scientific point of view—"there is no such thing as a Jewish race"—is an indication that the novel might have been intended as an argument against the social construction of ethnicity.

A look at Ferber's autobiography *A Peculiar Treasure* confirms this. Some of the very terms in which the novel defines "Jewishness" are taken up by her twenty-two years later. She asserts, "I have felt that to be a Jew was, in some ways at least, to be especially privileged. Two thousand years of persecution have made the Jew quick to sympathy, quick-witted (he'd better be), tolerant, humanly understanding" (9). The following passage is worth quoting in its entirety as it shows how constant Ferber's thinking about ethnicity remained; in addition, it nicely illustrates how certain kinds of social constructedness of ethnicity are not at all unlike essentialism:

> hundreds and thousands of years of continued ill-treatment must stamp its mark upon a people. Primarily, to be a Jew meant belonging to a religion, not a race. But a religious sect, persecuted through the centuries, takes on a certain resemblance, one to another, in countenance, in habits, in feeling, much as one often notes that a husband and wife, through years of common experience and companionship, grow to look alike. The Jewish eye is a melancholy eye, the mask is tragic. He has acquired great adaptability, nervous energy, ambition to succeed and a desire to be liked. It irks me to hear people say that Jews are wonderful people or that Jews are terrible people. Jews are wonderful and terrible and good and bad and brilliant and stupid and evil and spiritual and vulgar and cultured and gifted and commonplace. Jews, in short, are people. (*Treasure* 9)

Jewish traits are historically acquired but now inherent, she seems to say. At the same time, the passage exhibits a peculiar tension between two assertions: on the one hand, Ferber claims, certain traits distinguish Jews from other people; on the other hand, Jews are like everybody else. This tension also operates in the title of her autobiography and those to whom it refers. "A peculiar treasure," used both as title and epigraph to her autobiography, is a quotation from Exodus (19:5) and here clearly refers to the Israelites. When she requotes the passage in the middle of her autobiography, it denotes the American people as a whole.

Diane Lichtenstein has noted that, "[l]ike many of the writers who preceded her, Ferber validated her Jewish self by linking it to an American identity," thus not having to "[choose] one nation over the other" (131). Lawrence Rodgers claims that "she viewed herself more as an American woman who happened to be Jewish than as a Jew who lived in America" (xiv). However, that the ambivalent stance somewhere between culturally separatist (a position implied in the essentialism of the long quotation above and in the first use of the phrase "a peculiar treasure") and assimilationist tendencies (Ruth Wisse, for example, charges Ferber with lack of a specifically *"Jewish* energy" [21], whatever that may be) is not problematized in *Fanny Herself* has to do with the logic of cultural nationalism, a view of ethnicity as separate and special but with full claim to participation and citizenship in the given nation and without claims to a territory.

We have seen a similar ideological configuration in *The Autobiography of an Ex-Coloured Man*, where the narrator castigates American society for its exclusion of African Americans while the narrative also shows the latter group as ethically superior to the mainstream, so that an ethnic life is a better life than a mainstream one. At the same time, the Ex-Coloured Man also insists in the Americanness of African American art. But of that more in the final chapter.

Fanny, however, unlike her creator Ferber, does deny her ethnicity, and that at the crucial point where she perceives her choice as one between career and ethnicity: when her future employer asks her directly whether she is Jewish. Though she regrets her immediate "No" which comes after a "breathless instant" (136), she does not take it back. Paradoxically, her employer is passing as well, as Ferber strongly suggests (146), and the same scene that depicts two passing Jews also makes clear that their ethnicity accounts for what is best in them, according to the novel. Indeed, ethnicity is associated with the "finer things" in life (151) as, in a brief conversation about some etchings on Fenger's office walls, both are shown to be discerning when it comes to quality in art. An artistic sensibility on her employer's side is seen as an ethnic trait, just as in Fanny's case earlier. Knowing that he, too, passes, Fanny thinks to herself that she "understood this man now," divining that the "marvelous examples of the etcher's art" on his wall have not been bought "in the desire to impress" but out of a "craving for beauty" (146). Through this juncture, passing is subjected to a moral judgment, though couched in aesthetic terms. If ethnicity means refinement, non-ethnicity must tend towards the coarse. Thus it becomes clear that the novel objects to the individualist course of its protagonist. While the work can be seen as a typical Bildungsroman up to that point, the issue of passing and the judgment passed on it initiate the process that leads to the ethnic revision of the genre.

That passing is morally reprehensible is a judgment pronounced by Fanny herself when she remarks that lying to Fenger about her ethnicity "stamps her" (153). Passing is seen as the first step on a downhill slope, a lie that will necessitate others and that indicates her willingness to do anything for material advantage. Indeed, the result of this lie is a conscious effort by Fanny to distance herself from sense impressions, from things connected with artistic sensibility. When walking through Chicago, which she used to do to garner impressions, she thinks to herself: "Don't let it get you. Look at it, but don't think about it. Don't let the human end of it touch you. There's nothing in it" (159). According to the novel, to be ethnic or not is an aesthetic as well as a moral decision. This pairing of ethics and aesthetics proves to be pervasive throughout the rest of the novel.

Despite Fanny's attempts to deny both her ethnicity and her artistic sensibility, she repeatedly feels herself drawn to sketching. Consistently, the poor and socially disadvantaged provide inspiration for her sketches. Art, in this manner, is vaguely related to social consciousness, though at this point her drawings serve no social purpose. The fact that Fanny receives her inspiration primarily when witnessing want and poverty confirms that "Ferber stresses the connection between suffering and art" (Lichtenstein 133)—and between both and ethnicity. One is reminded of her early preference for novels of social protest (42). However, it is difficult to see in her excursions into the poor and working class areas of Chicago anything like social protest, particularly as these excursions take place on her days off from furthering the well-being of one of the companies paying starvation wages, as she herself becomes aware, to the inhabitants of those areas. What this somewhat voyeuristic gazing at misery and the resulting sketches are meant to remind the reader of is the ongoing struggle between materialism and ethnicity in Fanny herself.

A key element in that struggle is Clarence Heyl, a former classmate of Fanny's, once weak and helpless, now sportive and independent, and the whole transformation triggered through his humiliation by and admiration of Fanny's selfless intervention on his behalf in a childhood brawl. In an ironic inversion, he has come to return her to the selflessness of her earlier days, and his means of doing that is to serve as the voice of "ethnic essentialism." Repeatedly, he reminds Fanny that her artistic ability and her social conscience are related to her Jewishness, are in her "blood" (188). To Heyl, and, it seems, to Ferber, ethnic solidarity is a duty (189). Once that pronouncement has been made, it is possible to openly declare leaving one's ethnicity as wrong.

Interestingly, as the novel outlines it, listening to the voice of ethnicity is not only a communal duty but also leads to greater self-realization—a classic nationalist claim. A selfless course of the individual leads to a fuller (ethnic) individuation—an ethnic twist on the Bildungsroman. Accordingly, Heyl tries to convince Fanny not to deny her artistic gift, giving as a reason—somewhat tautologically—that she will not be able to deny it. But the reader has already witnessed this. Fanny is shown as being happier following her artistic calling than she is at work. Self-realization and ethnic solidarity are thus intertwined. Indeed, as Heyl declares, both are ultimately Fanny's "debt to humanity" (217). At moments like these, the novel attempts to embrace a kind of universalism while firmly advocating ethnic essentialism. For most of the novel, however, the latter firmly prevails.

This becomes clear in Fanny's relationship to Heyl, who serves as a kind of ethnic conscience, relentlessly reminding her of her artistic abilities, which she is supposed to put into the service not only of Jews but of humanity in general. When insisting that she should explore her artistic talent rather than be a success in business, he insists

You can't kill that kind of thing [her ability to sketch], Fanny. It would have to be a wholesale massacre of all the centuries behind you. I don't mind so much your being disloyal to your tribe, or race, or whatever you want to call it. But you've turned your back on yourself; you've got an obligation to humanity, and I'll nag at you till you pay it. (215)

Though he says that ethnic solidarity is not foremost in his mind, he does claim that she is disloyal not in passing, which he does not know about, but in not developing her inherent talents.

Here, the novel sounds like a fictionalization of Horace Kallen's vision of cultural pluralism:

> As in an orchestra every type of instrument has its specific timbre and tonality, founded in its substance and form; as every type has its appropriate theme and melody in the whole symphony, so in society, each ethnic group may be the natural instrument, its temper and culture may be its theme and melody and the harmony and dissonances and discords of them all may make the symphony of civilization. (*Culture and Democracy* 124–125).

Ethnic solidarity and essentialism on the one hand and universalism on the other thus emerge not as contradictory but ultimately as complementary, as in many declarations of ethnic nationalism.

Universalism is only the long-term goal, though. For the moment, Heyl attempts to veer Fanny away from a career shown to threaten her spiritual well-being and into his own arms. Since he is a naturalist and writing a perceptive newspaper column, the reader is to assume that—according to the logic the novel has established—he is fulfilling his debt to Jewry and humanity in following his artistic and journalistic callings, so that the union of the two reunites Fanny with her ethnic group. Marriage outside of the ethnic group is never considered. The only other self-appointed option, a man for whom Fanny has a certain fascination, is her employer Fenger, a passing Jew himself. In the choice between a man who has renounced his heritage for materialism and a man who, as we are to believe, realizes his ethnic heritage through a creative career, Fanny ultimately opts for the insistent Heyl, who has all along served as a kind of spiritual guide.

At the same time, in a different strand of the plot, Fanny's relationship with her brother serves to highlight her straying from her ethnic group and in part also causes her return. Of course, indirectly, he has also been instrumental in distancing her from her Jewishness, because she resents the sacrifices she and her mother made for his career as a violinist, indirectly blaming him for her mother's death, and choosing selfishness over sacrifice as a reaction. However, once she learns that he has written a musical piece expressing the essence of Jewishness, she repents of not having supported him more than she did. His piece is, in his words, "Jewish music. . . . As Jewish as the Kol Nidre. I wanted to express the passion, the fire, and history of a people. My people," to which she responds, "Ted—dear—will you ever forgive me?" (272).

Confronted with an ethnically committed life which, again, means an artistic life, she becomes convinced of the value of self-sacrifice. When listening to her brother playing the violin, she thinks to herself, "This is what my mother drudged for, and died for, and it was worth it. And you must do the same, if necessary. Nothing else matters" (282). This recognition of the value of the ethnic and artistic in her brother comes at about the same time as a revival of her own artistic instincts. In Carol Batker's words, "she is . . . forced to negotiate her Jewishness as a businesswoman. The traditional Jewish value of Tzedakah, or charity, becomes a central concern to Fanny," as she regrets not having supported her brother more and as she turns her artistic attention to the Jewish working class.

She finds the inspiration to draw her masterpiece when watching a women's suffrage parade, producing a drawing of a Russian Jewish garment worker whose face expresses, in Fanny's opinion, "the history of a people. . . . It spoke eloquently of pogroms, of massacres, of Kiev and its sister-horror, Kishineff" (250).[2] This confrontation with and inspiration by Russian Jewish working women provides interesting parallels to the life of Zionist leader and Supreme Court judge Louis Brandeis—who may have provided Ferber with Fanny's last name—which underline the ideological mission of Ferber's novel. Brandeis's connection to Judaism was rather frail before the turn of the century. "He never joined a synagogue or any of the fraternal groups, and while never denying his Jewish ancestry, neither did he advertise it" (Urofsky 114). Mediating in a garment workers' strike in 1910, however, brought him into contact, for the first time, with immigrant Jews from Russia. This experience was instrumental in awakening his interest in Jewishness and preceded his involvement in Zionism (Urofsky 115–116). Fanny's encounter with garment workers is also instrumental in her emerging Jewishness. As in earlier instances, art, ethnicity, and selflessness become interwoven, almost as if they were interchangeable. The act of drawing leads Fanny to feel ethnic solidarity (261) and to embrace Jews as "her people" (261), though not yet publicly.

In a discussion with her brother on what ethnicity means in the U.S. as opposed to in Europe, Fanny comes closer to a public articulation of what being Jewish means and will mean for her. Though there is less ethnic cohesion in the U.S., partly, as the novel claims, as a result of the relative lack of oppression but also because of materialism, of which Fanny herself is an example, each individual, the novel announces paradoxically, is even more responsible for the "image" of his or her ethnic group. As Fanny says, "They don't object to us as a sect, or a race, but as a type. . . . We're free to build as many synagogues as we like, and worship in them all day, if we want to. But we don't want to" (295). Similarly to *Haunch, Paunch and Jowl*, the novel suggests that the center of Jewishness has shifted—although Ferber proposes that the shift results from artistic endeavors rather than from socialism. This shift of the center is even reflected in prejudice directed against Jews: "The struggle isn't racial any more, but individual," as Fanny attempts to explain to her brother when pointing out the differences between European and American prejudice. "For some reason or other one flashy, loud-talking Hebrew in a restaurant can cause more ill feeling than ten thousand of them holding a religious mass meeting in Union Square" (294).

This, in turn, sounds almost like an ironic rephrasing of the ideology of ethnic pluralism. When Kallen asks, in "Democracy versus the Melting Pot," "What do Americans *will* to make of the United States—a unison, singing the old British theme 'America,' the America of the New England School? or a harmony, in which that theme shall be dominant, perhaps, among others, but one among many, not the only one" (*Culture and Democracy* 118), he clearly favors the latter answer. But Ferber seems to suggest that if one of those voices in the harmony sings a little bit too loudly, it will immediately incur the wrath of the rest of the choir.

On the one hand, Ferber says, there is an approximation of equality in the U.S., or at least no open persecution. On the other hand, this relative lack of outside pressure also leads to tendencies of disintegration. But Ferber's conclusion is somewhat difficult to understand; following Fanny's elaboration, her brother responds, "Then here each one of us is responsible. Is that it?" (295). First she denies that there is wholesale group prejudice but then argues that each individual's action potentially damages the entire group. That this necessitates that each ethnic individual feel a heightened responsibility for the ethnic image is only intelligible when considering the limitations of this freedom from prejudice: there may be no all-out persecution in the U.S., but ethnicity continues to be regarded as a liability by the mainstream, and any behavior by the ethnic individual going against the mainstream's cultural norm will immediately be registered against the group as a whole.

As a result, ethnic solidarity remains of utmost importance, which is why Fanny's brother, on discovery of her passing, remarks, "I don't know which is worse; my selfishness, or yours" (295). Since hostility against the ethnic group can always be expected, desertion in the interest of individual advancement registers as selfishness under the logic of ethnic solidarity. Hence the tension between the relative scarcity of negative experiences that Fanny makes on account of her ethnicity and the resentment she nonetheless feels against being Jewish. She feels restricted by the outside and by the inside, by the (internalized) expectations that are on her on account of being Jewish, by the voice of ethnic nationalism, in other words. And as we have seen, those expectations are given voice by both an insider (Heyl) and an outsider (Father Fitzpatrick).

The definition of ethnicity thus takes place in a kind of collaboration between mainstream and ethnic group—an issue on which the novel is in agreement with Kallen, who maintains that a group's "traditional social inheritance or *natio* . . . [reaches] consciousness first in a reaction against an antagonistic America, then assumes as an effect of the competition with 'Americanization' spiritual forms other than religious" (*Culture and Democracy* 103). Of the latter, Ferber's novel itself is an example. In *Fanny Herself*, the mainstream's expectations of or hostility against the ethnic group furnish one defining element, ethnic cultural traditions and responses to that hostility another. In Ferber's novelistic world, the individual has only very limited room in deciding what ethnicity means.

In addition, there is also the "automatic" pull of ethnicity, the ethnic essentialism that the novel subscribes to that makes every ethnic individual want to be ethnic, at least on a subconscious level. It is this biologism that makes Fanny yearn to do something different while she is pursuing her managerial career. Again and again, she feels compelled to go on sociological excursions, attracted to the aesthetic side of things, and to drawing, so much so that her boss remarks that she is as "wooden as an Indian while talking about a million-a-year deal, and lyrical over a combination of electric sign, sunset, and moth-eaten park" (254).

Ferber needs this "biological" pull for the articulation of the ideology that the novel announces: that ethnic solidarity is a necessity, because of a hostile outside world and because of inner drives, and that denial of ethnicity is selfish, wrong, and against nature. This underlying essentialism plays a crucial role in differentiating the work from a traditional Bildungsroman, since it leaves as the only logical conclusion, in terms of the ideology Ferber forwards, the union of the protagonist with her ethnic community. The course of her individuation is prescribed in communalist terms. Ferber also needs the biological pull to be able to bring the novel to the wished-for conclusion: Fanny has to end up happy and married in this sentimental narrative, and the reader has to be able to accept why her career cannot bring her happiness, starting, as it did, with a denial of ethnicity; this happiness is achieved in embracing ethnically committed art and her personified ethnic consciousness, Heyl. Novelistic and ideological needs both find their happy ending here.

Angela Murray expresses dissatisfaction with her station in life and her ethnicity very early in *Plum Bun*, though not at a much earlier age than Fanny. She sees being African American as a restriction and wishes to live on a larger scale than her parents:

> With a wildness that fell just short of unreasonableness she hated restraint. Her father's earlier days as a coachman in a private family, his later successful years as boss carpenter, her mother's youth spent as maid to a famous actress, all this was to Angela a manifestation of the sort of thing which happens to those enchained it might be by duty, by poverty, by weakness or by colour. (13)

Though color is listed as only one of the things that might cause restraint—and clearly, "restraint" has economic overtones here—the kinds of positions her father and mother occupy in the American labor market around the turn of the century and the use of the verb "enchain" point to the centrality that color occupies in Angela's thinking and to the parallels drawn with the history of slavery. "Colour or rather the lack of it," she concludes, "seemed to [her] the one absolute prerequisite to the life of which she was always dreaming" (13), and thus she identifies it as the single most important factor to hamper an individual's rise in the socioeconomic structure. In this she is unlike her sister Virginia who, as a child, "meant to live the same kind of life [as her parents]; she would marry a man exactly like her father and she would conduct her home exactly as did her mother" (22). Throughout the novel, Virginia will provide an alternative model of attitude towards ethnicity for Angela.

Fanny, like Angela, wishes to supercede the small town existence of her mother and to do business on a larger scale. But while Fanny does not often think of passing until her mother dies, Angela learns passing from her mother who, being very light-skinned, at times lets herself be taken for white, enjoying the advantages this occasionally brings with it, and because "it amused her when by herself to take lunch at an exclusive restaurant whose patrons would have been panic-stricken if they had divined the presence of a 'coloured' woman no matter how little her appearance differed from theirs" (15). Angela's mother is thus fully conscious of the social constructedness of race. Like Fanny's mother, Angela's mother stands out from her ethnic group while also being un-problematically rooted in it. In Mrs. Brandeis's case, it is partly her casual observance or nonobservance of Judaic rites and mostly the fact that she is a businesswoman, thus deviating from the role other middle-class Jewish women in her town play, which differentiate her some-what from the ethnic community. In Mrs. Murray's case, it is her light skin color and her love of luxury, maybe learned through her employment to an actress, which sets her apart. An unintended side effect of her lightness and love of luxury is that "her desire to consume products just like any other American results in a power hierarchy in the home where those who have less color have more privilege," as Carol Allen asserts (64). Though this hierarchy of privileges outside the home does not seem to translate into a color hierarchy within the home, it does have an effect on Angela.

Like her mother, Angela learns to love luxury, and access to luxury becomes associated with a denial of ethnicity, since that access becomes possible through passing. The connection between denial of ethnicity, materialism, and whiteness is symbolically expressed in how she deals with the house of her parents after their death: "Angela's attitude toward her heritage as a whole suggests that it exists or vanishes at her pleasure. She literally sells her inheritance (the parental home) to finance her adventure in passing" (Kubitschek *Claiming the Heritage* 108). This episode reminds one of the *Autobiography* and its exchange of "mess of pottage" for "birthright" and equally implies how bad a bargain she has struck. As in the *Autobiography*, the dichotomy established in this manner points to the ethnic nationalist elements of the novel.

What to her mother is a mere diversion—passing—becomes Angela's most important desire. Given that Mrs. Murray sees her passing adventures with a sense of irony, "[n]o one would have been more amazed than [her] if she could have guessed how her daughter interpreted her actions" (14). As far as Angela is concerned, she learns "the possibilities for joy and freedom which seemed to her inherent in mere whiteness" (14) from her mother's example. In a similar misunderstanding, what is a necessity for Mrs. Brandeis—business—becomes the sole goal in life for Fanny. For both protagonists, then, the directions their lives take are determined in part through a misinterpretation of their mothers' lives.

While this misinterpretation contributes to the protagonists' escape from ethnicity, their mothers also represent a strong bond to it, given that both mothers did not resent their ethnic heritage or contemplate rejecting it. Both Angela and Fanny thus only arrive at the ultimate decision to pass—though it has been latent for both of them earlier—once their mothers, and in Angela's case both mother and father, have died. And like Fanny, Angela also has to distance herself from her home geographically to facilitate her decision.

The parallels between Mrs. Brandeis and Mrs. Murray might suggest that color and religion serve as main markers of ethnicity in the respective novels, because the passing protagonists distance themselves from these markers, but that is not the case. As it is, what comes to define ethnicity turns out to be almost identical for Angela and Fanny. Like Fanny, Angela shows an early predilection for the artistic, as if to verify Du Bois's dictum that "[The Negro's] greatest gift to the world has been and will be the gift of art, of appreciation and realization of beauty" (Levering Lewis *Du Bois* 461). Even as a child, "[h]er eye for line and expression was already good and she had a nice feeling for colour" (13). And as in *Fanny Herself*, the protagonist's love of drawing focuses on sketching faces and people and finds its expression in portraiture, specifically in the portraiture of ethnic models—her favorite model being her and her sister's housekeeper, Hetty Daniels (66)—and of the socially disadvantaged.

For both Fanny and Angela, it is the expressiveness of their drawings that makes them distinctive, Angela's strength being the ability to "[interpret] on a face the emotion which lay back of that expression" (111); and that ability is implicitly explained through a heritage of suffering. Time and again, the novel reminds us that "race" is connected to "suffering" (341), and even before he knows she is passing, Angela's (white) friend Ashley remarks on her "aura of suffering, of the pain which comes from too great sensitivity" (321)—but it is just that sensitivity which allows her to interpret faces. The novels thus characterize ethnicity by essential traits or abilities, of which color or religion may or may not be symbolic.

Plum Bun is somewhat divided against itself on that question. A number of passages in the novel strongly suggest that Angela is not closely tied to her ethnicity and exhibits certain character traits because of her light skin color. This becomes particularly obvious in a comparison to her sister Virginia, the voice of ethnic nationalism, a comparison that the novel continually invites. Angela likes shopping while Virginia loves home (20); Angela is dissatisfied with her home life, but Virginia wants to be just like her parents (22); Angela embraces individualism as life philosophy, at least initially, while Virginia advocates ethnic solidarity (79–80). Eva Rueschmann argues that "*Plum Bun* uses the sister complimentarity in a critical way . . . to expose her [Angela's] 'passing' as a form of denial of her self and her African-American history" (122). But Rueschmann assumes as a given what the novel attempts to establish: that self must be ethnically and racially grounded. Virginia herself actually verbalizes this implied essentialism when she speculates on a cause-and-effect relationship between Angela's hurtful behavior towards her and Angela's color, or the lack of it. In a conversation between the two sisters after Angela has shunned Virginia in the presence of her white lover, Virginia tells her, "Perhaps you're right, Angela; perhaps there is an extra infusion of white blood in your veins which lets you see life at another angle" (168).

The most blatant conflation of color and character remains to be stated by Angela herself, though. In contemplating her own selfishness towards the end of the novel she thinks,

> Her father, her mother and Jinny had always given and she had always taken. Why was that? Jinny had sighed: 'Perhaps you have more white blood than Negro in your veins.' Perhaps this selfishness was what the possession of white blood meant; the ultimate definition of Nordic Supremacy. (275)

Though she immediately contemplates that her seemingly white admirer Anthony seems to be an exception to this rule, Anthony later turns out be passing as well. While Angela does have white friends who are

helpful to her, the equation of selfishness with whiteness remains ver-
bally uncontradicted; that is, Angela does not revoke her statement.
As Jacquelyn McLendon suggests, Fauset reverses stereotypes about
mulattoes as they had been circulated by white writers of the period
who "attribut[ed] their [mulattoes'] faults and failures directly to their
'black' blood and instead makes 'white' blood culpable" (28); in her
juxtaposition of Angela and Virginia, Fauset thus inverts "traditional
literary conventions" that associate light with good and dark with evil
(McLendon 35). While the fact that the novel ends with two light-
skinned African Americans marrying might appear to bolster existing
color hierarchies, both the marriage of Angela's parents and the symbolic valuation of color as the novel constructs it go squarely against
such a reading.

Through juxtaposing the sisters, Fauset also intervenes in a (still continuing) debate: what is the role of women in nationalism? Virginia,
who serves as an ideological role model, also appears to be more domes-
tically oriented than Angela, whose breaking away from tradition and
home has slight feminist overtones, though they are undercut by her
seeking security in marriage. From that position, the choices open to
her could be framed in terms similar to the "gender vs. race debate"
of the post–Civil War suffrage struggle: will she seek freedom and
opportunity as a woman (and deny her race), or will she subordinate
her socioeconomic goals to the ideal of racial and communal solidarity? It would appear that, just as Frances E. W. Harper,[3] Fauset decided
that when it came to the "question of race, she let the lesser question
of sex go" (Painter 231).

While Plum Bun does explore the limitations women faced economically—and even whiteness does not liberate Angela in that respect[4]—the novel appears far more interested in the racial aspect of
Angela's journey. Nonetheless, it must be noted that, once Angela decides to forego the economically secure but ideologically problematic
marriage to Roger, she becomes more independent and does not seek
marriage (though it comes her way nonetheless). To that extent, the
novel does not align the path of ethnic solidarity firmly with notions
of domesticity.

As the juxtaposition of the sisters implies, then, whiteness is suggestive of selfishness and blackness of altruism, something similarly
suggested by the titles of the novel's sections. "'Home' in Plum Bun is
thus first of all childhood and parents' love, and when those are gone,

is full acceptance and understanding of one's separate identity before one's full communion with others. The Market is the mistaken dream—wealth if one is poor; white if one is Black" (Sylvander 185). Home vs. Market equals black vs. white—blackness thus becomes associated with nonmarket values, whiteness with money and materialism. What is more, these two sets of values appear as mutually exclusive; just as in *Fanny Herself*, the protagonist must choose between ethnicity and materialism: she "can take advantage of the 'American market' in the 1920s only at a high cost, namely through 'passing,' which entails a denial of her entire past and her African-American heritage" (Rueschmann 121). In passages like Angela's contemplation of Nordic Supremacy (275), which imply that selfishness comes with "white blood," the distinction between black and white seems morally absolute.

Angela's thoughts on these matters are reminiscent of similar claims leveled against W. E. B. Du Bois by Marcus Garvey: "his mixed-race identity . . . was sometimes perversely charged against him by Garvey's circle as a sign of disloyalty to black nationalist concerns" (Sundquist *To Wake* 460–461). Because ethnic nationalism demands ethnic solidarity, a failure in the latter would also be a manifestation of selfishness. Why would Fauset, a close associate of Du Bois and herself light-skinned, contemplate these matters? In a 1920 short story, "The Sleeper Wakes," she explored this question:

> Amy in "The Sleeper Wakes" does not know if she is Black or white. When she recognizes in white people a coldness and cruelty toward the unfortunate that is foreign to her and to the Blacks she has grown up with, she concludes that she is Black. In *Plum Bun* Fauset is not so foolish as to extend the suggestion that kindness and cruelty can be biologically inherited. (Sylvander 134)

While the novel as a whole might not see the distribution of kindness and cruelty this way, inasmuch as it features kind white characters, the issue of biological essences is contemplated repeatedly and given a moral valorization.

Fauset appears to respond to a question asked by W. E. B. Du Bois in *The Souls of Black Folk*: "What if to the Mammonism of America be added the rising Mammonism of the re-born South, and the Mammonism of this South be reinforced by the budding Mammonism of its half-awakened black millions? Whither, then, is the new-world quest of Goodness and Beauty and Truth gone glimmering?" (57). Fauset's novel explores this very question, if in a Northern context, and the answer to it is that African Americans, through their upholding and, as Fauset's novel seems to suggest, embodiment of nonmaterial values, are positioned as keepers of light in a country otherwise benighted through its commercialism.

This essentialism allows Fauset, paradoxically, to stress the element of choice inherent in the concept of passing. If lighter skin color should permit entrance to privileges denied the darker members of the ethnic group, conscious revocation of that privilege figures as heroic. If it entails overcoming inherent tendencies towards selfishness and materialism, the heroic element becomes even more pronounced. According to this view, Angela is not a heroic character because she succumbs to the lure of whiteness before finding her way to ethnic solidarity. The character of sociologist Van Meier, however, who, as has been remarked by a number of critics (e.g., Sylvander 173, McLendon 35), represents Du Bois, does not make that same mistake. When whiteness is offered to him symbolically, in the guise of Angela's friend Paulette Lister's sexual advances to him, he coldly dismisses it and her (222), providing a role model for Angela. Though she is "conscious of a swelling pride" (222) when the story is related to her, she does not yet apply the lesson to herself. Both this incident and Anthony's revelation of his race, however, prefigure her eventual revocation of whiteness, and as she and Anthony are able, despite their whiteness, to do so, Angela's musings on the relatedness of color and character find their contradiction in their actions, a contradiction already apparent in the fact that her mother, too, chooses blackness over whiteness. In addition, "[s]everal of Angela's white friends reaffirm their friendship, so that individual personality and action are seen to have some effect on one's social reception" (Kubitschek *Claiming the Heritage* 110); conduct appears, then, as a matter of personal responsibility. But is it, according to Fauset?

As I have mentioned, the novel seems somewhat divided against itself on the question of whether color is symbolic of underlying characteristics or not. On the one hand, Angela's behavior is attributed to her light skin; on the other hand, she does eventually return to her ethnicity, exhibits those artistic abilities that are the sign of ethnicity in *Fanny Herself* as well (and Angela paints more once she decides to be ethnic again [317–318]), and is equally as drawn to ethnic models and to ethnic life as Fanny.

Throughout her experience of passing, Angela never loses the sense that, somehow, life in Harlem is richer and deeper than anywhere else; at Van Meier's lecture, for example,

> she sensed that fullness, richness, even thickness of life which she had felt on her first visit to Harlem. The stream of living ran almost molten; little waves of feeling played out from groups within the audience and beat against her consciousness and against that of her friends, only the latter were without her secret powers of interpretation. (216)

According to Amritjit Singh, scenes like these indicate that

> at one level there is an attempt to delineate a dimension of culture and values which the middle-class blacks shared with white Americans. At the same time, these novels [*Flight*, *Plum Bun*, and *Passing*] inform white readers that middle-class blacks have no intention or desire to relinquish the joy and abandon of black life for the dullness of the white bourgeoisie. (93)

Angela is privy to the "freemasonry of the race," to use the Ex-Coloured Man's term, and she can perceive the fullness of the life around her better than her white companions, Fauset suggests, implying that she has a built-in antenna, an inherent sense that allows her to do so. Even the discussions among her white friends appear shallow to her in comparison to what she heard at home in Philadelphia (117). It would seem, then, that, in *Plum Bun*, ethnicity goes beyond color, as Angela ultimately has a stronger connection to being black than her color would suggest.

At the same time, she is subject to temptation by the very qualities associated with whiteness, as was her light-skinned mother. In the end, *Plum Bun* suggests that color, as the outward sign of ethnicity, merely symbolizes potential deeper-lying traits—just as the absence of color hints at a different set of potential traits—but does not serve as a sure indicator of their actual presence. Angela does not have the help of the outward symbol to point her in what the novel perceives as the right direction. She must therefore struggle harder to arrive at "the burnt-offering of individualism for some dimly glimpsed racial whole" (117)—the subject of discussions in her Philadelphia home—than her sister Virginia who, because of her color, never has an option not to be ethnic. But confrontation with her sister's color marks a crucial point in Angela's ethnic career: "Angela's public denial of her sister forces her to rethink her inner conflict between her social ambitions and her attachment to her sister, and by extension her heritage" (Rueschmann 123).

Because of color, then, what is an option for both Fanny and Theodore—passing—is only possible for one of the Murray sisters. Color thus serves to establish a group cohesion that is more "automatic" than that established by a common history and religion. Or so it would seem. However, when one looks at the internal dynamics that compel both Angela and Fanny to return to ethnicity, one finds them similar enough to suggest that the emphasis, in both novels, is decidedly much more on the inside of ethnicity than on the outside—the outside, in Fanny's case, being Judaism, to which she has a rather distant relationship.

There is a wealth of material in *Plum Bun* linking character traits to ethnicity. Materialism, individualism, and selfishness are often associated with whiteness, while solidarity, depth of feeling, artistic ability, and altruism are associated with being African American. In this respect, the novel differs from *Fanny Herself*, because the latter, while always implying "organic" links between materialism and nonethnicity, does not spell them out as insistently, a difference also observed in the comparison of *Haunch* and the *Autobiography*. Nonetheless, *Plum Bun*, too, has its moments of universalism. Heyl, in *Fanny*, talks about Fanny's general debt to humanity, and Angela makes clear through much of her passing phase that she merely wants to be a human being with equal rights. The trappings she imagines for her being are those of the white middle- and upper-class society of her time, though, so that being human in its concrete form is shown to be always bound up with class or racial status. But when, at the end of the novel, after she has rejoined her ethnic group, Angela is snubbed by a black woman who mistakes her for being white (363), the arbitrariness of racial designation becomes utterly clear—it is in the eye of the beholder. Much of the novel affirms ethnic essences, however, as does *Fanny Herself*, and both novels are equally clear about certain kinds of attributes they claim as ethnic. They are also in agreement on what those attributes are: artistic ones. It is those artistic attributes that eventually cause both Fanny and Angela to return to their respective ethnicities.

In *Fanny Herself*, the links between art and ethnicity are strong. *Plum Bun* shows the same essentialist connection between those two. Though Angela does not acknowledge being ethnic because of a direct causal link to her drawing abilities, as is the case with Fanny, affirmation of ethnicity takes place in the context of her artistic endeavors. It is in an attempt to defend the right of another African American woman, Miss Powell, to receive an art scholarship to go to Paris that Angela reveals to the press that she, too, being the recipient of a scholarship, is "black" (346).

The connection of art and ethnicity is all the more striking as Angela, when passing, had denied her ethnic kinship to Miss Powell. When Angela is about to meet her white lover-to-be Roger, who she knows holds rabidly racist views, in front of the art school, Miss Powell catches up with her "and laid her hand on Angela's arm but the latter shook her off. Roger must not see her on familiar terms like this with a coloured girl" (148), particularly not on the afternoon on which she expects—futilely—a marriage proposal. At this point, the call of whiteness, money, and security is stronger than the call of blackness and art, and the fact that that drama is enacted in front of an art school further underlines the ethnic connotation of artistry. Not surprisingly, then, her interest in art flags considerably while she is involved with Roger. Angela, for whom marriage, rather than being a link to family and ethnicity, as for her sister, means an escape from it into individuality, seeks "money and influence" and because of this thinks "it would be better to marry . . . a white man" (88). "Angela Murray's desire to marry in accord with the plot of sentimental novels is but one facet of her overall desire for the isolate self, which she images as independent," as Missy Dehn Kubitschek explains (*Claiming the Heritage* 106). Angela imagines this independence from financial need and ethnicity, which she apparently sees as identical, as coming in the guise of whiteness and thus must avoid Miss Powell, who is a reminder of blackness. Consequently, her newly awakened interest in art, which follows the decline of her relationship with Roger, is also accompanied by a renewed interest in fellow ethnic artist Miss Powell, confirming essential links between art and ethnicity.

In *Fanny* and in *Plum Bun*, then, art has much to do with the ethnic revision of the Bildungsroman. Art serves not only as a marker of ethnicity but also as a motivating force in bringing the protagonists back to their ethnic groups. While the artist's quest is more (stereotypically) connected to a flight from society and to an attempt to realize artistic vision untrammeled by societal restrictions, the function of art in the ethnic Bildungsroman is quite manifestly the opposite: art connects the protagonists to their ethnicity and ultimately to their ethnic group.

However, even though Angela and Miss Powell have artistic ability, their art scholarships are revoked on grounds of race. Though art might be the natural expression of ethnicity in *Plum Bun*—and the fact that both scholarships are won by African American artists certainly underlines that message—that does not guarantee recognition of either art or ethnicity in white society. Incidents like these confirm Fauset's message that African Americans "were despised . . . simply because they were 'colored'; light or dark, ignorant or intelligent, cultured or not, black people living amid hatred and bigotry shared a common problem" (McLendon 7). Once art is recognized as the medium of ethnicity, though, recognition by white society becomes secondary or even unimportant. That Angela goes to France to study despite the denied scholarship points to an insight of that kind. But lest her trip to France be understood as an immersion into another kind of whiteness, albeit a European one, Fauset provides the reader with a clue—Angela's impending marriage to Anthony—that Angela's art-inspired rejection of passing has wider implications. More of that later.

Family ties prove to be as important as art in shaping the protagonists' attitudes towards ethnicity in both novels and thus also crucial for the communalist revisions of their genre. As discussed above, the decision to pass is connected to the protagonist's relationship with her mother in both novels, though it is based on an apparent misinterpretation of each mother's behavior. The return to ethnicity and the relationship to a sibling—brother Theodore in Fanny's case, sister Virginia in Angela's—are equally intertwined in both works. In *Fanny Herself*, the protagonist's brother's return and his ethnic commitment, expressed in his music, trigger feelings of guilt in Fanny about her passing, thus becoming one of the catalysts responsible for her return to art and Jewishness. In *Plum Bun*, Virginia feels guilt concerning her own conduct towards her sister. While Fanny thinks she has not supported her brother enough, Angela has denied her sister in public. For both protagonists, a willingness to sacrifice something for the sibling symbolizes the approaching readiness for ethnic solidarity, which is thus understood in terms of sacrifice as well. Fanny resolves to support her brother no matter what the price in the future and devotes considerable time to his career. Angela is ready to give up Anthony for her sister's sake and rejects the temptation of testing Matthew's (a former admirer who is now in turn admired by Virginia) attachment to her, resolving never to hurt her sister again (258). Because sibling relationships are a prelude to the regaining of a sense of ethnic solidarity for both protagonists, ethnicity is understood in terms of family relationship in both novels, or in terms of ties of "descent," as Werner Sollors would say.

According to Orlando Patterson, "They [ethnic groups] are the structural expressions of primary, extrafamilial identity. They resemble the family in the intensity of involvement of members and in the tendency to equate and rationalize relationships with other members in consanguineal terms" (308). One can observe the tendency of family relationships to determine how the protagonist feels about her ethnicity. In *Plum Bun* and *Fanny Herself*, the protagonists' misinterpretation of their mothers' ethnic allegiance or failure thereof sets the stage for both Fanny's and Angela's passing, as it does, arguably, in the *Autobiography* (and in *Brown Girl, Brownstones* and *Bread Givers*, as we shall see).

The idea of ethnicity as family, or as a descent relationship, in Sollors's terms, predominates in these works and is deployed deliberately, since it makes, of course, for much of the moral power that the appeal to ethnic solidarity has. The idea of family as essential connectedness of all members of an ethnic group overrides even the idea of shared geographical space, which becomes secondary in transnational appeals to "nationness" such as Emma Lazarus's:

> I do not hesitate to say that our national defect is that we are not "tribal" enough. . . . [W]e have not sufficient solidarity to perceive that when the life and property of a Jew in the uttermost provinces of the Caucasus are attacked, the dignity of a free Jew in America is humiliated. . . . Until we are free, we are none of us free." (quoted in Urofsky 44)

Marcus Garvey similarly stresses the "transnational" character of Pan-African nationalism: "As the Jew [sic] is held together by his religion, the white races by the assumption and the unwritten law of superiority, and the Mongolian by the precious tie of blood, so likewise the Negro must be united in one grand racial hierarchy. Our union must know no clime, boundary, or nationality" (Clarke 158). What provides the perceived basis for nationalism here are culture (art) and descent, both in Jewish and African American cultural nationalism.

At the same time, neither protagonist ever seems to lose the sense that ethnicity is something of a handicap, or at the very least connected to sacrifice. Even when in the throes of love, Angela still thinks of renouncing whiteness as a sacrifice, even if it is one willingly offered to Anthony: "No sacrifice of the comforts which came to her from 'passing,' of the assurance, even of the safety which the mere physical fact of whiteness in America brings, would be too great for her" (294). Of course, this passage entails a conscious critique of racism and its socioeconomic effects on Fauset's—if not on Angela's—part. Nonetheless, one has to remember that Angela's sister Virginia has a much more joyful attitude towards ethnicity; seen in that context, Angela's view of ethnicity is still far from enthusiastic when she contemplates ethnicity in comparative materialist terms. Her upper-class exposure in white society may be one explanation for the fact that Angela regards her return to ethnicity in somewhat condescending terms until the very end. The psychological preparation for her return takes place, befittingly, in the "Home Again" section of the novel. When she has reached the point of letting "the world take her as it would" (325)—which for her is a first step towards her ethnicity but also a phrase right out of the *Autobiography* and reflective of the Ex-Coloured Man's self-serving justifications—she contemplates the meaning of Harlem for her:

> Harlem intrigued her; it was a wonderful city; it represented, she felt, the last word in racial pride, integrity and even self-sacrifice. Here were people of a very high intellectual type, exponents of the realest and most essential refinement living cheek by jowl with coarse or ill-bred or even criminal, certainly indifferent, members of their race. Of course some of this propinquity was due to outer pressure, but there was present, too, a hidden consciousness of race-duty, a something if translated said: "Perhaps you do pull me down a little from the height to which I have climbed. But on the other hand, perhaps, I'm helping you to rise." (326)

This haughtiness may well reflect Fauset's "Talented Tenth" associations, but it is also expressive of the war between individualism and communalism taking place in Angela. While she considers communal self-sacrifice, she also regards the "refined" individual as self-accomplished, risen to heights on his or her own merit and beholden to others mostly by choice, not by necessity.

Nonetheless, Angela also comes to see only family relationships and friendships within her ethnic group as "permanent" and "real" (250). The idea of permanence is directly related to the notion of ethnicity as family, stressing the communal nature of ethnicity. Since familial ties are not voluntary but taken as a given, they cannot and—as the novel exhorts—should not be revoked. By contrast, Angela's relationship with Roger does not bind either one of them—which is why Angela wants marriage, a "consent" relationship which would give her the same protection and safety as a family relationship, but for the price of a rejection of her "descent" relationship to ethnicity. Early in the novel, she makes clear that safety is one of her reasons for seeking marriage (88). A white marriage, in her view, simply provides material comfort and, in that sense, more security. Later in the novel, after her relationship with Roger has failed, Angela comes to see security not so much in material as in emotional terms. Since the novel associates materialism with whiteness and emotions and solidarity with blackness, it is only logical that now Angela understands safety to reside in the familial circle of ethnicity, and there only.

By representing ethnic ties as family ties, both novels not only stress the inevitability of ethnicity but also strengthen the moral obligation that is associated with it in these texts. Ferber and Fauset thus present ethnic solidarity not merely as an ideal, but as a compelling moral duty. Thus, like *Fanny Herself*, *Plum Bun* exhibits passing not as a mere individualistic quirk but as a failure, as a first step down the "moral ladder," to be followed by others; once passing, Angela is ready to engage in an illicit affair with Roger when he reminds her that their relationship would "be all the sweeter for that secrecy" because she already has experienced that "stolen waters were the sweetest, she of all people knew that" (189). In Angela's case, the nadir of this course will be reached when she does not acknowledge her sister in public.

Regarding Angela's relationship with Roger, one must note that her material desires do not fulfill themselves, ultimately, through her strategy of passing, while that same strategy succeeds in the case of the Ex-Coloured Man.[5] Because he is a man, after having abandoned blackness, all business opportunities are open to him, though he, too, must forsake artistic endeavors. Angela can only obtain the material rewards of whiteness through marriage, it seems. Even then, class barriers prevent that from happening. As Vashti Crutcher Lewis has noted, "because she has no social class standing among the Eastern-seaboard nouveau riche, he can accept her only as his clandestine mistress. . . . It is ironic that she, as a refined white woman, qualifies only to assume the status of mistress, a role historically assigned to black women in white black liaisons" (381). One may wonder whether Fauset consciously confined Angela to this historic role and meant to show the ultimate inescapability of race, or whether the class dynamics are meant as a critique of class barriers in the U.S. The latter seems doubtful in a novel focusing on the injustice of the racist exclusion of African Americans from a middle-class luxury and lifestyle that the novel shows as desirable.

More likely, we are to read Angela's fate as indicative of how difficult it is for an African American woman to achieve or maintain middle-class status, her options being so limited—a truth of which Fauset's life itself was illustrative. In a comparison to *Fanny Herself*, one can see how *Plum Bun* focuses on ethnicity and color even more than on gender or class, because what are barriers for Angela are surmountable difficulties for Fanny. Though she has a boss who "never employ[s] a woman when [he] can use a man" (135), her career flourishes, thanks to her abilities and strength, and she has access to material possibilities without marriage. However, despite Angela's, and Miss Powell's, artistic ability, their art scholarships are revoked on grounds of race. The juxtaposition of the two novels highlights the role and status of whiteness in the American labor market.

Both protagonists opt not to revoke their ethnicity in the end, and the return to ethnicity is motivated similarly in both novels through a conjunction of abstract duty and personal feelings as the ethnicity-equals-family metaphor suggests. To no small degree, love by and of a man of their ethnic group provides an incentive for the return. Thus, both "consent" and "descent" bind the protagonists to their ethnic group, a double formula typical of nationalism (more of that in the concluding chapter). In Ferber's novel, Heyl's insistence, verging on preposterousness, on Fanny's duty to realize her "racial" gifts may only be the external impersonation of her repressed tendencies, but the fact that she does what he demands of her in the end lets his urgings and her actions coincide to a maximum degree, underlined by their romantic involvement.

Angela finds herself influenced by Anthony Cross before she knows that he is "black." His ideal of selfless love corresponds to the ideal of unselfish ethnic solidarity that the novel espouses. As she finds herself drawn to that kind of love after her quest for material comfort through marriage has failed, it just so happens that this love is to be found within her ethnic group. One is reminded of fairy tale plots—and their movement from "illusion to reality," as Carolyn Wedin Sylvander has noted (185), though the line between the two is thin in *Plum Bun*—in which the lowly turn out to be aristocratic in the end and thus make perfect spouses for princely suitors who do not have to cross class lines after all.

In *Plum Bun*, the conjunction of love and ethnicity serves as mutual reenforcement of the (nationalist) ideology advanced by Fauset (and Ferber): ethnic solidarity is personal love writ large. And it is very shortly after Anthony's public revelation of his race (338–339) that Angela sides with Miss Powell (346), so that personal love may also prompt ethnic solidarity. At the same time, as the novel has it, conjugal commitment to a member of the same ethnic group stands as a sign of ethnic solidarity, particularly when the other option is marriage to a nonethnic who despises African Americans and thus indirectly forces a denial of familial connections.

In this respect, *Plum Bun* outlines its ideological message with respect to ethnicity even more forcefully than *Fanny Herself*, where marriage to a nonethnic is not considered—because Fenger is a passing ethnic himself—and, as a result, passing does not assume Faustian dimensions to the same degree. However, the link of materialism to passing is equally stressed in both novels, as potential marriage to the non-or-passing-ethnic means considerable financial gain for both protagonists. The price for that gain would be a continued repudiation or downplaying of ethnicity, which establishes a Faustian dimension of passing in both novels, particularly given the moral equation of ethnicity with higher emotions and altruism and of nonethnicity with materialism and selfishness. The only right choice, in both novels, is to accept ethnicity, even though this may be accompanied by sacrifices.

However, it is those very sacrifices, these novels say, that have made being ethnic what it is: a richer, deeper state of being, and the only one the ethnic individual should embrace. *Plum Bun* propagates a belief in ethnic solidarity and ethnic distinctiveness just as *Fanny Herself* sees Jewishness as a "Peculiar Treasure," an inheritance the ethnic individual must accept for the good of Jewry and humanity, even if it means revoking worldly treasures. Both Fauset and Ferber explain the greater depth, artistic inclination, and sensitivity they see as ethnic potential through a legacy of suffering. As Ethan Goffman says, "certainly religious transcendentalism is crucial to many strands of black identity. Yet the same can be claimed of Jewish identity, of Jewish suffering" (182). But though this is a sociohistorical explanation, their novels claim that the revocation of ethnicity is both morally and inherently impossible.

Nationalism requires that the individual members of a group live up to the characteristics deemed peculiar to it. If they do not, they run the risk of being seen as betrayers of an (ethnic) national consensus. This moral judgment is facilitated by the fact that *Plum Bun* and *Fanny* (as well as *Autobiography* and *Haunch*) create, as it were, false dilemmas: either the protagonist lives up to an ethnic ideal as the novel constructs it, or she becomes completely absorbed in the pursuit of materialism. This extreme dichotomy had come into being before Du Bois described it so memorably in *The Souls of Black Folk*. Melvin Urofsky shows that "As early as 1885, the Russian Hebrew journal *Ha-Melitz* wrote: 'This new land is not prepared to receive the old Jewish religion. This agreement does America make with each new immigrant: "Give me your soul and you may take the material possessions."'"(Urofsky 74). Because that latter option is easily discredited by the plot in that it harms other members of the ethnic group and is shown to leave the protagonist feeling spiritually unsatisfied, the "ethnic choice" is attractive because the only other choice presented is so objectionable. An anonymous review of *Plum Bun* in the *Afro-American* of March 23, 1929, asked cleverly, "Can a Colored Girl 'Pass' and Be Happy?" (Bassett 109). Both Fauset and Ferber answer "No."

CHAPTER THREE

Brown Girl, Brownstones and *Bread Givers*:
Reconciling Ethnicity and Individualism

Although thirty-four years separate the publication dates of Anzia Yezierska's *Bread Givers* (1925) and Paule Marshall's *Brown Girl, Brownstones* (1959), and though significant historical events and social changes mark those years and the approximately three decades intervening between the plots of the two novels, they exhibit perhaps the most striking parallels of the three pairs discussed in this study. Both delineate immigrant communities in their early stages. *Bread Givers* describes a time span of about twenty years, presumably—because of the autobiographical nature of her work—from the 1890s to sometime before the 1910s, which roughly parallels Yezierska's own life history (Kessler Harris vii–ix). This period also marks the high point of Eastern European Jewish immigration, and the novel illustrates the economic and social hardships of that time.

Some of the Jewish immigrants who lived in dire poverty in the early part of the twentieth century have risen in the world and appear as employers of Barbadian immigrants in Marshall's novel, which chronicles the time from 1939 to about 1947.[1] While Hitler is referred to as "the worse person in the world" (184) and as "the devil-incarnate" (69) for his crimes against the Jews, there is also a sense that this does not really concern the Barbadian community, which sees World War II as "these white people getting on too bad" (69). As the Barbadians exist on the margins of American society, World War II itself is relegated to the margins of the plot as a "white man's war." The novel's focus remains on the Barbadian American context for which the war has mostly economic consequences, as it provides work in the defense industry. The novel's emphasis on community internal dynamics and on the friction between Barbadian America and the dominant white society offers much ground of comparison to *Bread Givers*. Ironically, though, Marshall's novel reflects the degree to which Yezierska's immigrants have become assimilated and moved up the social ladder: the Jewish employers or classmates featured in the novel are not distinguishable from the larger white world. Silla groans about having to clean the floors of Jewish homes, Selina appears to have a Jewish friend (Rachel), and some Barbadians see Jewish success as a model for their own aspirations; but the immigrant character of Jewish Americans appears to be a thing of the past in *Brown Girl, Brownstones*.

What makes for the eminent compatibility of both novels is not to be found in any sociohistorical similarities, though there are some, given the recent immigration of both novels' ethnic communities, but in their conceptualization of ethnicity. In both novels, the protagonists struggle with Old World roots (which are already New World in Marshall's case) that are closer than in any of the previous novels. Thus, *Brown Girl* attempts a definition of ethnicity somewhere between "Barbadian," "African American," and "American," while *Bread Givers* negotiates "Old World Jewishness," "New World Jewishness," and "Americanness." In both novels, the Americanness of the parent generation is recent and tenuous and, in part as a result, the protagonists, to some extent, struggle towards it, so that "Americanness" does not only or predominantly appear in the white materialist guise of the other four novels, serving as a threat against which an ethnic idealism has to maintain itself. However, both novels also reflect a dialogue with ethnic nationalism, though a more antagonistic one than the previously discussed texts. Ultimately, it is again the interplay between individualism and communalism, between idealism and materialism, and between ethnicity and mainstream that allows for a comparison, and this interplay, as I have shown and will discuss in greater detail in the concluding chapter, is in part endemic to the nationalist project and also a result of the tension between Bildungsroman and nationalism.

Both novels are about ethnic worlds which have a specific historical location, highlighted much more in *Brown Girl, Brownstones* than in *Bread Givers*, but which are also isolated to an extent from the outside world, though they are subject to its dynamics. This isolation reflects the immigrant status of both communities. In both novels, depictions of ethnic customs abound and create a world different from the "mainstream." This difference is primarily marked by language. Direct speech is often rendered in the distinctive vernacular (rendered in English, though, in *Bread Givers*) of the Barbadian or Eastern European (Russian-Polish Jewish) immigrant communities in juxtaposition to the narration, which is in American English. The duality of language use in those two novels reflects "the general idea of the interdependence of language and identity—you are the way you speak" (Ashcroft et al. 54)—and in this context, it is significant that the protagonists do not speak the vernacular of their communities in the latter parts of either novel. Nonetheless, the use of Barbadian and Jewish English highlights cultural specificity. At the same time, these texts "employ vernacular as a linguistic variant to signify the insertion of the outsider into the discourse" (Ashcroft et al. 57). The very rendering of the vernacular in written language gives it equal status to mainstream English and linguistically symbolizes the act of immigration. These culturally specific communities serve as background for the coming of age of two protagonists born into families recently immigrated to the United States.

That African American literature is far from monolithic and has immigrant elements is sometimes neglected. The *Autobiography* has been called a migration novel (see Farah Jasmin Griffin), *Plum Bun* is a domestic novel, and *Brown Girl* a novel delineating immigration and its consequences—but all three find equivalents in Jewish American literature, a fact that emphasizes "relatedness" when it comes to the conceptualization of ethnicity.

Of the six hybrid forms of autobiography and Bildungsroman examined in this study, *Brown Girl, Brownstones* and *Bread Givers* are the two that are most autobiographical in nature. More than any of the other novels, they render the life circumstances of their authors and the complicated relationship to their parents. As Alice Kessler Harris says in her foreword to *Bread Givers*: "All of the six books Anzia Yezierska published between 1920 and 1932 are in some sense autobiographical, but none more so than *Bread Givers*" (v): "Anzia Yezierska and Sara Smolinsky, the novel's narrator, are emotionally interchangeable" (xvii). In her afterword to *Brown Girl, Brownstones*, Mary Helen Washington notes that Paule Marshall, "in 1959, at age 30 . . . published that novel, which explores her own girlhood through the character of Selina Boyce"(322).[2]

Because both novels, to a significant extent, render their authors' lives, their protagonists may be somewhat less symbolic and more individualized than those of *The Autobiography of an Ex-Coloured Man* and *Haunch, Paunch and Jowl* and may fulfill less of an obviously didactic function than those of *Plum Bun* and *Fanny Herself*. This does not mean that the respective ethnic communities of these two novels do

not occupy a central place in the plot, because they do; but these stories are more individualistic in ideology than any of the four other works
and therefore see ethnicity predominantly as a social construct. At the
same time, both novels seem to fit the traditional Bildungsroman mold
better than the other four in their insistence on a right to individualism and in their protagonists' rebellion against their communities. But
almost as if to forestall the conclusion that individualism rules, both
novels devote considerable time to delineating other characters' lives,
particularly those of the dominant parent who comes to represent the
ethnic community. In this, and in many other respects, the novels can
be understood as a constant negotiation between individualism and
communalism.

Because the protagonists, Selina Boyce and Sara Smolinsky, feel as
outsiders in their communities, attempt to break away, and come to a
painful reconciliation only at the end, the range of being ethnic is expanded beyond the parameters set by the novels discussed previously.
Though all of the four earlier protagonists attempt to break away from
their ethnic communities as well, or actually do so in one way or another,
their behavior is implicitly condemned and the novels supply models
of what they recommend as better courses of action; these better courses
are embedded in essentialist conceptualizations of ethnicity. In *Brown
Girl, Brownstones* and *Bread Givers*, however, the protagonists try to
establish their own positions vis-à-vis their ethnic groups, and they
encounter other characters who have done so without these individuals being judged negatively by the protagonist or through authorial
comments. In this way, both novels show a wide range of possibilities
of being ethnic, not all of which have to play themselves out in the
ethnic community.

This is so because both works also depict their protagonists as experiencing the ethnic community as oppressive or confining at times. What
Carole Boyce Davies has said about autobiographical writings by black
women holds true for both of these novels: "The mystified notions of
home and family are removed from their romantic, idealized moorings,
to speak of pain, movement, difficulty, learning and love in complex
ways. Thus, the complicated notion of home mirrors the problematizing of community/nation that one finds in Black women's writing
from a variety of communities" (21). The traits of their communities
that the protagonists dislike are clearly shown to be responses to socioeconomic conditions, though, not essential characteristics of the ethnic

group. And, perhaps more importantly, because these novels, for the most part, do not see ethnicity in essentialist terms, the protagonists are not forced to decide between individualism and ethnicity—though those choices do present themselves in the respective plots, and even in those terms. The narratives do not portray Selina and Sara as betrayers if they lean towards individualism, even though both novels show an awareness of the possibility of seeing individualism as a betrayal of ethnicity and are indeed writing against that perspective. The constructionist bent in these novels can thus be interpreted both as the result of their stronger individualist leanings and as a way of making these leanings possible in the first place while not showing them, as the four earlier novels do, as an expression of unmitigated—and unethnic—selfishness. To that extent, these novels both uphold and modify the individualist bent of the Bildungsroman model.

As Carole Boyce Davies's remark implies, the struggle the protagonists have to go through to arrive at a hybrid form of individualism and communalism is expressive of the narratives' struggle with cultural nationalism. Carol B. Schoen sees *Bread Givers* "most of all [as an exploration of] the unresolvable tensions between the ancient Jewish mores that assumed male domination and the American ideal of individual freedom" (61), tensions which the novel does resolve, however uneasily. Accordingly, Sam Girgus has noted the similarity between the ideology Yezierska's narratives seem to embrace and Louis Brandeis's Zionism, which proposed the compatibility of Zionist aspirations and American citizenship (109).[3]

Paule Marshall, in "From the Poets in the Kitchen," explains the influence which the conversations of her mother and her friends had on her in her writing career. In these conversations, Marcus Garvey played a pivotal role: "If F.D.R. was their hero, Marcus Garvey was their God. The name of the fiery, Jamaican-born black nationalist of the 20s was constantly evoked around the table" (5). Small wonder, then, that his spirit, in the form of ethnic solidarity as ideal, hovers over the novel.

But far from simply subscribing to Zionism or Garveyism, both novels are locked in a dialectical struggle with the notion of ethnic solidarity. They are thus characterized by dualities: their protagonists rebel against a communally prescribed ethnic identity and yet come to a kind of reconciliation with their communities; the novels adhere in part to the individualistic plotline of the Bildungsroman and yet revise that model to accommodate the notion of ethnic solidarity; and they both harshly criticize and celebrate their ethnic communities.[4] The result for the protagonists: a reluctant but inescapable hybridity.

Brown Girl, Brownstones and *Bread Givers* both tell the story of a young girl (both Selina and Sara are ten years old at the respective novels' outsets) with immigrant parents growing up in a section of New York primarily inhabited by Barbadians and Eastern European Jews, respectively. Both protagonists' lives are lived partly in response to what they see as the model of ethnicity that one of the parents embodies for them. In the case of *Brown Girl*, that parent is Silla, Selina's mother; in the case of *Bread Givers*, it is Sara's father, Reb Smolinsky. Both of these characters dominate their respective households: they determine economic matters of the household, even against the resistance of the other parent, and they attempt to mold their children's lives. The novels depict both of them at times as ruthless and cruel. Resistance against them is apparently futile—but also becomes a mark of the protagonist's growth and character. In their attempts at resisting that parent's influence, in their fears of becoming like the dominant parent, and in their ability to reach a kind of peace with that parent, the protagonists each establish their individuality and their relationship to their ethnicity.

While the earlier novels suggest that individuality, the wish to live according to one's talents, desires, weaknesses, and strengths, is subordinate to ethnic solidarity, *Brown Girl, Brownstones* and *Bread Givers* reverberate with ambiguities. Carol Schoen says of *Bread Givers* that the "conflicting tensions that had marked both [Yezierska's] life and her work found here a successful expression—the wish to become part of America versus the pull of tradition and family; a woman's desire for self-fulfillment versus the wish for home, husband, and children; the desire for material comforts versus the demands for intellectual achievement" (62). As a result of such ambiguities, the novels recognize the necessity of ethnic solidarity, associated with the Old World, and affirm individuality, associated with the New, as equally important. Their protagonists are paradigmatic of a new and uneasy ethnicity— in Werner Sollors's words, "In the complicated American landscape of regional, religious, and ethnic affiliation, it could be very difficult to construct the self as autonomous individual and as fated group member" (*Beyond Ethnicity* 173).

One strategy through which the novels accomplish the affirmation of the equal importance of individualism and communalism is by establishing their heroines as characters a little apart from their families. Even though, as children, these heroines fully immerse themselves in their families and communities, they also feel, or are depicted as, somehow stronger, older, or wiser. This strategy bases itself on the assumption of the constructedness of ethnicity, allowing individuals to differ from one another without calling into question their "ethnicness"—as happens in the earlier novels—and without attaching any obvious judgment to their "intra-ethnic difference." However, the protagonists' difference also expresses their second-generation status: unlike their parents, they have not experienced the ethnic homeland, yet both family and community expect loyalty to ethnic customs. Simultaneously, there is also the lure of the "paradigm of 'progress' embodied by [the] host society, capitalist America," as Heather Hathaway (129) has said with reference to *Brown Girl, Brownstones*. In negotiating a path between the two, both protagonists have to prove whether they have the strength to realize the potential inherent in their second-generation status to "harmonize past with present to create a truly revolutionary 'New World' presence in the United States" (Hathaway 129). When the protagonists' personal peculiarities (which seem to symbolize intra-ethnic difference) first appear, as they do in the opening pages of both novels, they are seen as positive, quite in accordance with the Bildungsroman model of the youthful and rebellious hero/ine. Not until later in the plots do these differences become problematic and connected to the question of betrayal of ethnicity.

Both Selina and Sara show strength of character early on and appear old beyond their years. They are described as thin and wiry, yet strong and determined, each harboring the wish to escape from her environment. In *Brown Girl, Brownstones*, these traits are made explicit in Selina's first appearance:

a ten-year-old girl with scuffed legs and a body as straggly as the clothes she wore. A haze of sunlight seeping down from the skylight through the dust and dimness of the hall caught her wide full mouth, the small but strong nose, the eyes set deep in the darkness of her face. They were not the eyes of a child. Something too old lurked in their centers. They were weighted, it seemed, with scenes of a long life. She might have been old once and now, miraculously, young again—but with the memory of that other life intact. She seemed to know the world down there in the dark hall and beyond for what it was. Yet knowing, she still longed to leave this safe, sun-lit place at the top of the house for the challenge there. (4)

Selina's thinness suggests an ascetic side of her character and foreshadows her antimaterialistic outlook on life, which will fully emerge later. Her scuffed legs and strong nose reveal toughness, an orientation towards action also emphasized by the last sentence of the quotation, alluding to her curiosity about the world. But the conflict between these traits, which turn out to be her mother's, and her father's sensuality, hinted at through her "wide full mouth," is introduced here. This conflict makes her a dynamic character, one who is torn between two poles; it sets up a dialectic out of which will emerge Selina the grown woman as synthesis. The other young characters in the book, and especially Selina's sister Ina, are not as affected by conflicts, and their development is predictable. As the most dynamic character in the novel, Selina is set aside from other characters, a state to which her precociousness adds and which "the family photograph, which did not include her" (6) most aptly symbolizes.

Sara, too, is "thin and small" (7), yet full of energy and determination, as indicated by her nickname, "Blut-und-Eisen" [Blood-and-iron] (20). She, too, is precocious: "But from always it was heavy on my heart the worries for the house as if I was mother" (1). Mentally, she takes on the responsibilities of an adult. But while Selina's precociousness is described in terms of a kind of worldly wisdom, Sara is old beyond her years because of the pressures of poverty, the fear of being "thrown in the street to shame and to laughter for the whole world" (1). Although all her sisters share poverty with her, she is more enterprising than they are, insisting on peddling wares to make some money for her family. In this enterprise, her strong sense of her own individuality is revealed; indeed, her personhood becomes defined by her ability to do business like an adult. Upon a friendly neighbor offering her some fish for starting her peddling business, she replies: "No—no! I'm no beggar! . . . I want to go into business like a person. I must buy what I got to sell" (21). She is able to prove wrong her mother's doubt as to her ability to earn money, and she triumphs in her success: "And throwing the fifty pennies, like a shower of gold, into my mother's lap, I cried, 'Now, will you yet call me crazy-head? Give only a look what 'Blood-and-iron' has done'" (23).

Resenting having been treated condescendingly, she establishes her personhood by accomplishing adult feats. Through this act the novel also establishes her as a dynamic character; just as she, not her sisters, shows initiative in an emergency situation, only she will break the pattern of poverty and dependence on a man, while her sisters end up in marriages not too unlike that of their parents. Sam Girgus notes that the "ideology of the individual self at the core of Yezierska's writings represents basic American attitudes towards freedom, success, and culture" (111), and the fifty pennies episode establishes Sara as exhibiting this kind of individualism. Both of Sara's parents register her difference through nicknaming her "Blood-and-iron," and her mother explains the significance of that name: "When she begins to want a thing, there is no rest, no let-up till she gets it" (20). This description will prove to be an apt one for Selina as well.

Selina, too, has a moment early in the novel when she asserts her personhood. When her mother compares her to her deceased brother, who had died before her birth on account of a weak heart, Selina reacts spontaneously: "Suddenly Selina sprang forward and leaning close into the mother shouted, 'I keep telling you I'm not him. I'm me. Selina. And there's nothing wrong with my heart'" (47). While the motivation for asserting individuality differs in the two novels, both novels establish that their respective heroines show an early and strong self-awareness and differ from their siblings. Like the mother in *Bread Givers*, Silla notes the premature strength and self-awareness of her daughter: "'But look at my crosses,' she whispered, awed, as Selina disappeared. 'Look how I has gone and brought something into this world to whip me.'" (47).

For both Selina and Sara, their independence is linked to their attitudes towards values that the novels connect with their ethnic groups, specifically through the stronger parent. Because they are depicted as independent and strong-willed characters, it appears consistent—particularly in terms of the Bildungsroman genre—that they would rebel at some point against what the novels outline as the norm, and in this case as the ethnic norm. In *Brown Girl, Brownstones*, Selina perceives this norm to be a form of materialism, a single-minded devotion to the project of buying a house that pervades the Barbadian community. As a child, she witnesses her mother's friend Iris torture her mother with the latter's failure—which is attributed to Selina's father, Deighton—to buy a house by naming a seemingly endless list of women who have "bought house" (73–74). The community's insistence on "buying house" as a measure of respectability, even as a measure of the "proper ethnic spirit," is epitomized in a communal wedding scene where Deighton has to suffer "the rejection of the entire community" (Mary Helen Washington 317) because he has spent money for pleasure rather than on a down payment.[5]

Unable to see her mother's and the Barbadian community's obsession with "buying house" as an "epic struggle . . . to establish . . . a precarious foothold in an alien world" (Le Seur 113), Selina rejects such a value system, as becomes clear in the scene where Iris tantalizes Silla with names of house-owning families. Commenting on Selina's physical growth, one of Silla's friends brushes her hand over Selina's budding breast, remarking, "Tell your mother that you's no more little girl, but near a full woman like us now that you's filling out—and that you can hold your tongue like a woman" (77). Selina is to hold her tongue because Silla has just announced that she will wrest land Deighton has inherited in Barbados from him so that she may sell it for a down payment. Her mother's materialism and her own physical growth are thus conflated, and the value system embraced by the adults assumes inescapable proportions. But "the scene ends in a failed initiation" (Basu). Selina's initial reaction is to strike out at Silla's friend's hand and to threaten her with a broken glass. Later, she is "seized by a frenzy of rejection" and tries to rub off the "imprint," though it proves to be "indelible" (78).[6] Her attempt to rid herself of her mother's friend's "imprint" signals her intention not to be part of their plan or their value system.

Her rebellion against materialism recurs throughout the novel, as in her assertion to her mother that there are things that cannot be bought in stores, such as love and breath (104), or in her condemnation of her friends' other-determined and money-oriented career goals (195ff.). In the latter scene, Selina's wish to develop her own goals and not follow a norm set by her ethnic group expresses itself in her observation that her best friend "Beryl's face had somehow lost its individual mold, that soft pleasing form she used to gaze at" (195–196). As Heather Hathaway comments, "for Selina, as a character who is both representative of and yet also markedly different from typical second-generation immigrants, the demand to conform to community mandate is asphyxiating" (153).

Unlike her peers, Selina does not wish to fulfill her community's expectations. Though, for much of the novel, she remains unsure of the values she wants to replace materialism with, she is certain that she does not want to fit the mold that the community seems to have cast for her. Ethnicity, for her, appears to be a kind of conformity, a conformity to materialism of which the Association of Barbadian Homeowners and Businessmen is the most visible expression, an expression which she scathingly denounces when first visiting the Association. The Association, aptly called "the biggest thing since Marcus Garvey" (196), serves as the novel's most visible symbol of Selina's conflict with ethnic nationalism and as "a testament to the dawning political consciousness of a small black community determined to make its presence felt" (Denniston 21). Though she recognizes admiringly the communal force of her ethnic group and even finds its "surety of purpose . . . enviable," she also perceives that "they were no longer individuals" (222) and rejects them at that point as "Clannish. Narrow-minded. Selfish" (227).

Sara's rebellion takes religion as one of its focal points. Because her father devotes his life to studying the Torah, her rejection of the ethnic life she sees around her is strongly linked to the issue of religion. Yezierska responds here to the image of the "pious scholar" as it had "emerge[d] in American Jewish fiction by the turn of the century. . . . The figure of the reflective, otherworldly scholar struggling to survive in the harsh grind of the sweatshop and bemoaning his children's apostasy, serves as a metaphor for the tensions inherent in new conditions" (Baum et al. 189). While this metaphor still serves the same function in *Bread Givers*, Yezierska revises it substantially by making the scholar not only a victim of changed conditions but also an oppressor in his own small world. The focus thus shifts from the plight of the scholar, which the novel nonetheless depicts, if mostly unsympathetically, to those suffering under the tyranny of that scholar. In turn, this shift in focus emphasizes less—at least at times—the oppressive circumstances caused by economic conditions in America than the domestic oppression taking place within that larger framework. Not until the protagonist experiences the outside world does her resentment vanish and the ethnic world starts appearing in a different light. (As we will see, a similar progression of attitudes structures the plot of *Brown Girl, Brownstones.*)

Before that, however, Sara resents her sisters' and her mother's state of subjection to her father, a custom she connects with her ethnicity,[7] while linking greater freedom to a nonethnic state. Thinking of the men who court her sisters, she resolves that she wants "No one from Essex or Hester Street" but "an American-born man who was his own boss.

And who would let me be my boss. And no fathers, and no mothers, and no sweatshops, and no herring!" (66). Her rejection of these icons of ethnicity points to her wish to escape poverty.

But poverty, according to *Bread Givers*, appears in part to be caused by religion, at least for Sara's family. Her father's resolve not to work, his exploitation of his daughters, his inept selection of husbands for his daughters, and his failure in business all are results of his inexperience in the world of business, which he despises. To one of his daughter's suitor's suggestion that he work himself instead of having his daughter work for him, he replies, "What? I work like a common thickneck? My learning comes before my living" (48). As S. M. Dubnow has said of rabbinic education in nineteenth-century Russia, "The scholastic education resulted in producing men entirely unfit for the battle of life, so that in many families energetic women took charge of the business and became the wage earners, while their husbands were losing themselves in the mazes of speculation" (quoted in Baum et al. 55). Dubnow's quote adequately represents not only the role of Sara's father but also Sara's attitude toward that role. Sara thinks and says, and Yezierska has other characters say, that her father should contribute to earning a living for the family. In fact, though, having the women of the family earn its income on their own if the father was a scholar was not unusual in Eastern European Jewish communities (Baum et al. 67). Such scholars were respected in the Old World *shtetl* and supported by it (Rose). Thus, one might say that the extent of Sara's resentment of this arrangement illustrates the extent of her Americanization.

Sara's dislike of poverty, a poverty that she, as narrator, attributes in part to her father, then also leads to a rejection of religion:

> I began to feel different from my sisters. They couldn't stand Father's preaching any more than I, but they could suffer to listen to him like dutiful children who honour and obey and respect their father, whether they like him or not. . . . I'd wake up in the middle of the night when all were asleep, and cry into the deaf, dumb darkness, "I hate my father. And I hate God most of all for bringing me into such a terrible house." (65–66)

One can see how "father" and "God" are paralleled here in a conflation of her feelings of anger towards her father (the man of God) and God. Her anger also determines her attitude towards the religious injunction to honor and obey one's parents. Her feelings of difference and her independence thus come to be defined in relation to religion, which, in turn, is a sign of ethnicity. The Bildungsroman's course of the protagonist's initial rebellion against his or her society thus leads, in this case, to an initial rejection of a major sign of ethnicity. That the novel constructs religion as such a sign becomes clear when her father counters her assertion, after having left the family, that she is "not from the old country" but that, instead, she is an "American" with the exclamation, "You blasphemer! . . . Denier of God!" (138). He, too, sees no difference between a denial of religion and a denial of ethnicity. Thus, both Sara and Selina, in establishing their independence, refuse to embrace one of the core values that define their ethnic community and, in the process of doing so, they feel a sense of aloneness, of being different than others in their family or age group.

The two core values rejected—acquisitiveness and religion—turn out to be closely related in both novels. Several of the passages in *Brown Girl, Brownstones* dealing with Silla's plan to sell Deighton's land have strong religious overtones. Silla paradoxically invokes God for her plan and compares Deighton to Jesus Christ at the same time, while religious exclamations are sprinkled throughout the following passage in which she decides to sell Deighton's Barbadian property:

> "Be-Jesus-Christ, I gon do that for him then. Even if I got to see my soul fall howling into hell I gon do it. . . ." Silla stood calm, confident, almost smiling in their midst. Her eyes had clouded over and she had forgotten them. . . . "As God is my witness I know how to sell it for him. . . . I know I isn't to do a thing against your beautiful-ugly father. He's Christ to you. But wait. Wait till I finish with him. He gon be Christ crucified." (75–77)

Silla becomes a prophetlike figure in this scene in which she metaphorically sells her soul to her new religion: the acquisition of a house at any price. On that altar, both her husband and Christianity, and specifically its virtue of compassion, will be sacrificed. Once she has decided to steal from her husband, all moral barriers fall and she conspires against and evicts one tenant (Suggie) and drives another into death (Miss Mary). She confirms the metaphysical nature of this choice when Deighton finds out about the sale of the land and she triumphs bitterly, "Yes, Silla has done it. She has lied and feigned and forged. She has damned her soul but she did it" (114).

Bread Givers, too, interweaves religious and materialist elements until both seem inextricably connected. Reb Smolinsky, Sara's father, repeatedly preaches the value of poverty and the richness of a life devoted to religion. However, when it comes to his daughters, he exhibits a ruthless materialism that easily rivals Silla's. He wants to be paid for his oldest daughter Bessie by her potential groom and be set up in business by him, which turns the custom of offering a bride price on its head, according to the novel.[8] He despises a suitor of one of his daughters for his poverty, making clear that his concern is not the welfare of his daughter but his own reputation (75) and well-being (in reference to another suitor, he exclaims, "You'll see he'll cover Masha with diamonds. And through her riches, all of us will get rich quick"—[77]). Accordingly, once he has married off two of his daughters, he expects to be served better food: "'Woman!' Father frowned. 'Why have you no meat for my dinner this whole week?'" (81). "Acting as the agent for his own daughter's marriage, Smolinsky makes money both as a representative of traditional authority and as an individual father, literally selling off his daughter," says Thomas Ferraro (70). Indeed, one might say that while Silla practices materialism with religious overtones, Reb Smolinsky practices religion with materialist overtones.[9]

Because both novels associate the ethnic community with materialism in a number of passages, they can be read as a critique of the strategy adopted in the other novels examined in this study that suggest an organic link between idealism and ethnicity, an integral element of nationalist ideology. Both novels thus write against what William Boelhower has identified as a basic plot for most immigrant novels: "With construction as the master topic, goals are still relatively uncomplicated, cultural motives are few, simple, public in character, and usually agreed upon by all. The ethnic project inspires consensus, and consensus inspires the building of an ethnic community" (Glass 101–102). Selina and Sara do not subscribe to that consensus and demand room outside the parameters it prescribes. Edward Said claims, "Students of post-colonial politics have not, I think, looked enough at the ideas that minimize orthodoxy and authoritarian or patriarchal thought, that take a severe view of the coercive nature of identity politics" (219). Brown Girl, Brownstones and Bread Givers do exactly that: they explore the potential of coercion behind the notion of ethnic solidarity (which, at least in Bread Givers, also takes on a patriarchal guise).

Ironically, the novels' critique of coercive ethnic solidarity brings them closer to the ideology of individualism, which is both a feature of

"Americanism" and a mainstream nationalist self-definition the ethnic community finds itself excluded from. At the same time, individualism is a feature of the traditional Bildungsroman and autobiography model that ethnic works often revise. But are these novels therefore assimilationist? Or are they traditional Bildungsromane? The answer to both is no, because rather than accept the definition of ethnicity represented by the strong parent or reject ethnicity as a whole, they create new ethnic boundaries, illuminating, as Werner Sollors has said in a discussion of Mark Twain's *Connecticut Yankee*, "Frederick Barth's thesis that ethnicity rests on the boundary, not on the 'cultural stuff it encloses'" ("Ethnicity" 299). This shifting of boundaries, however, while creating distance between the protagonists' and the parents' version of ethnicity, does not result in an uncritical embrace of individualism.

Both protagonists attempt to establish their independence from the strong parent, whom the novels make symbolic of the coercive aspect of the ethnic community, through a refusal to conform to one of the main tenets of their ethnic communities, namely acquisitiveness and adherence to religious doctrine, respectively. However, this refusal is not equivalent to a renouncement of ethnicity, as it would have been in novels that construct ethnicity predominantly along essentialist lines, such as *Plum Bun* and *Fanny Herself*. Both *Bread Givers* and *Brown Girl, Brownstones* provide characters located between absolute ethnic solidarity and unmitigated individualism, and those characters are depicted in positive or sympathetic terms. This strategy becomes necessary because both protagonists still have to deal with the ethnic consensus described above and establish some kind of truce, since ethnicity, as the novels make clear, goes into the making of their personalities. As Barbara Christian has said of *Brown Girl, Brownstones*, "an appreciation of one's ethnic and racial community becomes necessary for black women in their commitment to self-development" (*Feminist* 178).[10]

The same awareness undergirds *Bread Givers*. Yezierska, in "We Can Change Our Moses But Not Our Noses," a story she never published, invented a protagonist who changed her name so she could get a job. She finds that she is unable to pass: "But I couldn't get away with it. . . . [T]he day I gave up my Jewish name, I ceased to be myself. I ceased to exist. A person who cuts himself off from his people cuts himself off at the roots of his being, he becomes a shell, a cipher, a spiritual suicide" (Schoen 7).[11] Here she voices unequivocally that the cultural ties to one's ethnicity are an integral part of an individual's personality and are beyond choice, since one, as the metaphors strongly suggest, leaves the realm of the living when one deserts one's ethnicity—an analogy presented in similar terms in the *Autobiography* when its protagonist makes the final decision to become white. Looking at *Bread Givers* through the lens of this unpublished story, one can see that the overall constructionism of ethnicity at work in the novel has its limits. One may choose not to follow one's ethnic group's mores and traditions to the full extent, as the short story's title suggests, but one cannot—indeed, should not—give up one's ethnic heritage.

In *Brown Girl*, one character located between individualism and the demands of ethnic solidarity is Selina's father, who does not meet the approval of his ethnic community because he does not save money for a house. This disapproval is expressed most notably in the communal wedding, but pervades the first third of the novel. Percy Challenor, who is Selina's best friend Beryl's father and something of a community leader, pronounces what the community thinks of Deighton: "I tell you those men from Bridgetown home is all the same. They don know a thing 'bout handling money and property and thing so. . . . I tell you, he's a disgrace!" (54). Though Deighton fully embraces his Barbadian upbringing, he does not meet all the standards for full community membership.

Suggie, one of the tenants in Silla's house, influences Selina in similar ways as Deighton. She, too, embraces Barbadian culture and fondly remembers the island. Yet the community regards her as an outsider because of her tendency to "live it up" and her promiscuity, and Silla evicts her, though she is one of Selina's best friends. Sensing her marginality but refusing to give in to community pressure, Suggie comments to Selina,

> My people! I's hiding from them with tears in my eyes. . . . You know what they want me to do? . . . I must put on a piece of black hat pull down over my face and go out here working day in and day out and save every penny . . . . I mustn't think 'bout spreeing or loving-up or anything so. . . . But they's sadly mistaken. . . . I gon spend my money foolish if I choose. (80–81)

Both Deighton and Suggie provide Selina with examples of following the course of life they have chosen for themselves. Though they both end up tragically—Deighton commits suicide, and Suggie moves on to an uncertain existence—they give Selina the warmth, affection, and sense of enjoyment of life that is missing in the community as the novel outlines it: one focused on work and acquisition. Their existence confirms for Selina and for the reader that there is more than one Barbadian standard, that being Barbadian is not defined by a kind of value-essentialism.

Sara does not have role models located between the conflicting demands of ethnic community and individualism to the same extent, though her mother does not adhere to the ruthless materialism exhibited by her father, supports her in her escape by giving her the family's "saved-up rent money" (136), and occasionally contradicts her husband. For most of the time, however, she accepts a subordinate role, and her posture when Sara leaves is indicative of her position: "As I put on my hat and coat, I saw Mother clutching at her heart in helplessness, her sorrowful eyes gazing at me" (136). In the conflict between father and daughter, her mother is an onlooker; while she is able to secretly slip her some money, she does not have a voice to take her side, only a "dumb look" full of the "suffering of her years" (136). To that extent, Sara's breakaway from her family, while prepared by years of resentment, appears a more solitary act than Selina's resistance to mother and community. As Irving Howe explains,

> For girls in the immigrant Jewish neighborhoods there were special problems, additional burdens. Both American and Jewish expectations pointed in a single direction—marriage and motherhood. But the position of the Jewish woman was rendered anomalous by the fact that, somehow, the Jewish tradition enforced a combination of social inferiority and business activity. Transported to America, this could not long survive. (265)

Sara is thus in a curious bind: her wish for a self-determined future goes against both traditional Jewish and, to a somewhat lesser degree, U.S. role expectations; she is supposed to develop her economic potential, but in the service of patriarchy, not for herself. As Gay Wilentz has commented, *Bread Givers* thus complicates the conflict between adherence to ethnic tradition and assimilation by Sara's "desires for independence as a woman."

Though Sara's mother and Muhmenkeh, a neighboring woman, to some extent provide alternative models to Sara's father's ruthless patriarchy by their unconditional acts of giving,[12] these are not the modes of behavior after which Sara patterns her own life, even if they do defy the notion that the novel embraces an overall—and stereotypical—ethnic essentialism. As both of the characters exhibiting complete self-lessness are women, however, the question of gender essentialism arises, since their altruism might be nothing more than an acting out of culturally ascribed gender roles, reintroducing a gender-informed ethnic essentialism alongside it. In this scenario, Sara would have to go up against a combined ethnic/gender cultural essentialism to completely invent a new role for herself.[13] However, this is not fully the case: not only her iron-willed father but also her sister Masha, whose stubbornness Sara often comments on in negative terms, live out before her eyes how to go up against the combined wills of the rest of the family and accomplish one's goals.

The character who most confirms Sara's course appears belatedly, when she has already finished her college education. His appearance is important, though, because, together with Sara's history, it maps out the course of a certain section of the second generation of Jewish immigrants, a course of which the novel approves. Both Sara's and Selina's stories take on a paradigmatic character in that respect: they are breakaways who integrate to a certain extent into the mainstream while retaining a strong awareness of their ethnicity. Sam Girgus has outlined this ideology in Yezierska's fiction and remarked on its similarity to Louis Brandeis's brand of Zionism:

> the immigrant appears trapped between wanting to be American and not wishing to betray her background and ties. Although it creates this trap for the immigrant, the ideology constructs an escape that Yezierska quickly perceives as another indication of how America creates unprecedented opportunities for Jews. It consists of the idea elaborated upon by Brandeis and others that with honesty about being Jewish one can be faithful to the principles of pluralism and diversity that ultimately bring all people together as Americans. By being true to herself as a Jew, she can set the example of what it means to be an American. She must compromise enough to achieve so-called Americanization but not change so much as to lose her ethnic identity. (110)

Americanization, of course, is a motto that is written all over *Bread Givers* (while being a subtler theme in *Brown Girl, Brownstones*). Consider the following description of Sara's principal Seelig (whose name, meaning "extremely happy" or describing a state of being blessed, indicates the novel's approval of this character), whom she meets after completing her education as a teacher, and who functions as an embodiment of the "unprecedented opportunities for Jews" which America offered, according to Yezierska:

> His face. The features—all fineness and strength. The keen, kind gray eyes. A Jewish face, and yet none of the greedy eagerness of Hester Street any more. It was the face of a dreamer, set free in the new air of America. Not like Father with his eyes on the past, but a dreamer who had found his work among us of the East Side. (273)

While the passage emphasizes Seelig's Jewishness, it also stresses the power of the environment to determine what particular face Jewishness will take on, at the same time flirting with projecting those traits that are perceived as negative on a particular past which is rooted in social circumstances and geography.[14] Old World ethnicity becomes personified by her father, whereas Seelig appears as a model for a New World ethnicity:

> Although Hugo Seelig is a Jewish immigrant, as a school principal he has also integrated himself socially into the new life without undue self-laceration. This figurative new American berth sustains him. It is also what makes him desirable to Sara. It is opposed to the lack of place in America for Sara's infuriated father. Quite reasonably, then, she thinks about Hugo's face and compares it favorably with "Father." (Wexler 171)

The novel constructs the new ethnicity as a hybrid between "American" and "Jewishness," embodied by characters like Sara and Seelig.[15] While this ethnicity is a hybrid one, it still maintains a boundary between "Jewish" and "American." Sara subscribes to this model of ethnicity, but her way to it is paved with the fear that she might be more like her father than she likes,[16] which puts her in an odd situation, because he has been a negative role model in the first third of the novel, the section titled "Hester Street." And two passages already quoted above have shown that "Hester Street" is Sara's label for what she does not like about her ethnic group. Thus, the reconciliation of Jewishness and Americanness does not come to Sara as easily as the Brandeisian formula seems to suggest.

Indications of her similarity to her father appear early on, as she stresses her strong will and her opposition to her father, which she verbalizes in direct confrontations. To that extent, she engages in a power struggle with her father and, like Selina, is involved in a dialectic of sorts which ultimately leads to a synthesis in which both protagonists combine the traits of their parents. Her sisters explicitly comment on Sara's similarity to her father when they come for a visit after she has left the family and started college; they expect to take her home for a visit with their parents:

> "My work goes on Sundays and holidays. I'm like a soldier in battle. I can't stop visiting, even with my own family." "You hard heart!" Fania threw up her hands at me. "Come, Bessie. Let's leave her to her mad education. She's worse than Father with his Holy Torah." (178)[17]

Development of the mind in study takes precedence over any other matters for her father as it does for her, and she cannot be moved by appeals to emotion or family feeling. Education becomes her god, an all-consuming concern that comes before any more worldly considerations.

But the novel creates ambiguity about this. Since Sara has broken away from her family because of an egotistical father, discovering the same trait in herself requires some explanation. Thus, when her father charges her with selfishness after she rejects a well-to-do suitor, she flings back, "All my selfishness is from you" (207). Having recognized the similarity, however, Sara needs further justification for her behavior in terms of her own value system. While her father justifies his selfishness with reference to his calling, she justifies hers by referring to her calling in a peculiar moment of hybridization of the two value systems, asking God to give her "the hard heart of reason" (230). The ultimate justification for her selfishness and independence—the two have become indistinguishable at this point in the novel—comes from the dean of her college, who assures her that "all pioneers have to get hard to survive" (232).

Sam Girgus notes that this strategy, similar to the one Yezierska used in "America and I," where she compares Jews to Pilgrims, provides "a vehicle for entrance into American culture" (109). Thus, from here on, selfishness and independence have become untangled again, because she can perceive herself as blazing a way for others, possibly—in an implicitly feminist construction—for other women, and specifically for other Jewish women. This implication is invited by the plight of her married sisters. Sara might be seen as (self-consciously) paving the way for women like them by proving to them that there are other options than marriage—the only problem with this interpretation being that she shows absolutely no concern for her sisters once she has left home.

While the feminist implications of her individualism remain questionable, the implications of her chosen course for her relationship to ethnicity are clearer. It appears that she attempts to combine individualism and ethnicity. Her intent of combining her individualist approach with the notion of ethnic solidarity becomes evident through her return to the Jewish neighborhood after her individualist goal has been reached, through her job as a teacher of Jewish children—although her attempts at having them speak "correct" English can be interpreted as a resolve to make them less "Old-World–ethnic"—and through her visits to her parents and particularly to her father once he becomes sickly.

Selina, too, has to discover that she is very much like the mother she rebels against, and the mother is repeatedly represented as an embodiment of the Barbadian Community ("She was confronting, she felt, not only the mother but all the others" [304]). When her boyfriend Clive, a virtual mirror image of her father, comments on how she seems to grab life by the throat, forcing it to give something to her, she is stunned:

> "But is that the way you see me? That's the way my mother is, not me!" "Then I guess it proves that you are truly your mother's child." She struck him on the chest and the hollow thud resounded in the night stillness. Her voice was sibilant with rage. "Do you know what my mother is like? The things she's done? What she did to my father?" (248)

At this point, she cannot bring herself to acknowledge her mother's heritage to her—a strong will and inexhaustible energy—having defined herself as "Deighton's Selina" in purposeful opposition to her mother and the Barbadian community.[18]

Because Selina perceives the ethnic community almost as a monolithic block, she derives a deviating self-definition from those whom that community explicitly condemns, namely characters like her father and Suggie. Like Sara, she shifts the boundaries of the definition of ethnicity. Her choice of boyfriend confirms this direction: Clive is a struggling artist who does not subscribe to the work ethic of the Barbadian community, but who is paralyzed by self-doubts and unable to create, much like Deighton. Thus, because the pronouncement of Selina's similarity to her mother comes from him, Selina has to confront the painful possibility that her oppositional course, in its very determinedness, might have brought her full circle, to the ruthless pursuit of goals that is her mother's mark, even though their goals may differ. Although her anger against Clive's remark may be read as an indirect acknowledgement of the truth in his statement, the direct acknowledgement does not come until later.

Before that, she proves to be fully her mother's child. When resolving to leave town with Clive, a plan which will never be carried out, she also finds a way of coming up with the necessary funds: winning the scholarship offered by the Barbadian Association. However, that scholarship is intended to fund schooling. Knowing this, Selina decides to be duplicitous, to "be contrite, dedicated, the most willing worker they've ever had" and is convinced that she will "get the money. It'll take some doing but I'll get it" (267). Her phrasing resembles Silla's vow to obtain the money for Deighton's land, no matter what it takes: "I gon do it. . . . Some kind of way I gon do it" (75). Here Selina most fully reveals how she has been influenced by her mother's ruthless determination.[19] But her mother's influence is not only negative. Selina's maturation is marked by her recognition of a multiplicity of viewpoints and value systems without necessarily condemning one and extolling others.[20]

Paradoxically, it is her individualism that, in the end, allows her to respect or at least regard with more tolerance the values of her mother and her ethnic group, even though those values do not really allow for individualism but demand ethnic coherence.[21] She can declare to her mother, "I'm not interested in houses!" (306). But she adds, "I don't scorn you. Oh, I used to. But not any more. . . . It's just not what I want" (306). By being clear about what she does not want and insisting on that as her right, she also has to respect that others want things different from her. Through her emerging selfhood, she may begin to see that the "dispossessed gain affirmation through possession because owning . . . is an economic as well as a political declaration of one's humanity, one's humanness, one's reality" (Dickerson 4), even though she wishes to express her own humanity differently.

The circle is complete when Selina recognizes that her mother herself, who is also a symbol of ethnic conformity and an enforcer of community values, was once driven by her own individualism. At that point, ethnic communalism and individualism do not appear as incompatible:

Everybody used to call me Deighton's Selina but they were wrong. Because you see I'm truly your child. Remember how you used to talk about how you left home and came here alone as a girl of eighteen and was your own woman? I used to love hearing that. And that's what I want. I want it! (307)

Interestingly, Selina uses a slight Barbadian English inflection in this passage ("was your own woman") that is not typical of her speech, which is otherwise American English. This denotes an embracing of ethnicity at the time when she verbalizes the possible coexistence of ethnicity and individualism, citing her mother—for her the symbol of the Barbadian community—as an example.

The peace the novel has her make with her mother also marks the synthesis of diametrically opposed ways of being she envisioned before: either you are like your father, i.e., completely different from your mother, or you become like your mother. Her worldview has become more complicated. The novel thus goes further than offering the dilemmas served up by *Plum Bun* and *Fanny Herself*: extreme materialism and egotism or subordination to communalist idealism. But what made this process possible for Selina?

Two factors play an important role here: one is a fuller experience of the world outside the home and outside the ethnic community, the other is the experience of racism. Once Selina leaves her immediate environment to go to college, the world there, at least at first, seems empty and shallow to her in comparison to the drama of the ethnic home life she knows, which she perceives as more dramatic and real: "The chill of utter desertion she had watching Suggie leave persisted through her first year of college. This was real while everything that happened at school had the unreality of a play viewed from a high balcony" (212). Sara's experience is almost identical and even rendered in similar terms, though her conception of ethnicity, at this point, is more positive than Selina's. After she learns to draw on her own experience in a psychology class, she looks down on the other (nonethnic) students: "I saw the students around me as so many pink-faced children who never had had to live yet. I realized that the time when I sold herring in Hester Street, I was learning life more than if I had gone to school" (223). To her, nonethnic life seems shallow, not like real life, while ethnic life provides her with deeper insights—a theme we also encountered in *Plum Bun* and *Fanny Herself*.

Both protagonists also encounter racism, an experience that confirms in them the feelings of marginality and separateness they have already known to a certain degree in childhood and adolescence by not fitting in with their peers. However, unlike in the *Autobiography* and *Fanny*, where this encounter leads to a decision to pass, experiencing racism makes Selina and Sara more fully aware of their own ethnicity, indeed of its character as boundary, and eventually leads them to feelings of ethnic solidarity—a crucial element in both novels which also brings them into the fold of the ethnic Bildungsroman. Encountering racism also enables them to better understand the parent they have rebelled against or at least to develop a bond of sympathy with that parent.

In *Brown Girl, Brownstones*, the recognition of ethnicity as an involuntary boundary, in this case, is rendered as a cognitive process that Selina undergoes and is aware of. After having been treated with cold condescension by the mother of a fellow dancer at a post-performance cast party, Selina reflects on her relationship to the Barbadian community:

> she was one with them: the mother and the Bajan women, who had lived each day what she had come to know. How had the mother endured . . . ? She remembered the mother striding through Fulton Park each late afternoon, bearing the throw-offs under her arm as she must have borne the day's humiliations inside. How had the mother contained her swift rage?—and then she remembered those sudden, uncalled-for outbursts that would so stun them and split the serenity of the house. (293)

Recognizing that her mother, too, has experienced racism, Selina not only acknowledges unity vis-à-vis a common oppression but also concludes that she has no right to judge her mother or the community: "Who are we to scorn them?" (293). She begins to understand the acquisitiveness of the Barbadian community as a defense mechanism against racism, the wish to own things as an attempt to fight back against exclusion. As Barbara Christian says, this defensiveness results in the community's "compelling, urging, insisting that every one of its parts bend to the common goal: the owning of a brownstone, the possession of property, as a bulwark against poverty, racism, failure" (*Black Women* 82). The novel suggests that the pressure to conform can be understood as a wish to protect and shelter the younger generation, hoping to equip them with better tools and more comfort in an essentially hostile white world.[22] Silla's gesture when hearing of Selina's plan to leave home bespeaks that wish: "Her arms half lifted in a protective gesture, and her warning sounded. 'Girl, do you know what it tis out there? How those white people does yuh?'" (306).

At the same time, the ethnic group's coerciveness expresses its insecure position and the resulting recognition that "individuality can be detrimental to a group needing to cohere in order to survive in a [hostile] nation" (Hathaway 132). Thus, there is something paradoxical about the fact that Selina's experience of racism, which makes clear to her that "American racism makes no distinctions in culture," that her color rather than her culture will determine her social and economic status (Denniston 24–25), serves as a kind of "Americanization" in that it blurs ethnic distinctions (between Barbadian and African American). While the racist incident helps Selina understand the motivation for ethnic solidarity, it also points out that color may assume greater significance than ethnic culture.

Sara undergoes this process of recognizing the pressures on the ethnic community less consciously but with similar results. She, too, recognizes her father's fragility—and by extension that of the Old World Jewish community. What before seemed an overwhelming pressure to conform has now lost its threat, and what remains are bonds of feeling and kinship. Acquisitiveness is understood as a fight against poverty and the coldness of Anglo Americans she has experienced at college ("beauty shining out of the calm faces and cool eyes of the people! Oh—too cool" [211]).

When her father remarries after her mother's death, she does not see him for a while. Just before their fateful encounter on the streets— poverty has driven him to become a peddler—she contemplates the fate of other peddlers:

> But as I walked along through Hester Street toward the Third Avenue L, my joy [over meeting Hugo Seelig] hurt like guilt. Lines upon lines of pushcart peddlers were crouching in the rain. Backs bent, hands in their sleeves, ears under their collars, grimy faces squeezed into frozen masks. They were like animals helpless against the cold, pitiless weather. Wasn't there some way that I could divide my joy with these shivering pushcart peddlers, grubbing for pennies in the rain? (281)

The symbolic (and naturalist) overtones of the passage are strong. Where before she saw greed, she can now perceive a desperate fight for survival in a hostile environment, a perception triggering feelings of solidarity and compassion. Her attempt to reach out for happiness now includes those around her, and she feels it her responsibility to include them in her "American Dream," symbolized by the red roses she has received from Hugo Seelig: "Hugo's red roses on my table—almost I could have wept for them. So full and rich with lovely colour, so heartlessly perfect, so shamelessly beautiful that it hurt to look at them. I didn't want them if they were only for me" (282). The description of the roses recalls her perception of Anglo American college students as beautiful but cold and implies a comparison of the East Siders' fight for survival with the empty but comfortable life of non-ethnics at college who, she says, "didn't even know I was there" (213).

Though she appears to have imbibed the value system observed at college to an extent, as her attitude towards clothing and appearance reveal, she is really only able to feel ethnic solidarity after her return from college. For her and for Selina, a "we-feeling" is only possible once they have experienced "them" and gained an appreciation of why tight ethnic in-group bonds are maintained. Sara's experience of what might be called a form of racism at college—mostly exhibited in the other students' distance and their laughter at her speech or "clumsiness"— does not have as shattering an effect on her as does Selina's (though Sara does shatter a hurdle in a gym class when she feels that she is the nonethnic students' "clown, and this was their circus" [217]). This may be due to the fact that the racism is not as blatant and is barely perceived as such, but one notices that after college, her Jewish identification is rendered in more positive terms than before. Seelig's description is one case in point, and her decision to teach in the Lower East Side another.

However, her acceptance of ethnicity, even of Old World ethnicity, can be observed most clearly in her relationship to her father. While she seems to dread the thought of having him be her responsibility for the rest of her life, she also feels a sense of tenderness and, most of all, of inevitability. Seeing him sick, she regrets her former dislike and affirms their oneness:

> How could I have hated him and tried to blot him out of my life? Can I hate my arm, my hand that is part of me? Can a tree hate the roots from which it sprang? Deeper than love, deeper than pity, is that oneness of the flesh that's in him and me. Who gave me the

fire, the passion, to push myself up from the dirt? If I grow, if I rise, if I ever amount to something, is it not his spirit burning in me? (286)

Because her father is, for her, the most powerful symbol of ethnicity in general and of Old World ethnicity in particular, her own conceptualization of her ethnicity is reflected in this relationship, which is considerably more complex than the simplistic Old World/New World dichotomy advanced several times earlier in the novel.[23] Rather than merely leaving behind one kind of ethnicity and adopting another, both interact continuously, as also manifested by her suitor's request to her father to teach him Hebrew. While Sara has achieved the goals set by her individualist strivings, duty and love are bonds that tie her irrevocably to family and community.[24]

Ironically, "She alone effectively challenges her father's authoritarianism but also becomes the only daughter capable of internalizing and accepting responsibility for his model of authority" (Girgus 114). What remains is ambiguity: on the one hand, Sara fully experiences feelings of ethnic solidarity, but only to come to see her ethnicity as a burden. To that extent, Gay Wilentz's comment that "the novel ends as a Jewish lament rather than in a happy ever after" aptly warns against overemphasizing a reconciliation between ethnicity and Americanization. The novel ends with Sara and Hugo's decision to have her father live with them. And although she will marry the representative of a Jewish American ethnicity, she perceives her father's presence as a "shadow still there, over me. It wasn't just my father, but the generations who made my father whose weight was still upon me" (297). Acceptance and alienation thus go hand in hand, mirroring the struggle between individualism and the demands of the ethnic community that pervades the novel.

In *Brown Girl, Brownstones*, a similar ambiguity prevails at the end as well. In rejecting the scholarship from the Barbadian Association because she acquired it by pretending false motives, Selina first feels the burden of love and experiences a strong sense of ethnic solidarity, maybe for the first time. On her way to the podium to receive the scholarship award that she will decline, Selina reflects on her community:

Selina moved . . . down the aisle, scanning those myriad reflections and variations of her own dark face. And suddenly she admired their mystery. No, not mystery . . . but the mysterious source of endurance in them, and it was not only admiration but love she felt. A thought glanced her mind as Cecil Osborne held her face between his ruined hands and kissed her: love was the greater burden than hate. The applause burst afresh and she gazed wonderingly over the smiling faces, which resembled a dark sea—alive under the sun with endless mutations of one color. (302–303)

Her newfound admiration of her community's resilience in the face of adverse circumstances comes at the moment that she recognizes herself to be one of them, her own purposefulness being rooted in theirs ("reflections . . . of her own dark face"), so that her individualism can now be understood as a variation of a theme rather than standing in opposition to it.

At the same time, however, she knows that she is not willing to do the community's bidding, and thus she feels utter alienation. Somewhat paradoxically, recognizing her own strength and her community's strength to be the same "underpin[s] her purpose" (303) to reveal that she does not share in their goals. This revelation, coming at the moment of greatest harmony between the community and herself, opens up the divide between communalism and individualism afresh. After declining the award as "something I don't want for myself," Selina leaves the hall:

The words rang hollow throughout the hall as she hurried down the platform and through the perplexed and unforgiving silence. The loud rustle of her gown bespoke her final alienation. And as the familiar faces fell away behind her, she was aware of the loneliness coiled fast around her freedom. (303)

Here it seems as if individuality can only be bought at the price of rejecting ethnic solidarity and communalism.

Her final gesture at the end of the book—the flinging away of one of the silver bangles signifying ethnicity ("silver bangles . . . which every Barbadian-American girl wore from birth" [5]) while keeping the other—bespeaks a more complex relationship between those two concepts and puts Selina on a similar middle ground as Sara: while ethnicity is accepted as inevitable, something new and different emerges, a kind of hybrid ethnicity that is the product of the Old World ethnicity represented by the strong parent and the influences of the New World environment.[25] In the terms of Werner Sollors's consent and descent model, ethnicity, particularly because it is represented by a parent, appears as an inescapable descent relationship (but not the form that ethnicity takes), while individualist strivings may represent the sway of the U.S. environment and are experienced as consensual.

However, U.S. influences are not specified. Both protagonists' lives are lived mostly within an ethnic community, and their contact with nonethnics is relatively limited. Indeed, the nonethnic world is perceived as lifeless and shallow, and first-generation ethnic models for individualist strivings do exist in both novels, making an American derivation of individualism less compulsory. Nonetheless, the presence of that almost stereotypically American value as an American value cannot be ignored in stories which tell of second-generation protagonists moving away from Old World definitions of ethnicity. The emergence of individualism can be explained in part by the relative easing of those extreme pressures of the Old World and/or New World, economic, social, or otherwise, which made for the cohesiveness of the Jewish and Barbadian communities, and for the emergence of ethnic nationalism, pressures to which both works allude.

At the same time, the individualist bent of the Bildungsroman has some sway here, allowing the protagonists to invent their own ethnicity. In the case of *Bread Givers*, the muted rejection of ethnic nationalism might well also be partially grounded in autobiographical considerations, such as Yezierska's relationship to her father and her ambitions as a writer and self-promoter. As for *Brown Girl*, the later 1950s marked a waning of ethnic nationalism (which was not to make a return until the late 1960s and would have a marked influence on Marshall's later novels). It must be remembered, though, that the novel reflects an earlier time period. Both novels, though, are useful reminders that a complete communal consensus of any kind is likely to remain elusive.

Though neither *Brown Girl, Brownstones* nor *Bread Givers* claims that individualism should completely overrule ethnic communalism, both novels recognize a struggle between those two ideologies. The hybrid ethnicity of Selina and Sara, arrived at against the resistance of strong parent figures, is in an ironic sense the outcome of those parents' decision to flee more oppressive circumstances to allow for a fuller development of (ethnic) life, not expecting that this decision also might give their children expanded opportunities to decide what shape their own ethnic lives will take. And it is the resulting hybridity that makes necessary the simultaneous assertions of and uneasy reconciliation between communalist ethnicity and individualism.

Both *Brown Girl, Brownstones* and *Bread Givers* thus record ethnic adjustments in the New World. Their protagonists figure as pioneers who point the way for implicitly inevitable developments within the community. However, the novels outline this development not as one from ethnicity to nonethnicity or Americanness but to a new kind of ethnicity that recognizes the necessity of solidarity in an adverse environment but rejects the absoluteness of a communal claim to solidarity that is the hallmark of nationalism (and which the other four novels affirm).

Because these two works support individualist aspirations, they cannot construct ethnicity in an essentialist fashion as nationalism would, as that strategy would force the implausible claim that the individualist protagonist is simply not ethnic any more but American. This, in turn, would align the novels' sympathy with Americanness, which cannot be the intent in works that outline in great detail an ethnic world with characters the reader is supposed to like, that point out that racism remains a highly significant factor in the life of the ethnic group and the individual, and whose major antagonists—the oppressive parent figures—are redeemed through the movement of the plot, which has the heroine embrace the antagonist. The simultaneous assertion of ethnicity and individualism must thus be accomplished through a constructionist rhetoric of ethnicity that allows one to see ethnic solidarity as a response to a hostile environment rather than an essentialist mandate. This constructionist approach allows for a wider range in definition for the ethnic character and makes possible "a satisfactory synthesis of the best . . . assets where multiple heritages are involved," as Joyce Pettis has said of *Brown Girl, Brownstones* (33).

At the same time, both novels respond to the ideological pressure of cultural nationalism in that they recognize that the course of individualism needs justification. This need to justify creates a tension alluded to before: certain features of their ethnic communities must appear as oppressive in order to legitimize the heroines' quest for individualism. Overly negative depiction of the ethnic community, however, would mean playing into the hands of a potentially biased readership; first and foremost, it would put the protagonist into an almost self-destructive bind, since, having ethnic ancestry, she would have to create herself out of nothing if she wanted to acquire a positive self-image while creating a negative one of her own community. The resulting tension is partially resolved by the depiction of ethnic individuals who are selfless and/or on good terms with the heroine, such as Muhmenkeh,

Bessie, Suggie, and Deighton, and by the reconciliation between the strong parent as symbol of the Old World ethnic community and the protagonist. I say "partially resolved" because both heroines experience unease with the realization that ethnicity is inescapable for them. They stand half-willingly in the tradition of the other four novels, a tradition that holds ethnic solidarity as the highest duty. While they partly strive to alter this tradition, they are bound to it to the extent that their individualism requires constant justification.

In this, and in their accommodation of communalism, these novels differ from the traditional Bildungsroman. The latter takes individualism for granted or extols it as a positive virtue; Marshall's and Yezierska's novels work within the framework of the ethnic Bildungsroman and thus need not establish ethnic solidarity and communalism but take those notions as their point of departure; instead, they have to justify their infusion of individualism. Rather than being responses to the traditional Bildungsroman, these novels converse with its ethnic revision.

But in the way in which this conversation is conducted, a difference between the two novels surfaces: they both integrate communalism and individualism but with differing overtones. Selina, like Sara, experiences ethnic solidarity as a burden, but her final departure for Barbados signals a kind of curiosity and acceptance at which Sara never arrives: for her, ethnicity remains a shadow. Having never understood the historical causes for her ethnic group's separateness as Selina has, and having never experienced racism as consciously, or a racism of the same intensity, her reconciliation has strong overtones of pity. The condescension with which she regards her community until the end, despite her involvement in it, prevents the healing comprehension Selina performs. But while the hue differs, the color is the same: both protagonists accept ethnic communalism to some extent while pursuing individualist agendas, creating a new conceptualization of ethnicity in the process, fusing America and ethnicity as they do the Bildungsroman with ethnic nationalism.

CHAPTER FOUR
Ethnic Nationalism and Ethnic Literary Responses

*Nations are Destroy'd, or Flourish, in proportion as Their Poetry
Painting and Music, are Destroy'd or Flourish. (William Blake)*

Julia Wright has said that "Blake, in his own inimitable way, is articulating one of the fundamental precepts of the nationalism that emerged in Europe in the late eighteenth century, namely that culture is the tie that binds a nation together into a coherent, populist entity." After examining the six novels of the preceding chapters closely, one sees that more than culture serves as the glue the novels concoct to bind together the ethnic nation. The debate over what the ethnic group is or should be and how its members should orient themselves towards their ethnicity, however, is conducted through literature, and so literature and nationalist ideology depend on one another here. I do not mean to imply that any of these works, in all their complexity, can simply be reduced to mouthpieces of a specific political position. Nonetheless, recurring themes pervade the novels, most prominently the oppositions of materialism and idealism and of individualism and communalism.

These oppositions also play a role in the ethnic revisions of the Bildungsroman genre: in exhorting their protagonists to be more communalist—and more idealistic—than they initially want to be, these novels depart from the more individualist plotlines of their traditional counterparts. Genre-related and ideological matters are thus intertwined. One could think of the ideological formation of which the above oppositions are a part as a kind of background theme for these literary works that can always be heard, no matter what melody is played over it. Sometimes, this background theme will be in harmony with the melody, sometimes it will not. If it is in harmony, then it becomes a part of the melody; if not, the melody sets itself off against it. The predominant note this background theme sounds is nationalism. What nationalism is, how ethnic nationalism can be distinguished from it, and why ethnic nationalism and the ethnic Bildungsroman make a happy marriage is the story of this concluding chapter.

I have shown how African American and Jewish American authors have revised the Bildungsroman, but in order to understand what makes ethnic nationalism ethnic, some features of European and U.S. American nationalism may prove a useful point of departure. Ethnic is a relational term, after all, and since both African Americans and Jewish Americans, through constant contact with European and European American developments, were likely to have been influenced by them, ethnic nationalism is, ultimately, a response to the ideological ferment surrounding and affecting the ethnic group.

> A nation is a soul, a spiritual principle. Two things, which in truth are but one, constitute this soul or spiritual principle. One lies in the past, one in the present. One is the possession in common of a rich legacy of memories; the other is present-day consent, the desire to live together, the will to perpetuate the value of the heritage that one has received in an undivided form. (Renan 19)

This is how Ernest Renan defines the nation in 1882. Striking in this definition is the emphasis on both spirituality and volition. The shared past alone does not suffice to found a nation: only the conscious and willed continuation of that past can constitute "nationness." The spiritual emphasis betrays the links of nationalism to Romanticism. While the earlier Enlightenment nationalism, as expressed by Rousseau, believed in the nation as a "social contract," many nineteenth-century thinkers distanced themselves from rationalistic conceptualizations of the nation and turned to more mystical notions of national essences.[1]

Advocates of nationalist movements referred to the idea of a "national soul" (Urofsky 10) that was to supply the bond that would hold the nation together. While the "belief in the existence of a 'national character' was present from the beginning of modern nationhood," the attempt of Romantics to find an "organic" vision of life discarded the more universalist—at least in form—aspirations of the Enlightenment (Mosse 122).[2] In the U.S., the universalist trappings of revolutionary rhetoric and the Declaration of Independence, while often claimed by ethnic writers, were also understood not to extend to them, so that a turning to ethnic nationalism can, in part, be understood as a response to such exclusion.[3]

This tension between universalism and essentialism was apparent in early American nationalism. While Crèvecoeur, in his famous third letter in *Letters from an American Farmer*, stresses the various (European) ethnicities which make up America as he sees it, he is also looking for a common national character, a defining characteristic of what it means to be an American, a kind of national essence, in other words. Even if that essence is ultimately defined in terms of culture, as Romantic ideology usually did, the line between culture and biology is often a thin one when one looks at how the term culture is deployed. We have seen this in the novels discussed here, and the boundary between culture and biology was particularly blurry in the period under discussion (and, in popular culture, continues to be to this day), as Walter Benn Michaels has shown. Michaels demonstrates that the notion that a certain culture is appropriate to a certain individual or group always depends on the underlying idea that, somehow, race and culture are really one:

> It is only if we think that our culture is not whatever beliefs and practices we actually happen to have but is instead the beliefs and practices that should properly go with the sort of people we happen to be that the fact of something belonging to our culture can count as a reason for doing it. But to think this is to appeal to something that must be beyond culture and that cannot be derived from culture precisely because our sense of which culture is properly ours must be derived from it. This has been the function of race. (60)

Thus, even a nationalism that does not overtly advocate unity on an essentialist basis, such as race or descent, might well do so implicitly through an appeal to culture. The six novels discussed here illustrate how the authors attempt to negotiate this tension between racial definitions of belonging and membership based on choice.

Given this inherent bent in nationalist philosophy towards monoculturality, nationalism seems like an odd choice as an ideology for ethnic groups. Nation states have usually, and with varying degrees of coercion and force, "adopted various 'nation-building' policies aimed at giving citizens a common national language, identity, and culture" (Kymlicka and Straehle). Why would ethnic groups embrace a philosophy that might not leave them a (cultural) space in the "nations" they inhabit?[4] If one is not a member of the group which makes up the majority of the population of a state and which has defined its institutions, laws, and ways of life, it may be difficult to feel like a member of a nation-state which does not see one's culture and institutions as valid and constituent parts of itself. As Uri Ra'anan says, in "multinational states it may be possible to be a patriot and a nationalist simultaneously—provided one happens to be a member of the Staatsvolk [the ethnic group which dominates and defines the nation]" (9).[5]

In most communities, both in the past and present, and in most areas of the world but the contemporary West and other industrialized societies, membership of a nation is primarily determined by blood or culture rather than through legal or territorial criteria.[6] At the same time, this is also one feature which distinguishes ethnic nationalism from mainstream nationalism in the context of this study: mainstream nationalism claims a territory and the hegemony of an often racially defined group in that territory, while ethnic nationalism is both a response to that exclusion and an attempt to preserve cultural identity under pressure of assimilation.[7] It is exactly this form of nationalism that one finds at work in the novels examined here, and it is also one of the reasons why passing, the obliteration of ethnicity under assimilationist pressure, is repeatedly problematized in ethnic works of the period—and usually rejected on nationalist grounds.

Despite U.S. American claims of exceptionalism, the "United States was no different from other nations in discriminating against those who had been traditional foils of modern nationalism, and whose imagined or potential non-conformity seemed to menace the stability of society: the blacks, the Jews, and those who did not conform to the established social norms" (Mosse 36). Since the early nineteenth century, at least European nationalism defined itself not so much through political boundaries but on racial grounds. To that extent, nationalism has a tendency to exclude ethnic groups if they are not willing to forego their allegiance to whatever cultural traits define their ethnicity.[8] Ethnic groups are well aware of this. For example, those Jews who were most successful in the U.S. in the nineteenth century—German Jewish merchants—were not only themselves assimilated but also worked towards the speedy assimilation of Eastern European Jews, fearing that the cultural difference of the latter might highlight their own difference—which they themselves had successfully downplayed—from the national norm. As a result, upper-class German Jews and Reform Jews resisted Zionism for much of its early history, because Zionism seemed to question their allegiance to the U.S.[9]

Even if American nationalism, for obvious reasons, could never adopt racial terms in exactly the same way as European nationalisms (Pan-Slavism, Pan-Germanism, etc.), several developments in the U.S. around the turn of the century clearly indicate a race-oriented approach to the concept of nationality. In John P. Roche's words, "this period [the pre–World War I era] saw the enthronement of racism in American public policy (the 'separate but equal' doctrine, confining blacks to the 'Jim Crow' car, was formulated by the Supreme Court in *Plessy v. Ferguson*, 1896) and in 'social science'" (64). Other indications of this were budding anti-Semitism, hostility towards Catholics, and the adoption of highly restrictive codes for Asians (Roche 60).[10] "The spirit of Vice President Calvin Coolidge, who in 1921 noted that 'biological laws show us that Nordics deteriorate when mixed with other races,' had triumphed in the land" (Roche 71–72). Similar pronouncements were heard with some regularity from within the highest circle of government: "As president, Warren G. Harding praised Stoddard's *Rising Tide of Color*, which repeated the old slanders that Africans had 'vegetated in savage obscurity,' had contributed 'virtually nothing' to civilization . . . and were 'widely addicted to cannibalism'" (Philipson 94). U.S. conceptualization of the nation in the early twentieth century equated nationality with race: being American meant being white.

Horace Kallen saw in this a shift in American national feelings: "To the dominant nationality in America 'nationality' in the European sense used to have no meaning: for it had itself been the measure of the country's excellence, and had been assimilating others to itself. Now that the process seems to be slowed down, it thinks it finds itself confronted with the problem of nationality just as do the Irish, the Poles . . ." (*Culture and Democracy* 93). According to Kallen, nationalism in the U.S. emerged only when national cultural homogeneity, the definition of the nation as Anglo-Saxon, was perceived as threatened by the Anglo American establishment. Inherent in this account is a complete and glaring dismissal of the Native American population and of African Americans—which called the national self-definition into question. (One might also say that those ethnic groups occasioned the national self-definition.) Due in part, paradoxically, to their greater cultural similarity, Southern and Eastern European immigrants were seen as a greater cultural threat. Non-Europeans were simply perceived as incapable of adding to or modifying the Eurocentric definition of Americanness.

At the same time, however, American cities experienced a massive influx from the South of African Americans, who, particularly in large cities in the East, also threatened to unbalance Anglo American predominance. Both migrations thus converged to bring about a crisis in the self-conceptualization of Anglo America. As the freedom and equality of white Americans was defined against an unfree and unequal population,[11] as well as against England until the twentieth century, in the late nineteenth and early twentieth centuries, being an American could also be defined against the differences of the new immigrants, among whom Eastern European Jews were conspicuous because of differences in culture and religion.

If nativist definitions of being an American tended to exclude everyone who was not white (a term the definition of which underwent significant change during the first half of the twentieth century) and not Protestant, ethnic groups had an incentive to express their own nationalisms as positive definitions of what it meant to be ethnic other than to be relegated to the margins of American society. To some degree, the novels examined here do two things: while they claim an ethnic right to, and show ethnic involvement in, America, they also depict ethnic separateness and particularity, based on moral difference. And that moral difference is based on the by now familiar opposition of spirituality and materialism and its many derivatives.

This differentiating move is, in and of itself, consistent with nationalist philosophy. Since hard facts about differentiations between population groups are difficult to come by, the characteristics that make the nation what it is (or is asserted or envisioned to be) are often claimed to be found in psychological or moral traits. What makes these traits important, or the very reason why nationalism searches for such traits, is primarily the mere fact of difference itself.[12]

The novels discussed here embrace or respond to this conceptualization of ethnicity and nationhood. They, too, construct specific, if mystical, features that set the ethnic group apart from the people around them. Fauset and Ferber highlight artistic ability and sensitivity that grow out of a tradition of suffering and persecution. Johnson and Ornitz claim that some form of idealism or spirituality, whether it manifests itself in music, political activism, or ethnic solidarity under duress differentiates (or, to take account of the novels' didactic intentions, ought to differentiate) members of the ethnic group from the materialist mainstream. Marshall and Yezierska, while maintaining that the individual can attempt to go her way apart from the ethnic group, also suggest that ethnic ties will not allow the individual to break away entirely. Their novels, too, are informed by the ideal of ethnic solidarity, a moral and spiritual link between all members of an ethnic group.

Two of the most prominent expressions of ethnic nationalism in late nineteenth-century and early twentieth-century America (and beyond) are Zionism and Black Nationalism, in all their various appearances, most of them (quasi-)religious in nature.[13] The exact role that the nation should play, however, was interpreted differently by various proponents of nationalism. In its more extreme forms, ethnic nationalism was the answer to everything. Marcus Garvey, in "African Fundamentalism" (1925), would say, "Remember always that the Jew in his political and economic urge is always first a Jew; the white man is first a white man under all circumstances, and you can do no less than being first and always a Negro, and then all else will take care of itself" (quoted in Clarke 158). Race is the answer to all questions. Know who you are racially, and you know what to do.

What underwrites both the more radical and the more moderate forms of nationalism is the idea of solidarity, an idea that is of importance in all of the works discussed here. Black Nationalism, Pan-Africanism, or Negritude all "begin with the assumption of the racial solidarity of the Negro" as Kwame Anthony Appiah says (6). This is most obvious in Marcus Garvey, where race becomes a program in and of itself. Echoes of it are also to be heard in Du Bois's view, elaborated in *The Souls of Black Folk*, of the gifts that every race had to contribute to humanity. In this view, one's race determines one's special capabilities. *Plum Bun* elaborates this conceptualization of ethnicity, and so does *Fanny Herself. Haunch* and the *Autobiography* subscribe to it in a more adumbrated way.

In the early twentieth century, the influential German-born anthropologist Franz Boas, teaching at Columbia University, pioneered an understanding of culture that sought to undermine the idea that culture was somehow connected to race, while his "antagonists assumed a close and even determining relationship between race and culture" (Hutchinson *Harlem* 65). George Hutchinson argues that "Boasian views are partly responsible for the dramatic change from the racialist concept of black nationality held by Alexander Crummell and the early Du Bois to the 'culturalist' concepts usually informing the Harlem Renaissance" (*Harlem* 65). However, except for the mostly non-essentialist *Brown Girl, Brownstones* (in part because it was written later than the other novels, in part because it depicts ethnicity within the larger U.S. national framework of "blackness"), that shift is simply not complete in the novels discussed here, which are replete with hints at, implications of, or outright assertions of a direct connection of culture and race. Though they also embrace constructionist conceptualizations of ethnicity, it is the influence of (cultural) nationalist ideology that has left its traces through essentialist "pre-Boasian" notions.

Several of Zionism's proponents claimed that nationalism and spirituality were mutually supportive of each other. The German-Jewish Zionist Abraham Isaac Kook, for example, "saw nationalism not in the secular mode of the nineteenth century, but as part of the spiritual heritage of Israel. 'The national sentiment is holy and exalted in itself,' he wrote, and part of 'the very foundation of Judaism and essential to it.' . . . By reinforcing nationalism, Zionism would contribute to spiritual progress" (Urofsky 38). Separateness thus fosters spirituality—clearly an anti-assimilationist sentiment that, in this outright form, was not necessarily shared by a majority of American Jews.[14]

Nonetheless, despite organizational disunity, certain ideological formations were prominent. While in its beginning modern Zionism, with Theodor Herzl's *Der Judenstaat* (1896) as one of its founding documents, always insisted on an actual territorial Zion, the nationalist feeling that underwrote Zionism had a broader basis, namely the idea of the essential unity of the Jewish people, regardless of geographical location. This idea was shared by Reform Jews, who were otherwise non- or even anti-Zionist, and by people who firmly believed in Jews as citizens of their respective countries, such as Emma Lazarus or Supreme Court judge and Zionist leader Louis Brandeis. When many Reform Jews in the U.S., for example, rejected territorially-based Zionism because they "had long forsaken the idea of return to Zion," this did not preclude them from subscribing to one of the philosophical bases of nationalism: "They had taken the concept of the Dispersion as Exile (a punishment for sins) and converted it into the ideal of Mission, with Israel chosen to spread the knowledge of God among the nations" (Urofsky 29).[15] What is important, then, is not necessarily the numerical strength of classical nationalist movements such as Zionism[16] and the Garvey Movement but the degree to which some of their underlying notions saturated a culture. And since the underlying notions are similar, there are many parallels between Zionism and Pan-Africanism or Black Nationalism.

Several of African America's foremost thinkers and founders of Black Nationalism have found inspiration in "the concept of 'Diaspora nationalism,' the idea that Jews—despite the lack of a geopolitical homeland—still constitute a distinct nationality" (Urofsky 33). As Paul Gilroy has said,

> It is often forgotten that the term 'diaspora' comes into the vocabulary of black studies and the practice of pan-African politics from Jewish thought. It is used in the Bible but begins to acquire something like its looser contemporary usage during the late nineteenth century—the period which saw the birth of modern Zionism and of the forms of black nationalist thought which share many of its aspirations and some of its rhetoric. (205)

This connection between Zionism and Black Nationalism can also be seen in the work of Martin Delaney, who saw the Jewish experience as a model on which to base a colonization scheme for Nicaragua (Gilroy 23); in the work of Wilmer Edmot Blyden, who admired Zionism and is widely regarded as an influence on W. E. B. Du Bois (Gilroy 209); and in Du Bois's work, as Anthony Appiah explains in *In My Father's House*. We have earlier seen the parallels Marcus Garvey drew between Jewish American and African American ethnic solidarity.[17]

The parallels were duly noted by participants in the debates: "Extending a central analogy of antislavery rhetoric—the slaves' delivery from pharaonic bondage—Du Bois would write in 1919, for example, that 'the African movement means to us what the Zionist movement means to the Jews, the centralization of the race effort and the recognition of a racial fount'" (Sundquist *To Wake* 559). In the case of Jews, hundreds of years of Diaspora and separateness because of religious and cultural traditions and involuntary exclusion provided an instant basis on which to construct a nationalist ideology. George L. Mosse has said, in reference to European nations, that a "ready-made historical past was essential in order to provide the nation with its roots" (96).

In the case of African Americans and Jewish Americans, the past that was recalled was one of exile and suffering, which provided a common historical bond and was seen as pointing to a common future which was to be free (or freer, at any rate) of suffering. For African Americans, the diaspora nationalism of Jews served as a useful model in the absence of an indigenous one, since the dispersal of people of African origins also included the fading or at least the attenuation of older group traditions, be they Fulani, Yoruba, Ashanti, or otherwise, particularly in the U.S., where African cultural practices were widely restricted. Indeed, African American and Pan-African nationalism had to leave aside such older traditions in order for nationalism to come into being, since the racial unity it envisioned was one superceding other group identities, just as Jewish nationalism disregarded the national origin of Jews in favor of religious and cultural homogeneity.

Two influential American philosophers of the early twentieth century, Horace Kallen and Alain Locke, were not only connected by a lifelong friendship but also subscribed to forms of nationalism with striking parallels in their philosophical approaches to ethnicity. While they favored a fostering of ethnic culture—Kallen was a Zionist, Locke a signal force in the Harlem Renaissance—they also rejected biologist definitions of race and instead embraced a view of race indebted to Boasian anthropology. Alain Locke, in an essay written in 1924 ("The Concept of Race as Applied to Social Culture"), affirms that "race is a fact in the social or ethnic sense." Therefore "it must be explained in terms of social and historical causes" rather than by recurrence to physical type (Harris 192).

While race is not rejected as a concept per se, its definition is shifted from a biological, and thus virtually unchangeable, basis to one that emphasizes human agency and environment. Thus, Locke claims that "[r]ace operates as tradition, as preferred traits and values" (Harris 195). That, for the most part, is exactly the view of race all six novels discussed here propose—away from physical traits and towards metaphysical ones, though essentialist elements remain: Johnson, Ornitz, Fauset, and Yezierska all imply that certain talents and inclinations are inherent to ethnicity.

Horace Kallen, in an 1910 essay titled "Judaism, Hebraism, Zionism," maintained that "Hebraism is the particular inheritance of the Jews, their tradition and culture" (*Judaism* 39). While this shift from biology to culture appears as a shift from essentialism to constructionism, the real change only consists in the way in which race manifests itself. I say "only" because at "the root of [Kallen's] cultural pluralism is a notion of the eternal power of descent, birth, natio, and race" (Sollors "Critique" 260). Because race is still said to possess "That peculiar selective preference for certain culture-traits" (Harris 195), there remains a kind of racial bedrock that allows for absolute distinctions—but only in the intermediate sense.

Both Kallen and Locke envision a long-term goal of universalism: "The conservation of no social object whatever is morally justified unless it is an actual synthesis of instrument and end, unless by being most itself, by making the most of its individuality, by perfecting itself in its natural function, it most avails the rest of mankind" (Kallen *Judaism* 36). Locke, too, in a 1930 essay entitled "The Contribution of Race to Culture," expressed his support for a "racial sense," for a stimulation of the "racial consciousness" and a revivification of "lapsing racial traditions" under the precondition that these were compatible with the "future development of internationalism and the approach toward universalism" (Harris 202). But like Kallen's, Locke's position on the relation between culture and race remained ambiguous. While he affirmed that

> there is no organic or causal connection between race and culture . . . he differed with the denial of Robert Lowie, in particular, of "all significant connection between racial and cultural factors." To Locke this contention was premature; he believed that eventually race would be necessary in a restricted form to explain cultural differences. (Hutchinson *Harlem* 91)

This ambiguous and transitional essentialism embraced by cultural pluralists like Locke and Kallen is highly reminiscent of Du Bois's "gift theory" in *The Souls of Black Folk*, which, in 1903, saw each race contributing its best towards the development of a larger unity—the American nation: "Actively we have woven ourselves with the very warp and woof of this nation. . . . Our song, our toil, our cheer, and warning have been given to this nation in blood-brotherhood" (187). This passage, in its fusion of ethnicity and Americanness, anticipates Louis Brandeis's assertion that Zionism and Americanism are entirely compatible. This compatibility is grounded in cultural pluralism.[18] As we have seen, though, cultural pluralism often tended towards essentialist definitions of culture more in keeping with nationalist thinking, a tendency revealed in the phrase "a nation within a nation." African American and Jewish American views of ethnicity were thus part of a web of common and mutual influences, inextricably intertwined.

The idea of ethnic solidarity, with its strong overtones of redemption through suffering, is a quasi-religious one. The spiritual component of nationalism arises from the essentially mystical nature of the nationalist idea. As in Zionism, the nationalist trend among African

Americans was closely aligned with issues of spirituality. Thus Cyril V. Briggs, a West Indian black nationalist, could appeal to the idea of sacrifice for a greater cause, to denial of self, and to asceticism—expectations one usually finds in religious orders. In his *Race Catechism*, Briggs asked:

> Question: What are one's duty to the Race? Answer: To love one's Race above oneself and to further the common interests of all above the private interests of one. To cheerfully sacrifice wealth, ease, luxuries, necessities and, if need be, life itself to attain for the Race that greatness in arms, in commerce, in art, the three combined without which there is neither respect, honor nor security (quoted in Sundquist *Contexts* 180).

Despite its stress on suffering, ethnic nationalism could also be informed by the materialist goals of the dominant mainstream ideology. Thus we find two of the causes to which Briggs's appeal meant to enlist its readers to be patently materialist ones: arms and commerce. They are only spiritualized by serving an essentially abstract and almost metaphysical entity: the "Race." Similar mingling of materialism and ethnic solidarity can be observed in *Plum Bun*, *Fanny Herself*, and *The Autobiography of an Ex-Coloured Man*, which take middle-class trappings quite for granted; at least Fauset and Ferber do not appear to see a contradiction between the "good life" and an ethnic one, while the other four novels arguably raise that question. Nonetheless, ethnic nationalism, both for Jewish Americans and African Americans, could serve as a form of resistance to the increasing encroachments of the capitalist spirit on American national life as a whole, even if it was informed by it.

For the American scene at the beginning of the twentieth century, the affirmation of the spirituality of nationalism rings more true for ethnic nationalism than it does for mainstream nationalism in a country which, by observers as politically diverse as Henry James (in *The American Scene*), Ezra Pound, Mark Twain, and W. E. B. Du Bois, was chided for its materialism. Ethnic nationalism positioned itself in opposition to materialism because it claimed to preserve, or rather— in what one might call a counterhegemonic move—usurp the spiritual element of the nationalist momentum, taking it over from a nation where it had lost its original impulse and turned into a strategy to maintain the status quo. The appeal of Fauset, Ornitz, Johnson, and Ferber to some form of spirituality or idealist notions is typical for and expressive of the nationalist impulse, but more convincing as a differentiating move than when occurring in mainstream nationalism.

The various intellectual connections between Zionism and Black Nationalism serve as one explanation for parallels between African American and Jewish American literary works—if two of the dominant ideological models of their time are intricately connected, it is not surprising, then, to find these ideological formations reflected, discussed, and responded to in the contemporary literary production. Yet, despite being grounded in or responding to ethnic nationalism, many writers have chosen a European genre to illuminate an ethnic world; this may show that there is no essential connection between ethnicity and race on the one hand, and literature on the other, and that any genre can be used by anybody for any purpose, given some cultural adjustments both by the writer and by the literary form.[19] A "universalized" literary genre may thus be employed for particularized resistance to cultural disintegration of an ethnic group.

The idea of literature as a whole has long been connected with the idea of race or ethnicity. Kwame Anthony Appiah has said, "the nation is the key middle term in understanding the relations between the concept of race and the idea of literature. . . . European nations conceived of themselves in terms of descent . . . all that happened was that descent came in the mid-nineteenth century to be understood in terms of race" (48). But since the nation is seen as the ultimate outward political expression of racial culture, a national literature is at the same time a racial literature, at least in the nineteenth-century understanding of the term "nation."[20] One only has to put two and two together, add the idea that a nation finds cultural expression in its literature to the racialized conceptualization of the nation to perceive the connection between the concepts of "race" and "literature" (Appiah 51).

Until postcolonial critics started doing so, though, this link between race and literature had been little discussed in literary criticism, even though nineteenth-century ideologues in the West were quite direct about the idea of literature as expressing a national spirit. Indeed, literature was seen as a teaching tool to inculcate nationalism in its readers.[21] One reason for the former silence on the connections between race, nationalism, and literature is that much of the erstwhile canon does not, on the surface, appear to put race in its center.[22] African American literature, however, differs greatly in this regard:

the major proportion of the published writing of African-Americans, even when not directed to countering racist mythology, has been thematically concerned with issues of race, a fact that is hardly surprising in a country where black people were subjected to racial slavery until the mid-nineteenth century and then treated legally as second-class citizens in many places until the 1960s. (Appiah 53)

While race, at least since the eighteenth century, was almost always connected with the idea of literature in the West, African American and Jewish American literature foregrounded this issue and made explicit what had always been implicit. Mainstream literature did not need to talk about race explicitly because race was only of interest as a distinguishing feature between the dominant and the marginal, the oppressor and the oppressed. And by the time the novel had become the major literary form, that difference had already assumed hegemonic status, and mainstream novels merely needed to depict it as an unquestioned part of literary reality to further assist in the "normalization" of that status quo. The foregrounding of race in ethnic novels thus had a disruptive function, a function that was complementary to the ethnic novel's purpose of "writing into existence" the ethnic subject.[23]

Edward Said says that narratives do not only serve the needs of a society that wants to "normalize" imperial ventures, "they also become the method colonized people use to assert their own identity and the existence of their own history" (xii). The fact that an oppressor uses a genre does not bar it from use by the oppressed. The opposite is more likely: because the colonizer or oppressor uses the form, it is a particularly apt vehicle to assert identity, because the form allows entrance into the dominant culture. In addition, as Benedict Anderson has shown, the novel is uniquely qualified as a vehicle for "nationness" since it can depict various strata of the ethnic community as if they existed simultaneously in time and thus make real a connectedness between its members through their very depiction on the pages of the same book (31ff).

Nonetheless, if the British novel as a genre had as "one of its principal purposes [to sustain] . . . almost unnoticeably the society's consent in overseas expansion" (Said 12), the novel might still strike one as an odd ethnic genre, since American mainstream novels, too, tended to normalize quasi-colonialist relations (a trend most easily observed in Southern apologist literature, but subtly present in much canonical literature, as Toni Morrison has shown in *Playing in the Dark*). If one accepts that the realistic novel is related in this way to imperialism, and thus to the oppression of non-European peoples, then one may wonder as to ethnic authors' aesthetic (and ideological) choice. The reason for this choice might lie in the fact that the novel, and particularly the coming-of-age novel, lends itself easily to ideological reinterpretation. Not, however, until a paradox at the core of this choice has been resolved.

The form lends itself easily because of its focus on the self. Rather than having to explain societal structures or rather than putting them in the center, as, according to Said, a novel like *Pride and Prejudice* does, the Bildungsroman focuses on the development of the self often, at least initially, against societal structures.[24] This oppositional element in the form offers itself for use for ethnic authors, who, because of the very nature of ethnicity, occupy an oppositional space vis-à-vis the mainstream.

The Bildungsroman's focus on the self also injects a strongly subjective element into the genre of realism. From the very start, it is clear that one sees society through the eyes of the protagonist, experiences it as the protagonist experiences it.[25] Autobiography and Bildungsroman have lent themselves well to ethnic purposes because they are subjective forms, telling of an individual's experience in the world. However, the deceptively subjective intentionality of the genre opens it up for use by any writer on any subject and invites views of society from any angle. Here lies the paradox mentioned above: because of its apparent subjectivity, the form is individualist in nature and thus conforms to a European world view that is foundational to modern capitalism, the very system which in turn often arises on the backs of ethnic groups and colonized people.

We are now in a position to understand more fully the genre revisions discussed in the introduction. Rather than only being expressive of an individualist world view, ethnic autobiographical novels come to embrace communalism in the form of ethnic solidarity. Kwame Anthony Appiah, in speaking of African novels, claims "that though the European may feel that the problem of who he or she is can be a private problem, the African asks always not 'who am I?' but 'who are we?' and 'my' problem is not mine alone but 'ours'" (76). One finds a similar distinction between mainstream and ethnic autobiographical novels. In the latter, ethnic solidarity is held high as an ideal and belonging to the ethnic group is seen as a mainstay of identity. The community becomes as important as the individual—if not more important. In part this may be a reaction to outside pressure, discrimination, and Diaspora, all of which produce an "us/them" dynamic. Ethnic forms thus communalize individualist forms and are answering to different, more communalist demands. The "I" becomes a "We"—if not, at least the work has to justify why this is not so, and even then the individualization of the protagonist takes place within an ethnic framework. Selina still travels to Barbados, the ancestral home, to find herself, and Sara works within and for the Jewish community and marries Jewish, even while advocating a kind of assimilation.

This does not mean, of course, that the novels present only two absolute choices: rampant individualism and unmitigated communalism, though *Fanny Herself* and *Plum Bun* come close to it; they show that there are various in-betweens, and both *Brown Girl, Brownstones* and *Bread Givers* clearly advocate a kind of individualism, though a new, ethnic individualism. In discussing R. K. Narayan's *The Vendor of Sweets*, the authors of *The Empire Writes Back* note that "a continuing dialectical pattern emerges between a traditional insistence on the collective, family, group, and society, and the opposed demands of the European ideology of the independent 'individual' whose social inflection is one of the strongest trace marks left by Europeanization on the post-colonial world" (Ashcroft et al. 114). This is the dialectic at work in ethnic autobiographical novels: they have to balance the individualist tradition of the form, visible in its focus on a protagonist, with the more communalist orientation of ethnic nationalism.

One way in which the individualist tendency of the form may be mitigated is by giving voice to other characters in a substantial way, as all of the works do and none more so than *Brown Girl* and *Bread Givers*, not least to counterbalance their otherwise more individualistic tendencies. What goes for *The Vendor of Sweets*, then, also goes for these two novels: "We do not have to decide between the generations [who stand for individualism or communalism, respectively] in a moral way any more than we have to endorse or reject their actions." Instead, "the novel's paradoxes and pluralities" are not reduced to a singular vision (Ashcroft et al. 114).[26]

Ethnic solidarity, as a survival tactic, is one of the values dominant in the ethnic communities as the novels depict them, and to that extent, the novels contribute to formulating and holding together a community.[27] The ideology a work of literature espouses may help to define race or nation; in turn, the position of an ethnic group, both in the larger nation and in the literature of that nation, has a lot to do with what ideology ethnic literary works will espouse. Lennard J. Davis has said this about the relationship of literature and ideology:

> Ideology is in effect the culture's form of writing a novel about itself for itself. And the novel is a form that incorporates that cultural fiction into a particular story. Likewise, fiction becomes, in turn, one of the ways in which the culture teaches itself about itself, and thus novels become agents inculcating ideology. (24–25)

For ethnic cultures, the relationship of ideology and literature is even more complicated, since ethnic literature, simplistically speaking, has to deal with (at least) two mutually contradictory sets of ideology. The dominant culture may demand assimilation while the ethnic group may expect adherence to tradition. If the ethnic novel teaches ethnic culture about itself and is informed by an ideology arising out of the historical experiences of that ethnic group, it also has to confront or respond to mainstream ideology about the ethnic group.[28]

This returns us to the definition of nationalism: "Man is a slave neither of his race nor his language, nor of his religion, nor of the course of rivers nor of the direction taken by mountain chains. A large aggregate of men, healthy in mind and warm of heart, creates the kind of moral consciousness which we call a nation" (Renan 20). If one overlooks the customary male bias of the statement, Renan—uncharacteristically—forwards a wholly constructionist idea of the nation here, though the incorporation of "morals" into the formation of a nation hints at the potential for essentialism, for declaring a nation "morally superior" not based on any actions but on supposedly inherent character.

The works under discussion do suggest that there are specific traits that define an ethnic group (nation). At the same time, they insist on commitment, knowing fully well that the biologist or culturalist definition of the group does not a nation make, i.e., does not create ethnic solidarity. Essential ethnic traits, such as Blackness or Jewishness variously defined, serve as a useful symbol, though. On the one hand, the essential traits embraced by the novels tend to be the very ones that have been used as justification for the ethnic group's marginalization (e.g., an emphasis on emotions over rationality). On the other hand, because they have been used as tools of denigration, their reinterpretation in positive, assertive terms makes for a very accessible and dramatic propaganda effect. After all, these novels may be seen as guides to being ethnic in America, providing maps, showing ways to be and ways not to be, and attempting to assist in a continued "ethnogenesis," to use Sollors's term.[29]

The peculiar tension between essentialist and constructionist positions in these novels is thus endemic to the nationalist project, a project which attempts to create something by claiming that it is already there (Brennan 44). As we have seen, ethnicity is often conceptualized in terms of descent, according to Sollors's model, in the novels under discussion here, stressing the seemingly inescapable aspects of nationness. At the same time, all of the protagonists have and exercise a choice in their allegiance or non-allegiance to ethnicity. Without this element of choice, the novels would have nothing to convince their readers of; thus they differentiate between simply being ethnic (inescapable) and actively being ethnic (subscribing to ethnic solidarity). Rather than being defined in essentialist or constructionist terms, the works under discussion configure ethnicity as a relationship of descent *and* consent. Being aware of its (partly) volitional character while claiming its inescapability and trying to convince their readers to subscribe to their ideological project, authors often had to prevaricate on the exact nature of ethnicity, varying their approach even within the same text.

There is, however, a further complication in entering the terrain of nationalism. While ethnic groups may exhibit ideological tendencies towards separatism or nationalism, which is thought to bring more economic independence and communal self-sufficiency vis-à-vis those mainstream forces which exploit, threaten, or denigrate the ethnic community, ethnic nationalism is always in danger of looking like mainstream nationalism, which often poses a danger to ethnic groups. Various nativisms in the early part of the twentieth century, anti-immigrationism, and the strength of the Ku Klux Klan also derive themselves from nationalist sentiment, from the perception that "foreigners" or "strangers," people who are not truly "Americans," are supposedly gaining influence or posing economic competition.

If literature is connected with the idea of the nation, then any literature that espouses a form of nationalism must face the dilemma of promoting a mode of thought that is just as easily turned against the ethnic group which that very literature attempts to guard. One way to confront this dilemma is to inject ethnic nationalism with values differentiating it from the mainstream while at the same time harkening back to ideas which can be seen as prototypically American. In other

words, if communalism and spirituality of some sort are seen as ethnic and materialism and selfishness as mainstream, one can claim that
ethnic group members now represent "American values" better than
Americans, a strategy Mary Antin adopts in *The Promised Land*, a book
that implies that new immigrants may be closer to being prototypical
Americans than Anglo Americans.[30] One can see the same strategy
in Louis Brandeis's Zionism: "Addressing the 1915 Zionist convention
in Boston, he proclaimed: 'The highest Jewish ideals are essentially
American in a very important particular. It is Democracy that Zionism represents. It is social justice which Zionism represents, and every
bit of that is the American ideals [sic] of the twentieth century.'"
(Urofsky 119).

In a slight variation of this argument, Horace Kallen maintained
that the U.S., while making material progress possible, "has turned the
minds of people and government to wealth alone, and in the haste to
accumulate wealth considerations of human quality have been neglected
and forgotten" (*Culture* 116–117). As a result, ethnic groups have to create or maintain their own spiritual and cultural life to fill that void.
Kallen thus came to encourage ethnic cultural nationalisms within a
larger political union. But as is the tendency of nationalist ideas, his conception of cultural nationalism was based in essentialism, his phrasing
of which nicely mirrors his fusion of ethnic nationalism with political
Americanism: "The selfhood which is inalienable in them [ethnic
groups], and for the realization of which they require 'inalienable' liberty is ancestrally determined, and the happiness which they pursue
has its form implied in ancestral endowment" (*Culture* 123). Similar
notes are sounded by W. E. B. Du Bois as well:

> there are to-day no truer exponents of the pure human spirit of the
> Declaration of Independence than the American Negroes; there is
> no true American music but the wild sweet melodies of the Negro
> slave; the American fairy tales and folklore are Indian and African;
> and, all in all, we black men seem the sole oasis of simple faith and
> reverence in a dusty desert of dollars and smartness. (8)[31]

White Americans do not represent America's true nature any more, and
ethnic Americans now occupy the morally central position previously
held, one assumes, by the Founding Fathers.[32]

What this reversal accomplishes is thus a kind of decolonization on
a metaphysical level: the ethnic group may be marginalized when it

comes to the material and political relations of the U.S., but it is dominant in the sphere of morals, ethics, and ideals. Political ideals and characteristics usually seen in terms of consent thus become "ethnicized" and defined in terms of descent, i.e., as being inherent traits of ethnic groups. Accordingly, the protagonists of *Fanny* and *Plum Bun* eventually embrace the idealistic/artistic/communalist ideal which becomes the sign of ethnicity in those novels, a sign which sets them above the more shallow, prejudiced, and materialist currents that implicitly represent mainstream society in the novels.

Though the quasi-religious quality ethnic nationalism assumes is a hallmark of nationalism in general, the insistence with which one finds the differentiation between materialist mainstream and spiritual ethnicity is remarkable.[33] Both *Plum Bun* and the *Autobiography* ask their protagonists to make the "right" choice as do, in related ways, *Haunch* and *Fanny Herself*, nor do the protagonists of *Bread Givers* and *Brown Girl, Brownstones* find themselves entirely able to ignore this moral imperative. The pervasive fact here is a strong moral valorization of ethnicity.

This idea reverberates in several of the novels, and all of them respond to it. Ethnic solidarity assumes a kind of religious significance; it does not need any explanation but is a good in and of itself. Any deviation from it can be called heresy by the ethnic community, as it is in *Bread Givers* and indirectly in *Brown Girl*, where Deighton's and Clive's fates indicate what happens to individuals who do not live up to the quasi-religious work ethic of the Barbadian community and thus forsake their "ethnic duty"—though the novel deplores such a despotic insistence on group cohesiveness. In all the novels, however, desertion of ethnicity leads to feelings of emptiness and spiritual dissatisfaction.

It is in this sense that the novels are imbued with the spirit of Black Nationalism or Zionism—not as an expression of literal emigration or the call for the creation of a homeland, but as a kind of spiritual internal emigration, a separation from values that are associated with the mainstream and an espousal of an idealist, moral kind of ethnicity. The nationalism of these works is a transcendental one.[34] There is still a connection between nationalism and literature here, and a more or less essentialist definition of the values or characteristics which make the nation a nation, but nationalism aims at a metaphysical territory here, not a geographical one. Accordingly, Du Bois would regard Zionism not so much as territorialism but as a "synonym for Pan-Africanism, a spiritual rather than a geographical idea—a 'nation' that consisted primarily of a transhistorical consciousness outside of property or the literal black body" (Sundquist *To Wake* 559).[35]

One can begin to understand the pressures that are bearing on these novels. Given that they work against stereotypical perceptions of ethnicity, they have a vested interest in asserting ethnic presence, and the individualist form of the autobiographical novel, blurring the boundary between fact and fiction as it does, lends itself well to that end. But the forces of individualism threaten to splinter ethnic culture while leaving the ethnic individual vulnerable in an environment hostile to her or him in a nation that defines itself often to his or her socioeconomic exclusion. The dominant nation, then, which establishes itself ostentatiously on individualist principles also carries a racialist (and nationalist) agenda that qualifies its "universalist" (by Enlightenment definitions) individualism. The ethnic nation serves as a counterbalancing force here. It makes a virtue out of exclusion, building on cultural traits that are claimed to differentiate the ethnic group from the mainstream. But given the heterogeneousness of the ethnic group along class lines, geographical origin, level of commitment to ethnic culture, etc., only very generalized traits will serve to bind all members of the group. The distinction between materialism and spirituality comes to bear at his point. As both Ferber's and Fauset's novels show, diaspora Jews and Africans share a legacy of suffering which is intricately connected to their spirituality and is indeed seen as spiritualizing. This legacy forms a counterpoint to the expanding capitalist economy of the U.S.

The Bildungsromane studied here, then, try to establish the ethnic individual while maintaining group coherence and attempt to counter stereotypes by forming a positive, while often normative, image of ethnicity.[36] They describe, circumscribe, and define the ethnic nation and call for ethnic commitment. They are fully aware of the volitional nature of ethnicity; after all, an "ethnic group only exists where members consider themselves to belong to such a group; a conscious sense of belonging is critical" (Patterson 309). The African American and Jewish American works discussed here attempt to build ethnic nations and are therefore freighted with the tensions of the nationalist project. One has only to remember Israel's flight from Egypt: left behind were fleshpots (materialism) in favor of religious freedom and against the danger of acculturation (idealism).[37] Ethnic nationalism may be a response to oppression and marginalization, but nationalism is also an attractive ideology for ethnic literature because it embodies many of the tensions inherent in the ethnic situation. One might say that if double-consciousness marks the ethnic condition, then this double-consciousness also finds formal and ideological expression in ethnic literature. The Bildungsroman, an individualist form, is rewritten for communalist purposes and becomes the vehicle for an ideology which uneasily combines essentialist and constructionist views of ethnicity, inasmuch as it has to summon to life what it claims is or should be alive already—group cohesion based on similarity of traits.

The Bildungsroman, with its genre-specific pressures, and the ferment of nationalism provide the parameters for the stories these works tell. The first four works depict their protagonists' attempt to assimilate into the mainstream or their adoption of mainstream methods (as in *Haunch*) as the wrong moral choice, while the espousal of artistry, idealism, and ethnic solidarity is seen as morally right. On the other hand, mainstream, in the novels, means hostility, denigration of the ethnic individual, materialism, often a lack of vibrancy and life force. The characteristics that define ethnicity in the works discussed here—artistic sensibility, experience of and empathy with suffering, communalism, spirituality—provide a useful standard against which the materialism of the mainstream can be measured. When Tacitus wrote *Germania*, he did not expect his Roman readers to adopt the exact lifestyle and virtues he was describing in Germanic tribes, but he meant the latter as a mirror in which Roman society should see the degree to which it had become decadent. While I do not claim that the authors discussed here necessarily had a similar end in mind, their narratives certainly lend themselves to such an end. After all, Samuel Ornitz insisted on the Americanness of his novel, saying that his book should not be "regarded in any other way than a book of Americans by an American" (Miller "Samuel Ornitz" 210); according to Ornitz, his protagonist thus meant to exemplify an American problem, not a Jewish one; however, solutions for this problem are offered in several altruistic Jewish characters. Selina's individualism can be seen as American, but she also reminds her mother that neither air nor love can be bought with money, thus rejecting the materialism her ethnic community has adopted when coming to America both as a defense against American racism and as a first step towards Americanization. Fanny exemplifies an American corporate success story but finds happiness and fulfillment only when she rejects a business career in favor of what the novel depicts as an ethnic and more communally oriented calling.

The ethnic cultural nationalism that imbues these works to a lesser or greater degree thus has a double message through which it differentiates itself from hostile anti-ethnic nationalism: it warns the ethnic community not to relinquish values which it posits as traditionally ethnic, and it holds a mirror to the mainstream, implying that the latter may have things to learn from both African Americans and Jewish Americans—and because of the way the lessons are packaged, the content proves to be similar.

NOTES

1. The discussion continues with an ever-growing number of publications, such as *Mutual Reflections: Jews and Blacks in American Art* by Milly Heyd, *What Went Wrong? The Creation and Collapse of the Black-Jewish Alliance* by Murray Friedman, and *African Americans and Jews in the Twentieth Century: Studies in Convergence and Conflict* edited by V. P. Franklin and Harold M. Kletnick. See, for example, David Brion Davis's review of six such books in the December 2, 1999, issue of the *New York Review of Books*. See also the special issue of *Society* 31.6 (1994) devoted to a debate about African American and Jewish American relations.

2. The discovery of African American/Jewish American parallels is not necessarily a thing of the past, either. When conducting a faculty seminar involving African American and Jewish American professors at the University of Massachusetts, Amherst, Maurianne Adams and John Bracey noted that "black participants were struck by the pervasive, recurrent issues of identity among the Jewish participants that seemed to parallel their own concerns about those issues" (B9).

3. Such a debate has taken place, for example, in the pages of the *New York Review of Books* concerning the meaning of the holocaust for subsequent generations. See Eva Hoffman's review of Peter Novick's *The Holocaust in American Life* (March 9, 2000), Peter Novick's and Steven Katz's comments with Eva Hoffman's reply (June 15, 2000), and another comment by Irving Greenberg (November 2, 2000).

Another discussion revolving around the nature of anti-Semitism followed Gordon Craig's review of Daniel Goldhagen's *Hitler's Willing Executioners* (April 18, 1996). Goldhagen's book explains widespread German participation in the holocaust by claiming that an eliminationist anti-Semitism had developed in Germany that was unlike anti-Semitism elsewhere and had to be understood through German history. Craig's review sees the book's merits but doubts the inevitability that Goldhagen ascribes to German developments. See also the debate between Marion Gräfin Dönhoff and Gordon Craig in the May 23, 1996, issue and Gordon Craig's review of—among other books—Saul Friedlaender's *Nazi Germany and the Jews*, which also contests Goldhagen's thesis.

A third debate between R. J. Tyndorf and Istvan Deak on whether Maximilian Kolbe was or was not an anti-Semite appears in the September 25, 1997, issue; it addresses what anti-Semitism is and how someone's anti-Semitism should be judged and measured. In addition, public debates about Israeli-Palestinian relations in the wake of the second intifada often involve the question of whether criticism of Israeli policies is ipso facto anti-Semitic or not.

4. As Leon Yudkin says, "By 1925, the great wave of immigration into America had come to an end, and was henceforth to be curbed into a thin trickle. But the Jews could now crystallise some of their earlier tendencies into a shape of a community with a character of its own. The literature written up to 1934 naturally evinces the contours of this peculiar but vibrant experience" (28).

5. I agree with Laurence Mordekhai Thomas's conclusion, in his 1993 study *Vessels of Evil: American Slavery and the Holocaust*, that both are "entirely different evil institutions" (12), for example in their ultimate goals and in their conceptions of their victims. This, of course, does not mean that no comparisons can ever be made. In making it impossible to compare either American slavery or the Holocaust to any other historical event, one would severely curtail understanding of them.

6. The first decades of the twentieth century saw a small African American movement spring up which may serve as an illustration of the degree to which Jewish American and African American nationalist concepts could become enmeshed. I am referring to the Church of God, also known as "Black Jews" or "Black Hebrews" founded by prophet F. S. Cherry in the late 1910s (Joseph R. Washington 134, 155). Cherry claimed that African Americans were the Jews of the Biblical tradition. His church followed some Orthodox Jewish practices but restricted its membership to African Americans (Arthur Huff Fauset 32ff.). Interestingly, then, unlike Judaism, which allows conversion, Cherry made a racially exclusive claim for followers of the true religion. The Black Jews existed in several geographical locations, some of the communities being independent of one another. The Harlem section of the Black Jews, incorporated in 1930, saw Judaism as the true religion. Its members claimed to be Ethiopian Jews and maintained contacts to the Jewish community. The Church of God is an expression of African American nationalist tendencies in the early twentieth century and shows an intriguing link between Jewish and African American diaspora nationalism.

7. As Janet Helms notes, social science literature has often disregarded ethnicity when discussing people of African descent, focusing instead on their shared Africanness, while studies of white ethnics in the U.S. often do not take into account their shared "whiteness" (4). Fanny, the protagonist of Edna Ferber's novel *Fanny Herself*, can take advantage of that shared whiteness and pass—but Ferber does not let her. The reasons why Ferber thinks she cannot

and should not are configured both in terms of ideology—what does Jewishness mean—and in terms of race as it has been tragically conceptualized for much of the nineteenth and twentieth centuries: as essential difference. The boundaries between ethnicity and race are blurry here, because Jewishness is configured by the novels in terms of choice and ideology *and* in terms of essence, and the same is true of the African American novels discussed here. For this reason, and for others discussed in the body of the introduction, as well as for the almost wholly negative use to which the term race has been put in much of its history, I will use ethnicity as the overarching term in this study.

8. After critiquing the ethnicity paradigm for its insufficient attention to structural and qualitative differences in oppression for racially defined groups as compared to European immigrants, Omi and Winant still come to the conclusion that the "ethnicity school can document in rich detail the contingency and adaptability of racial identities (considered of course in ethnic group terms)" and that "[e]thnicity theory, especially its post-1965 incarnation, comes closest to our concept of 'racial formation'" (53). In short, of the various paradigms under consideration, Omi and Winant consider the ethnicity paradigm as best suited as a basis for the study of identity formation even of groups defined in terms of race.

Steve Fenton, prefers ethnicity to race because of the latter term's "analytical ambiguity" and its implication that it describes "people who are inescapably different and between whom relations are essentially problematic" (ix). Fenton claims one can avoid the main danger of the ethnicity paradigm— "seeing ethnicity and ethnic groups as everywhere the same phenomenon"— by speaking of "different modalities of ethnicity" (x): "It is possible to show that ethnicity is constructed by showing how ethnic categories shift their ground, import and content as circumstances change. But ethnicity also has a 'real' social basis in the enduring significance which people attach to ancestry, cultural difference and language" (xi). According to Fenton, ethnicity should thus be thought of as "a *social process*," a fluid and ever-changing phenomenon that is a way for groups and individuals to tell themselves who they are in terms of culture. As Fenton emphasizes, "Central to this process is the production and reproduction of culture" (10).

9. William M. Phillips Jr. defines this latter term as follows: "a minority group is held to be a social aggregate whose solidarity is both a response to external pressure forcing it to live in some degree of isolation, conflict, and ostracism and a response to internal pressures forcing it to create a distinctive collective consciousness. The African American and Jewish American communities, therefore, are identified as minority groups" (x).

10. Among them are such well-known works as Houston A. Baker Jr.'s *Blues, Ideology, and Afro-American Literature*, Hazel V. Carby's *Reconstructing Womanhood*, Barbara Christian's *Black Feminist Criticism*, Henry Louis Gates

Jr.'s *The Signifying Monkey*, Bernard Bell's *The Afro-American Novel and Its Tradition*, and Farah Jasmin Griffin's *Who Set You Flowin'?*, just to name a few.

11. Another of Wong's criticisms of an interethnic approach to literature has to be taken into account as well. In discussing William Boelhower's *Immigrant Autobiography in the United States*, she observes that "Boelhower's omnibus term *immigrant autobiography* signals a conceptually problematic telescoping of first and second generations into a single 'immigrant experience'" (147). This conflation is problematic because "the historically-situated voyage that transforms foreign nationals into American immigrants separates the first and second generations quite drastically" (Wong 148). I have tried to heed Wong's advice by selecting only protagonists that are at least second generation, particularly in order to facilitate the comparison between Jewish American, Barbadian American, and African American works. Though obvious differences in terms of socioeconomics remain, the ethnic situations of the protagonists compare in that none of them has any experience of the geographic locale that their ethnic culture claims as its place of origin. At the same time, all of them are aware of a difference between themselves and members of the dominant culture that is at least in part based on their ancestry and its geographic origin. In addition, many African American writers and protagonists of the period in question might be considered "second generation" inasmuch as their parents came from the rural South with its significantly different socioeconomic climate. Language does not become a problem area through a limitation to (at least) second-generation protagonists; as Wong says, "immigrant writers who compose in English tend to do so by choice; the American-born, by right and necessity" (151).

12. Neither does a comparative approach necessarily privilege the dominant group any more than does a cross-ethnic approach. Though admitting that "benefits can be achieved when a critic examines ethnic literature using a transethnic approach" (27), Adam Meyer criticizes Sollors for studying ethnic literature in relation to the dominant culture: "In some ways, Sollors' transethnicity perpetuates the very majority-minority bias it sets out to go beyond. Cross-ethnicity, on the other hand, provides a true study of the relations between and among ethnic minorities. The distinction between the two approaches is analogous to the distinction between the theories of 'separate but equal' and 'integrationism'" (27). Meyer speaks as if by looking at literary references of ethnic characters to other ethnic groups somehow a truer picture of ethnicity emerged, as if the overall cultural context for those references were not there anymore. Even the reactions of ethnic groups to each other are often influenced by the conceptualizations of the dominant culture. Because the ethnic situation as I understand it in the context of this study is always one of contact between cultures (a Pole in Poland is not ethnic, but

a Pole in the U.S. is) and—in the U.S.—contact that is predominantly characterized by the positioning of ethnic group and mainstream, much interethnic contact will bear the mark of the social situation the respective ethnic groups find themselves in with regard to the dominant society. In comparing specific ethnic authors, their relation to the dominant society as imagined in their works is the most important indicator of how they conceptualize ethnicity since, after all, their very ethnic situation has come about because of, but does not exclusively consist of, their difference from the dominant society.

13. R. Radhakrishnan has aptly formulated the concerns that underlie much of the criticism of comparative approaches to ethnicity: "No sooner do we say 'post-ethnic' than legitimate fears creep in about the kind of theory that we should employ in historicizing ethnicity. . . . How could any theory be 'post-anything' and still serve a specific constituency? Aren't theories of the 'post-' incapable of engaging in identity politics? . . . Does not the theory of the 'post-' (with its strong European formation) eventually operate as a mercenary mode that overlooks the value as well as the necessity of historical commitments?" (16) Though this study does not attempt to be in the business of identity politics, it will try to study identity formation—not to reach for some *post*-ethnic space, not to go *beyond* group-specific identities and their literary and historical expressions, but to analyze the common ground they create and to look for reasons for this common ground as far as the texts will yield them.

14. Naomi B. Sokoloff has noted, for Jewish literature, that "as Jews have dealt with assimilation, the Bildungsroman has taken on tremendous importance. This genre, with its partial attention to childhood, emphasizes the relation of . . . the familiar Jewish environment to the wider social milieu" (8). Elizabeth Schultz maintains that in African American autobiographies, too, (African American) ethnicity in white America is a central concern, as the autobiographical protagonist achieves knowledge of self in the context of a society that has embraced a racialized worldview (87).

15. Indeed, Kessler Harris sees "Anzia Yezierska and Sara Smolinsky, the novel's narrator, [as] emotionally interchangeable" (xvii).

16. In recent years, critics of ethnic fiction have been employing the term Bildungsroman with more regularity and genre considerations have received more attention. See, for example, Geta Le Seur's *Ten is the Age of Darkness: The Black Bildungsroman*, Louis F. Caton's "Romantic Struggles: The *Bildungsroman* and Mother-Daughter Bonding in Jamaica Kincaid's *Annie John*," or Glynis Carr's "Storytelling as Bildung in Zora Neale Hurston's *Their Eyes Were Watching God*."

17. As early as 1922, Wilhelm Dilthey, in *Das Erlebnis und die Dichtung*, mentioned both Bildungsroman and autobiography in conjunction (394), and Spengemann and Lundquist note "the striking coalition which these two

genres have formed in our own time" (501). The practitioners of the craft themselves point out the kinship of the genres: Thomas Mann says that "[the Bildungsroman] is at the same time an autobiography, a confession" (quoted in Swales 159), and autobiographers themselves "seldom make a distinction between autobiography, autobiographical novel, memoir, memories, or reminiscence, genres with different ideas of truthfulness" (Adams ix).

18. Philippe Lejeune, in discussing autobiography in France, sees an even closer kinship between factual and fictional life stories, virtually obliterating genre boundaries. According to him "modern autobiography was . . . born . . . in the wake of the appearance of a new biographical form, the autobiographical novel" (quoted in Fleishman 197). In making the (modern) autobiography an offspring of what Avrom Fleishman calls "pseudoautobiography" (198), Lejeune stresses the fictional, imaginative characteristics of the genre: "the novel of experience imitated a situation of interiority on the fictional level— actually the same situation as the autobiographer's. . . . [H]ere, too, authenticity began to be imitated in the novel before it was retrieved and interiorized by autobiographers: the autobiographer came into his own only by imitating (novelists) as they imagined what it was to be an autobiographer" (quoted in Fleishman 197–198). Because both genres typically revolve around one central character, all other elements of the plot hinge on their relationship to the protagonist. For the Bildungsroman, Franco Moretti, in commenting on Goethe's *Wilhelm Meisters Lehrjahre*, maintains that "what interests us about Lothario and the others is not their autonomous existence, but only the effects they have had on Wilhelm" (21).

Even without offering detailed genre-specific or historical explanations, a number of studies have, in their critical practice, also chosen to disregard genre boundaries. Susanna Egan, in *Patterns of Experience in Autobiography*, works in the "grey area where autobiographical novel and poem overlap with the formal autobiography" (3), and Albert E. Stone includes the "mock autobiography" (2) in his province when studying *Autobiographical Occasions and Original Acts*.

19. For autobiography, James Craig Holte offers an explanation that sees a linkage between literary production and sociopolitical stability or the absence of it. According to him, societies in upheaval often see a flourishing of autobiography because the writing of the self creates an order that the outside world lacks. When the established hierarchies that define an individual's position are threatened, it becomes more important to justify and explore that position ("The Representative Voice" 29). For the Bildungsroman, Susan Gohlman maintains that "the truly significant Bildungsromane are the products of periods of intellectual instability"; the reason for this is "that it is the absence . . . of an objectively definable cosmos that provides the greatest stimulus for the composition of such works" (19). Given that Bildungsromane are often autobiographical,

one might apply the same explanation for this phenomenon that Holte offers for the autobiography. However, the process of Bildung itself, which has given the genre its name, provides further insights as to why instability produces such works. Gohlman defines Bildung as a "reciprocal, creative exchange between inner man and external environment, . . . a process in which the individual actively influences what he absorbs" (21).

20. Some critics, though, subscribe to a view—proposed by Francis Russell Hart—that sees autobiography as closer to history than to fiction, which is concerned with meaning, not with "historic identity" (Stone *Autobiographical Occasions* 6). "The struggle to see and state one's 'circumstanced' location in time and social space, and thereby to discover one's historical self, marks the commonly accepted difference between autobiography and fiction" (6), says Stone. But for critics of the Bildungsroman, or the autobiographical novel, the distinction does not seem to be as clearly demarcated. Roy Pascal, for example, identifies "the relationship of man's innate personality with social circumstance" as "the central problem" (148) of both autobiography and the autobiographical novel. Lothar Köhn, too, in discussing tendencies of twentieth-century Bildungsromane, notes that they are dedicated to the present and discuss contemporary problems (41); and Susan Gohlman finds that Goethe's *Wilhelm Meisters Lehrjahre*, the prototype of all Bildungsromane, is closely tied to its historical context (20). However, since Bildungsromane revolve around the development of a protagonist, and since they tend to be at least partially autobiographical, one might say that the Bildungsroman explores historical identity of an (invented) self. And that the self of autobiography is an invention is nicely reflected in titles of critical works like *Fabricating Lives* (Herbert Leibowitz) or *Telling Lies in Modern American Autobiography* (Timothy Dow Adams) and has become almost a critical commonplace. Mutlu Konuk Blasing's words thus hold true for both autobiography and Bildungsroman: they "represent the point at which a particular relation between the self and the collective experience can be marked in . . . time" (xvii).

21. James Craig Holte's explanation as to why autobiography is a popular ethnic genre connects well with that fact: he claims that ethnic Americans have felt in an even more pronounced manner the disconnection from ancestral culture and past that is typical for many Americans and that that is the reason for their attraction to a genre that "impos[es] order on change" ("The Representative Voice" 33).

22. As Susan Stanford Friedman notes, "the emphasis on individualism does not take into account the importance of a culturally imposed group identity for women and minorities" and thus prevents a realistic depiction of the individuation process (34–35).

23. Michael G. Cooke has commented on the "[p]aradox inher[ing] in the form [autobiography], which calls for personal uniqueness and yet depends

on a cogent general category" ("Modern" 255); Bella Brodzki and Celeste Schenck, in talking about the "(masculine) tradition of autobiography," remark on "the mirroring capacity of the autobiographer: *his* universality, *his* representativeness, *his* role as spokesman for the community" (1). This, of course, calls for adjustments from female autobiographers and for an insistence on female subjectivity. For Jewish American authors, autobiography and Bildungsroman have served to explore the question of what it means to be Jewish in a non-Jewish environment: "[Gershon Shaked] argues in his book *The Shadows Within* that the most important characteristic of Jewishness in modern literature is the very struggle with the issue of identity itself. Narratives of childhood, concerned with a young figure's search for a personal voice, are keenly attuned to such matters and contribute to a wider phenomenon in modern Jewish literature of restless seeking for self-definition" (Sokoloff xi). For African American authors, "autobiography is a revolutionary act," as David L. Dudley says of African American men's autobiography specifically: "it asserts the author's ego against all 'others' in the world" (167). This assertion of the ego plays an important role in the African American literary tradition: according to Sidonie Smith, the creation of a textual self undermined and contradicted the ideologies of slavery and racism, which sought to deny individuality to people of African descent. And this assertion of self remains an impulse driving African American autobiography (Sidonie Smith 10).

24. This political dimension of autobiography and Bildungsroman intimates that utilizing those forms makes a statement about the relationship between reality and the written text. The ethnic writer of autobiography or the Bildungsroman attempts to show his or her readership what it is like to live as a member of a particular ethnic group. If her readership consists of members of her own ethnic group, the text may serve as a different type of teaching device, as a sort of socialization primer, by providing models so that texts may also be understood "as codes for a socialization into ethnic groups and into America" (Sollors *Beyond Ethnicity* 11).

This didactic tendency of both forms has been commented on repeatedly by genre critics. In about 1820, Karl Morgenstern gave the Bildungsroman its name because of that didactic bent. According to him, the genre deserved its name "primarily because of its subject, because it depicts the hero's Bildung at its beginning and up to a certain degree of its completion. . . . but also because it [the Bildungsroman] fosters the reader's Bildung through this depiction to a higher degree than any other kind of novel" (quoted in Köhn 5 [my translation]). Autobiography, too, features a certain degree of didacticism, simply because the protagonist becomes a potential identification model. The frequent choice of forms with teaching or model-providing potential bespeaks ethnic authors' reliance on a belief in referentiality and their optimism regarding the likelihood of their audiences sharing that belief. But since the Bildungsroman has been the genre of choice almost as frequently as the autobiography, Albert E. Stone's often quoted words, "*Life* is the more inclusive sign—not *Literature*—which deserves to be placed above the gateway to the house of autobiography" (19), seem unnecessarily exclusive. Maybe *Life* and *Literature* should be placed above the houses of all genres with a demonstrable trust in referentiality, and the Bildungsroman is certainly among those.

25. Elizabeth Schultz agrees that "black Americans continue to feel that the autobiography is an efficacious means for conveying their views of their relationship with society" (81). The Jewish Bildungsroman, too, stresses the interaction between the Jewish community and the surrounding world, as Naomi Sokoloff asserts. Particularly when they focus on childhood, "the plot actions and the act of storytelling . . . involve dynamic interactions between mature and immature voices. The result: oscillating perspectives that bring about an exploration of clashing cultural codes" (Sokoloff ix).

26. According to Elizabeth Schultz, "Traditional autobiography . . . focuses emphatically upon the individual. . . . Characteristic of the black autobiography, however, is the fact that the individual and the community are not polarities; there is a community of fundamental identification between 'I' and 'We'" (81).

27. As Glynis Carr says of *Their Eyes Were Watching God*, which she pronounces a Bildungsroman, "Janie's discovery of her personal identity is thus closely bound to her exploration of cultural identity" (199). In her dissertation on Jewish American and Chinese American literatures, Ruth Yu Hsiao concludes that the "search for self-identity in Afro-American works . . . always implies a communal identity as well. . . . The self in ethnic fiction argues for its legitimacy as selfcreated, but is also cognizant of its attachment to its ethnic roots" (24). Bella Brodzki and Celeste Schenck discover a similar tendency in (white) women's autobiography. The "female autobiographer takes as a given that selfhood is mediated" (1) and therefore recognizes the influence of others.

28. "Goethe, whose *Wilhelm Meister* is generally regarded as the prototype of the Bildungsroman, developed a definition of *Bildung* . . . [which] includes the idea of reciprocal growth or change in which the individual and the environment are engaged in a process of mutual transformation, each shaping the other until the individual has reached the point where he or she experiences a sense of harmony with the environment" (Gohlman x).

29. Sondra O'Neale is one of them: "While aquiescence in the quest of what Roy L. Ackerman calls the young man's drive for 'complete personal freedom' would seem minimal for survival to a character who is racially acceptable to the 'established order,' and who can thus find arenas for some exercise for freedom in that order, such a compromise would be a repudiation of historic ethnic aspiration in this country. To allow a character to surrender to dominant

group mores which exclude his humanity or to validate an established order that wants to destroy him has never been the choice for protagonists within the protest canon" (26). Naomi B. Sokoloff maintains that the Bildungsroman contains "a code of understanding to be entered into or reacted against" (26), and William Boelhower claims that ethnic autobiography "consciously re-elaborat[es] or simply rewrit[es] the received behavioral script of the rhetorically well-defined American self" ("The Making of Ethnic Autobiography" 125).

30. Naomi B. Sokoloff says for Jewish narratives with a child protagonist that "the status of the child as an outsider on the margins of adult activity proves congenial for the purposes of the artist whose aim is critique or reinterpretation of status quo" (7). But also Bildungsromane with protagonists growing beyond childhood years emphasize critique.

31. In addition, one transformation Esther Kleinbord Labovitz claims as exclusive to the female Bildungsroman occurs in ethnic works (both female and male centered) as well; according to her, "there [in the female Bildungsroman] emerges a whole new fictional world depicting a female culture of engagement, commitment, and conflicting ideologies" (255). As Sidonie Smith, Roger Rosenblatt, and John M. Blassingame have shown for African American texts, political engagement is a crucial feature of African American literature in general and not exclusive to works by women.

32. Ellen Morgan finds that for women, whether ethnic or mainstream, the Bildungsroman offers an expression of this search for authenticity and selfhood: "The novel of apprenticeship is admirably suited to express the emergence of women from cultural conditioning into struggle with institutional forces, their progress toward . . . full personhood, and the effort to restructure their lives and society according to *their own* vision of meaning and right living" (185 [emphasis mine]). Raleigh Whitinger has noted that, since the beginning of the twentieth century, such female Bildungsromane appear to dominate the tradition. Quoting Rita Felski, Whitinger maintains that such "narratives of female development [anticipate] . . . an awakening consciousness of the female identity as 'potentially oppositional force to existing social and cultural values'" (464).

33. The Bildungsroman appears to have some universalist appeal (at least when it comes to cultures that put some premium on individualism); Susan Gohlman notes "that *Bildung* should be associated with a process rather than a genre and . . . this process manifests itself in novels of any nation or culture" (228). It must be said, however, that if authors of any nation or culture choose the Bildungsroman as a form, certain historical processes are likely to have preceded that choice; the specific literary genre "novel" or Bildungsroman is not likely to emerge spontaneously. Bonnie Hoover Braendlin identifies this near-universalist appeal as one reason for the genre's popularity with ethnic

authors: "The current revival of interest in the *Bildungsroman* by American marginality-group authors . . . presumes a theoretical genre, one governed by widely shared, if not universal, experiential phenomena and interpersonal relationships that figure prominently in the formation of personality" (76–77).

I. TWO VERSIONS OF PASSING

1. This connection is even more explicit in *Plum Bun* and *Fanny Herself*.

2. Samira Kawash argues that "it is no more natural to define the narrator of *The Autobiography*, with his few drops of black blood, as black than it is to define his childhood friend 'Shiny' as black" (134). Of course, it is also no more natural to define him as black than it is to define him as white. According to Kawash, "While the mulatto challenges the myth of racial purity, the figure of the passing body goes a step further, challenging the stability of racial knowledge and therefore implicitly the stability of the order that has been constructed on that knowledge" (131).

3. Samira Kawash has said that, "Although the narrator is able to decide whether he will be taken by others as being black or white, he does not ever claim to be simply black or white, and there is always an uncomfortable dissonance between what others take him for and his own sense of himself. For others, the narrator appears as white and black, but for himself, he feels neither white nor black" (139–140). But the narrator cannot really decide what he will be taken for, since his looks make him appear white. His only choice is to announce or not announce what others would take to be blackness. And until the moment in school, he feels white, though his narrative also attempts to trace a hidden blackness through his early musical affinities. Later passages in the novel also hint at his identification with whites.

4. The protagonist's good opinion of himself remains unaffected to a large degree after he discovers that he is categorized as "coloured": "I was accustomed to hear remarks about my beauty; but now, for the first time, I became conscious of it and recognized it" (17), as he says recalling standing in front of a mirror searching for his blackness. Michael G. Cooke has noted the "narcisso-homosexual overtones of his description" of himself in that passage (*Afro-American* 48). This very self-centeredness facilitates his decision to live as a European American later on, and it is significant that he looks at his mother "searching for defects" (18), projecting his negative conception of his own ethnicity outward, away from himself. At this point, however, he is still able to perceive his mother's beauty, his double-consciousness not fully developed yet, meaning that, in this case, he is capable of perceiving himself and his mother objectively, without a distorting racist filter, with his conception of beauty not yet essentially connected to the notion of race. Years later, having passed for much of his life, even his visual self-perception has undergone

change, bearing witness to a kind of inverted psychological growth (or shrink-age) in the narrator. When revealing his blackness to his wife-to-be, his reaction to her initial silence indicates that his double-consciousness has cancelled out his youthful self-perception: "Under the strange light in her eyes I felt that I was growing black and thick-featured and crimp-haired" (204). The wording of this description shows that his adult "schooling" in racism has been even more effective than his white childhood years in which his mother had at least some restraining influence. Beauty is now, in his mind, linked to whiteness.

5. Donald C. Goellnicht also notes that the protagonist "frequently chooses to adopt the gaze of white society" (20). Kathleen Pfeiffer critiques Fleming (and others) for "presuppos[ing]—like Jim Crow laws—that his fundamental alliance *should* be with his 'black' blood, and view[ing] it as a moral failure when the protagonist feels otherwise" (409). This critique neglects to notice that the text itself very much guides the reader in this direction (of seeing racial solidarity as a good thing) by presenting the narrator as a racist before he realizes his "race," as an opportunist, and as a materialist—and even as a coward, who voices only muted criticism of racism but eagerly exonerates or approves of whites. Thus, to extol, as Pfeiffer does "The Ex-Coloured Man's individualism" as "uniquely American" (405), to claim that the novel's "whole mission is to expose the narrow demands of group loyalty" (406), and to wind up the argument by asserting that "through his racial vacillation, the Ex-Coloured Man locates his self-invention in an identity which is both sympathetic to many races and independent of any single racial affiliation" (417) seems to me to be doing quite a bit of violence to the novel. Though the protagonist's individualism might be "American," the novel hardly celebrates it; the protagonist's prejudices are so obvious that I doubt he can be seen as "sympathetic to many races," and if anything, the novel's mission is to expose the protagonist's *lack* of loyalties, not "the narrow demands of group loyalty."

6. Even when he witnesses a lynching, he does not judge the crowd according to the standards he applies here. As Eugenia Collier has shown, his observations of African Americans are those of an outsider and, in their orientation towards stereotypes—such as his description of an innkeeper as a kind of "Aunt Jemima," his perception of mulatto women as prettier than darker women, and of the African American male "as splendid physical specimen"—they resemble the perspective of a patronizing white person (Endless Journey 368). Even after having lived in Jacksonville for a while, and "though he begins to appreciate black music and dance . . . [he still] refers to black people as 'they,' not 'we.' He is still an observer rather than a participant" (Collier "Endless Journey" 368).

7. Just like the doctor, the narrator concerns himself with race consciousness on "a subjective note" (Barton 138). His own position matters to

him, not so much the position of African Americans (or European Americans) as a whole. Though he is "a crude appraiser of groups," both of different classes of African Americans and of European nationalities (Faulkner 150)—but not, interestingly, of European Americans, presumably because he identifies more with them than with any other group—he does not see himself as part of any group, which makes him a kind of embodiment of "anti-essentialism."

8. The Ex-Coloured Man "has no foundational principles from which he cannot be swayed," which is "the reason for . . . his success in society" (Brooks) and also for his unreliability as an observer both of himself and of the society around him.

9. Gayle Wald cites Walter White's autobiography *A Man Called White* as an example: "Walter White . . . depicts his own encounter with a white mob during the 1906 Atlanta riots as a benchmark of his identity formation as a raced subject. . . . Culminating in White's declaration of pride in 'the knowledge of my identity,' which is inseparable from his critical disidentification with 'those whose story is the history of the world, a record of bloodshed, rapine, and pillage' (12). The scene of the riot thus establishes his text as the antithesis of the ex-colored man's autobiography" (29).

10. In commenting on the "one-drop rule," Samira Kawash argues that, "although whiteness certainly could be described in terms of its visual characteristics, whiteness could not be 'invisible'; whiteness then is the absence of both visible and invisible blackness. But if whiteness depends on the absence of something that cannot be perceived, then whiteness becomes increasingly precarious" (132). In Johnson's novel, however, blackness becomes as desirable and as precarious as whiteness.

11. On one level, the protagonists' detachment from their ethnic groups seems to make them good observers, as it allows them to move in many circles, emotionally beholden to none. On another level, one cannot trust their observations as they show only superficial grounding in and understanding of ethnic culture, expressed in sometimes facile rejections of it and in the protagonists' lack of commitment. For both of them, unreliability as narrators and detachment from their cultures are functions of their character flaws: selfishness and materialism. In both novels, too, the narrator's unreliability emerges at the very opening of the narrative and puts the reader on guard. The Ex-Coloured Man compares himself to a criminal and highlights his secretiveness; *Haunch* opens with, "I begin my history. I want to tell everything. Everything: so that even if I tell pathological lies the truth will shine out like grains of gold in the upturned muck" (13). While both narratives promise to reveal something, *Haunch* announces that the revelations promised have to be sorted out by the reader herself. In Meyer Hirsch, then, one finds selfishness, materialism, and unreliability in a much less mitigated form than in the Ex-Coloured Man, as far as both his narration and deeds are concerned. He openly denounces

any signs of selflessness in others as weakness, calling the idealists "dream-stupefied" (188), and he is often proud of his ability to exploit and deceive. While the Ex-Coloured Man looks for justifications for passing, Meyer Hirsch has no compunctions about using friends and community for furthering his career while only pretending to serve their interests.

12. Werner Sollors also notes of the Ex-Coloured Man and of Cahan's David Levinsky that they "perceive themselves as victims of circumstance, unhappy cowards, and traitors to kin and authentic, inner descent-self" (*Beyond Ethnicity* 171).

13. Jeffrey Melnick discusses Ornitz's treatment of music in terms of Jewish "flexibility" and of Jews as "Americanizers" of African American music through successful, though sometimes self-serving, "mixing" of ethnic and racial traditions (*A Right* 80–93). However, in specifically making Jewish agency appear as natural, Ornitz also leans on a rhetoric compatible with ethnic nationalism.

2. ART AND ETHNIC SOLIDARITY

1. Gayle Wald shows this (41–46) in reference to Fauset's short story "The Sleeper Wakes," which served as a sort of blueprint for *Plum Bun*.

2. One source for this scene may well be the "Uprising of the 20,000"—a general strike on November 22, 1909, as response to working conditions at the Triangle Waist Company and the Leiserson shop, companies which employed predominantly women. Another probable source was the March of 50,000 following the fire at the Triangle Waist Company on March 25, 1911, which caused the death of 146 workers (Baum et al. 140f.).

3. Frances Ellen Watkins Harper (1825–1911) was a noted African American archivist, author, and social reformer and a founding member of the National Association for the Advancement of Colored Women in 1896.

4. As Gabrielle Foreman has noted, "Because Angela understands that it is power, not whiteness per se, which she ultimately desires, she also recognizes that there are other signs, other badges which stand in its stead." Angela also finds out that gender restricts her in ways that whiteness does not overcome.

5. Concerning "The Sleeper Wakes," Gayle Wald comments that "unlike the ex-colored man, Fauset's protagonist cannot look to the public sphere of the market place as a gendered refuge from the contradictions of her raced citizenship" (42).

3. RECONCILING ETHNICITY AND INDIVIDUALISM

1. This juncture indicated, as Jeffrey Melnick says, "the troublesome reality that one important point of contact for Jews and African Americans has been the employment of African American women as domestics in . . . Jewish

homes, particularly via the notoriously exploitative "Bronx Slave Market" of the 1930s, where African American women were often constrained to accept absurdly low wages for a long day's work (*A Right* 11).

2. See also Barbara Christian, *Black Feminist Criticism*: "She [Marshall] wrote the novel not primarily for publication but as a process of understanding, critiquing, and celebrating her own personal history" (177).

3. See also Carol B. Schoen about Yezierska: "Her response to her heritage was ambivalent, but whether she was lauding its virtues or condemning its restrictiveness, she was continually reacting to its pressures. . . . Yezierska was seriously concerned with the American stress on individualism and the dichotomy between the nation's ideals and its actual practice" (iv). Schoen thus also comments on Yezierska's constant thematizing of the relationship between ethnicity and Americanization/individualism.

4. In an article focusing on the quest of Marshall's heroines, Missy Dehn Kubitschek arrives at a similar conclusion from a different angle: "An adolescent, Selina separates from her parents without rejecting them, acknowledges her community while denying its right to determine her personality" ("Marshall's Women" 59).

5. "The novel . . . measures the spiritual prices that many of them paid to advance economically or even to survive—a primary one being their need to expel or destroy any one of them who did not pursue their common goal" (Christian *Novelists* 82).

6. See also Collier, "The Closing of the Circle," pp. 300–301.

7. "In a religious civilization like Judaism, ritual obligations were prized and one derived communal honor from their fulfillment. Women, having fewer religious responsibilities, were consequently assigned a religious and communal status inferior to that of men" (Baum et al. 5).

8. "In the Russia-Poland of Mrs. Smolinsky's memory, fathers exercise nearly complete authority over their daughters' marriages, but they are obligated to provide as opulent a dowry as possible. . . . While deriving his authority to intervene from tradition, Smolinsky reinterprets the obligation to provide a dowry as an opportunity to secure economic peace" (Ferraro 68).

9. It is exactly the materialist aspect of his religious practice that alienates Sara from him. She points out his double standard concerning his view of poverty when he ignores the poet Lipkin as his daughter Fania's suitor by reminding him: "Father! . . . didn't you yourself say yesterday that poverty is an ornament on a good Jew?" (70). In the course of the conflict over Fania's suitor, she asserts the value of love over materialism by implying that Fania should have been allowed to marry for love: "'What are you always blaming everything on the children?' I burst out at Father. 'Didn't you yourself make Fania marry Abe Schmukler when she cried she didn't want him? You know yourself she ate out her heart for Morris Lipkin—'" (85). Her insistence that

love is more important than money is identical, though the circumstances differ, to the stance Selina takes opposite her mother. The dualistic value of materialism vs. idealism is an important factor in the estrangement between Sara and her father (e.g., 135).

Her mother's heartlessness towards her father is a reason, or even the main reason, for Selina's alienation from her mother. But the conflict between Deighton and Silla is symbolic of the materialism-idealism dualism to a high degree as well. When she visits her childhood friend Beryl a year after her father's death, Selina is dismayed at their superficiality and materialism, but unsure how to oppose it. Beryl and her friends talk about the gifts they expect from their parents for finishing college while Selina senses that Beryl's father has "transferred his acquisitive spirit to her [Beryl]" (196). In contemplating what it was her father had given her, she remembers: a "cold March afternoon long ago . . . she had found him stretched on the cot in the sun parlor in his shirt sleeves, his head cradled in his arms and humming. 'Is it spring?' she had asked, her breath coming in cold wisps. He had drawn her down beside him, loosened her arms and said, 'Yes.' And suddenly she had sensed spring in the air, seen it forming beyond the glass walls and had not been cold any more" (197–198). The exact nature of his gift to her can only be circumscribed because it is a metaphysical one. While Deighton, too, often thinks of material things, Selina mostly remembers him for his warmth, playfulness, and imaginativeness. Her rebellion against her mother is thus expressed through her embrace of what she sees as her father's values, so that her first sexual encounter becomes a symbolic rejection of her mother's and her community's goals and she enacts it in part "so that they might witness how utterly she renounced their way, and have the full proof that she was indeed Deighton's Selina!" (239).

10. See also Susan Willis: "In *Brown Girl, Brownstones*, Silla asks her daughter the critical question that Marshall will continue to demand of all her characters: 'But who put you so?' . . . As Selina discovers . . . the answer to this question cannot be obtained by a simple review of personal history, because the personal is inextricably inscribed within the history of black people in this country" (63).

11. Yezierska phrased this similarly in her autobiography: "I had to break away from my mother's cursing and my father's preaching to live my life; but without them I had no life. When you deny your parents, you deny the sky over your head. You become an outlaw, a pariah" (quoted in Dearborn 113).

12. Carol Schoen has noted that Muhmenkeh exemplifies the communal spirit of ghetto life (73).

13. Ron Ebest documents latent or overt anti-Semitism in the debate over the "Jewish Question" in even the most respected contemporary magazines, which tended to see Eastern European Jews as noisy tenement dwellers and/or

socialist agitators—in any case, as close to unassimilable. According to Ebest, sympathetic commentators explained supposed "Jewish traits" they objected to by pointing to environmental influences, a theory Yezierska seems to have embraced. As a result, rather than contesting stereotypes, she "sought to alter the meaning of the image of the greedy Jew." Though some of her stories see "greed as an American pollution," *Bread Givers* appears to divide the blame between Old World customs and New World poverty.

14. Sara's relationship to Seelig also undermines the novel's feminist potential, showing that Sara's development as a woman is subordinated to her Americanization (which is clearly not synonymous with female independence). As Ruth Wisse points out: "How meekly our heroine yields to her principal, Mr. Seelig, when in front of the public school class she has been hired to teach he tries to correct her tell tale immigrant pronunciation" (273).

15. To some degree, Yezierska/Sara do have to invent a new role for themselves. According to Mary Dearborn, "In a move that was almost unheard of at the time, Yezierska left her family in 1900 and began to live independently" (110). However, there are also indications that hers was not a completely unique fate: "Working Girls in Evening Schools, a study conducted in New York City during 1910 and 1911 by Mary Van Kleeck . . . provides a guide to what was going on among Jewish women during this period. . . . [A]ccording to this study, about 40 percent of the women attending evening schools in New York were Jewish. . . . If most first-generation immigrant women seemed to be living within the confines of the Old World traditions, Van Kleeck's study indicates many were breaking with the customs of the past, and indeed some of them were in open rebellion" (Baum et al. 129).

16. "As a modern, educated feminist who rebels against her father by refusing to accede to his authoritarian demands, Sara seems to be not only his archenemy but his exact opposite in terms of values and ideals. In fact, however, they are most like each other as character types" (Girgus 113).

17. The phrase "hard heart" connects her to her sister Masha, who, according to the narrator has "no heart" (6) because she single-mindedly invests her money in clothes or towels while her family starves; as opposed to Masha, also called "Empty-head" (6), Sara invests in her personal education, but also to the neglect of her family. Masha's single-mindedness provides her with a role model, as mentioned above.

18. As Geta Le Seur has said, "For the first time Selina sees her own capacity for evil as she reflects her planned duplicity of the scholarship community [sic]" (116).

19. Gavin Jones argues that *Brown Girl, Brownstones* "proposes a wider, creolized, prismal sense of identity which contains many different facets" (601).

20. "Because Selina sees herself as her father's daughter, she resists not only her mother's attempts to possess her but the Barbadian community's as well"

(Christian *Novelists* 100). However, her encounter with racism leads her to an insight: "Selina has been jolted into consciousness of the shared bond between herself and her people, necessitated by the imperative of conquering racism in order to enable full development of human potential. In this sense, Selina begins to comprehend what lies behind her mother's harsh outbursts and actions and her people's need for coalition" (Le Seur 120–121).

21. While the acquisition of brownstones is an ethnic goal, Susan Willis demonstrates how this oppositional materialism is at the same time a move towards assimilation: "Marshall demonstrates deep political understanding in *Brown Girl, Brownstones* by showing that the desire to own property may well have represented an initial contestation of bourgeois white domination, but because property ownership is implicit in capitalist society, the momentum of opposition was immediately absorbed and integrated into the context of American capitalism" (74).

22. Carole McAlpine Watson has commented on the protective side of ethnic communalism: "Silla comes to represent not only a certain limited approach to life but also the protective and nurturing aspects of the ghetto. Silla and the striving West Indians, represented by The West Indian Home-owners and Businessmen's Association, are one" (85). Heather Hathaway sees the Barbadian obsession with "buying house" as indicative of an understanding "that their greatest weapon against poverty and discrimination lay in property ownership" (146).

23. Laura Wexler notes that Sara's relationship with Hugo is also based on a link to Old World ethnicity: "But does facing the Old World and keeping one's 'eyes on the past' really lose out in *Bread Givers*? Hugo and Sara are 'of one blood.' But what this means to them is not some external and essentialized concept of 'race.' It is that they share a history, a memory, a social past, and the responsibility not to forget what has happened to their people" (171).

24. "Sarah analyzes her options with great care and makes a decision that is not only defensible but persuasive: to seek freedom within a (changing) community rather than outside of it" (Ferraro 77). However, I disagree with Ferraro's assessment that Sara virtually reenacts the entrapment of her youth by taking her father into her new home (Ferraro 779ff.). I would argue that there has been a significant shift of power, which makes hers more an act of compassion than a submission to her father's renewed tyranny (though that element is present).

25. Susan Willis has commented on that scene and described the dual meaning of Selina's gesture: "One bracelet thrown, one bracelet kept—Selina, Marshall's figural self, bids goodbye to her childhood and the Chauncey Street tenements and brownstones where she grew up. The bracelet, whose arc she traces across the moonlit sky and whose sharp clash marks its fall, gives testament to Selina as she has been formed by her community; it also represents

her gift to those who remain behind. The bracelet Selina keeps is her visible link to her Carribean heritage" (53). Joyce Pettis stresses the affirmative side of the gesture in that she interprets Selina as "symbolically acknowledging the people and the environment that have contributed to her development" (15). However, I believe the gesture, while one of giving, also symbolizes an act of giving something up. Gavin Jones reaches a similar conclusion: "That Selina removes from her wrist, at the end of the novel, only one of her two Barbadian bangles is emblematic of her final ambivalence and self-division" (604).

4. ETHNIC NATIONALISM AND ETHNIC LITERARY RESPONSES

1. In a fascinating study entitled *The Identity Question: Blacks and Jews in Europe and America*, Robert Philipson analyzes the discourse on Blacks and Jews and their respective responses to it in both Europe and the U.S., using an Enlightenment philosophical framework as the overall parameter which determines how both groups defined themselves: "Eighteenth-century Europe engaged in a discussion about the nature of Black and Jewish identity that set the terms of response by the intellectual representatives of those groups. Drawing from a legacy of classical literature, Christian ideology, and the *realpolitik* of the nation-state competition, eighteenth-century discourse coalesced around new theories of race, human nature, and environment that were to remain thematically dominant as long as Enlightenment assumptions defined the political will of the West" (xviii). Eighteenth- and nineteenth-century ethnic writers in the U.S. utilized the Enlightenment presuppositions of the Declaration of Independence to frame their arguments for their place in the U.S., but it is my claim that in the twentieth century, at the very least for a good number of literary works, Romantic nationalism, which is not least a reaction against Enlightenment universalism, is a more important touchstone than the latter. I encountered Philipson's book only after I had finished this manuscript. While I focus on detailed readings of texts and the implicit inter-action between texts, Philipson's work largely discusses the philosophical and ideological framework of Black and Jewish self-definitions. Philipson, in keeping with his Enlightenment focus, sees nationalism as an eighteenth-century phenomenon, whereas I concentrate on the Romantic racialism of nationalist ideology as it dominated the nineteenth and twentieth centuries. It is pre-dominantly *that* form of nationalism that leaves its traces in the novels I discuss. However, the Bildungsroman, as an Enlightenment genre, provides the opposing pole that contributes to some of the tensions in the novels. None-theless, occasionally Philipson and I reach some similar conclusions when it comes to textual comparisons. As he says of Equiano's *Narrative* and Maimon's *Geistesgeschichte*, "these autobiographies reveal a consciousness that is as deeply informed by ethnic particularity as by its participation in a so-called universal

culture" (31). This duality, however, mirrors the tensions between essentialism and constructionism and between communalism and individualism that I
highlight in my study and which I argue are endemic to the project of ethnic
cultural nationalism as it is indebted to Romantic nationalism. Romantic
nationalism thus serves as a better explanatory framework for the texts I discuss than does Enlightenment universalism.

2. Often, this turning away from universalism can be understood best in
local circumstances. In Germany, for example, Johann Gottfried Herder, one
important source of modern nationalist philosophy, rejected the French universalist Enlightenment ideas in favor of a more indigenous and local cultural
development in part under the influence of the French military occupation
of Prussia (see Brennan 52–53).

3. An emphasis on national essences thus meant that "regardless of the unity
in diversity advocated by some nationalisms, cohesion and uniformity were
always potentially present" (Mosse 122).

4. One might say that, legally speaking, "allegiance to the state, . . . residence
therein, and submission to its jurisdiction, are the hallmarks of the Western
idea of nationality" (Ra'anan 9) and that, therefore, there is no requirement
with regards to race in nationalism. But as the idea of the nation builds on
the idea of essences, be they spiritual, cultural, or otherwise, and because the
national territory is rarely, if ever, inhabited by a homogeneous ethnic group,
"loyalty and commitment to the state and to the nation often not only are
not synonymous, but may be in direct conflict with one another" (Ra'anan 9).

5. Given, then, that ethnic groups in the U.S. reside in a "national" territory, the relationship between geographic territory and ethnic nationalism is
a problematic one. Some expressions of Black Nationalism, such as specific
forms of Pan-Africanism or the Garvey Movement, claim Africa for Africans
(or African Americans), and Zionism, in most of its forms, claims Palestine
as a Jewish nation. Ethnic nationalism, however, as it manifests itself in *Fanny
Herself, The Autobiography*, and the other works under discussion here bases
itself on sociological and cultural concepts only. The two ethnic groups in
question live in a "nationally" defined territory that none of the authors question; thus the literary works discussed here envision a culturally defined ethnic
territory.

6. As Uri Ra'anan explains, "it is not *where* an individual resides and which
state has jurisdiction over him that determines his nationality, but rather *who*
he is—his cultural, religious, and historic identity, i.e. his ethnicity, a heritage
received from his ancestors and carried with him, in mind and body, irre-
spective of his current place of domicile. Consequently, one is dealing here
with a *personal* (as opposed to Western *territorial*) criteria of nationality" (10).

7. In *Beyond Ethnicity*, Werner Sollors shows how ethnicity as such may self-
consciously function as boundary. See, e.g., pp. 26ff.

8. "The nation by its very nature demanded a thorough assimilation by Jews long before the civic religion of nationalism threatened their membership in the community" (Mosse 121).

9. See Urofsky, chapter 3.

10. The 1924 Immigration Act, which attempted to insure that the United States would always remain Northwestern European by reserving 75 percent of the immigration quota for immigrants from that region of the world, was perhaps the most prominent expression of nativism. The other 25 percent of the quota was not, as one might assume, to be divided up among immigrants from the rest of the world, but only among immigrants from the rest of Europe; other continents were granted merely nominal immigration quotas of a few hundred individuals.

11. Toni Morrison, in *Playing in the Dark*, has recently explored this issue in regard to American literature. As she says, she started out wondering "whether the major and championed characteristics of our national literature— individualism, masculinity, social engagement versus historical isolation; acute and ambiguous moral problematics; the thematics of innocence coupled with an obsession with figurations of death and hell—are not in fact responses to a dark, abiding, signing Africanist presence" (5).

12. Timothy Brennan explains this in reference to German philosopher Johann Gottfried Herder: "Herder transformed Rousseau's 'people' into the Volk. The significance of this latter concept is its shift from Rousseau's Enlightenment emphasis on civic virtue to a woollier Romantic insistence on the primordial and ineluctable roots of nationhood as a distinguishing feature from other communities. Each people was now set off by the 'natural' characteristics of language, and the intangible quality of a specific Volksgeist" (53). It is useful to quote W. E. B. Du Bois in conjunction with this definition of nationalism to appreciate the extent to which one of America's foremost thinkers was, at the time, influenced by nationalist ideology. W. E. B. Du Bois claimed that "while race differences have followed mainly along physical lines, yet no mere physical distinction would really define or explain the deeper differences—the cohesiveness and continuity of these groups. The deeper differences are spiritual, psychical, differences—undoubtedly based on the physical, but infinitely transcending them" (quoted in Appiah 29). Werner Sollors categorizes this moral ethnic difference as a typological rhetoric of "chosen peoplehood" which may "serve to define a new ethnic peoplehood in contradistinction to a general American identity" (*Beyond Ethnicity* 49).

13. George L. Mosse claims that "Toward the end of the nineteenth century . . . many people came to perceive the nation as a civic religion that determined how people saw the world and their place in it" (Mosse 1).

14. "Despite numerous attempts in the nineteenth century, American Jewry had been unable to agree on a single body or group as its spokesman" (Urofsky

160), and despite Zionist and non-Zionist cooperation starting after World War I, this continued to be true in the first decades of the twentieth century— to no one's surprise, since nobody would expect a whole people to be adequately represented by any one organization.

15. Here we have a version of nationalism with a heavy emphasis on spirituality, an essential connectedness in a mission. Even many Zionists put more emphasis on the cultural and spiritual effects of Zionism than on territorial goals. Thus, Solomon Schechter, president of the Jewish Theological Seminary, which was closely aligned with the leadership of the Federation of American Zionists, explained that for him, Zionism was "the great bulwark against assimilation. . . . I belong to that class of Zionists that lay more stress on the religious-national aspects of Zionism. . . . The activity of Zionism must not be judged by what it has accomplished *in* Zion and Jerusalem but *for* Zion and Jerusalem, by awakening the national Jewish consciousness" (quoted in Karp 249).

16. Until World War I, the Zionist movement had a relatively marginal existence in the U.S., with only 20,000 members in all of the various Zionist organizations out of a Jewish population of 1.5 million.

17. Both African Americans and Jewish Americans were involved in debates over the question of a homeland. Should America be accepted as the new home or should the ethnic group as a whole desire a return to an ancestral country or continent? This debate involved, of course, tricky issues, such as the question of one's present position in the U.S. and how agitation for a homeland would affect it. Not without justification, opponents of a return to an ancestral home worried that the (white) general public might view such agitation as a sign of insufficient loyalty to the U.S., thus further weakening the socioeconomic and political position of African Americans or Jewish Americans. "There were those who warned about potential accusations of dual loyalty: 'Is not America our Zion, Washington our Jerusalem?' they proclaimed" (Karp 248). Proponents of territorial nationalism, be it African American or Jewish, would naturally interpret the very fragility of one's position as the best reason for the foundation of a nation of one's own.

18. As sociologist Robert E. Park observed in 1925, "The Negro race, as Booker T. Washington used to say, is a nation within a nation. For somewhat different reasons the Jews in this country are in a similar situation. The Jews are seeking to preserve their culture while accommodating themselves in other respects to the conditions of American life. Different as they are in other respects, the Negro and the Jew are alike in this" (quoted in Hutchinson *Harlem* 55). Because of this assessment, he saw both groups as "the two outstanding illustrations of the impending cultural pluralism so interestingly advocated by Horace Kallen."

19. As the authors of *The Empire Writes Back* maintain, "The perspective of

cross-cultural literatures has given explicit confirmation to the perception that genres cannot be described by essential characteristics, but by an interweaving of features, a 'family resemblance' which denies the possibility of either essentialism or limitation. Any writer may extend the 'boundaries' of a genre. . . . In one sense, the European forms created a basis on which the indigenous literature in English [sic] could develop. But this is more a marriage of convenience than a deep cultural commitment to the received genres. . . . Inevitably, the sensibilities of individual writers will be influenced by the literary and aesthetic assumptions of their own cultures" (Ashcroft et al. 181–182).

20. Herder, in Germany (or rather in Prussia), called for a national literature that would express the spirit of the nation, just as language was inextricably tied to the Volksgeist.

21. Literary critic Trevor Ross proposes that in eighteenth-century Europe, the idea arose "that literature operates within a vast complex of human activities, and, if properly disseminated, contributes to the formation of a national culture" (quoted in Wright).

22. In *Playing in the Dark*, Toni Morrison shows this for such canonical figures as Cather, Hemingway, and Poe, bringing to light how much some of their work was, indeed, concerned with race.

23. The novel creates a "unified and coherent subject," says Firdous Azim. She says that, however, while explaining the connection of the creation of a unified imperial subject to the domination of the colonial one. The unified novelistic subject, in metropolitan novels, is also seen as a citizen of a nation. And only the citizen of the nation is endowed with the rights that the nation guarantees (215). According to that logic, then, the only way to claim a basis for equal rights—except for the religious argument, which occurs frequently in premodernist ethnic literature—is membership in a nation. Of course, this creates problems if one is an individual who is already *formally* part of a nation, even if that nation does not extend to one its full rights. The novel as a genre, however, offers the attractive possibility of creating a unified subject that is part of an *ethnic nation* and has full rights in that nation, especially if the ethnic national subject in the U.S. outside the novel still awaits mainstream national rights.

24. This resistance may be overcome in later stages, leading to a kind of integration, as happens in the classical German Bildungsroman—and in *Plum Bun* and *Fanny Herself*, though the integration is a kind of reintegration into ethnicity which the protagonists had rebelled against initially.

25. Because of this feature of the Bildungsroman tradition, the ethnic author can break through one "of the most persistent prejudices underlying the production of the texts of the metropolitan canon[:] that only certain categories of experience are capable of being rendered as 'literature.' This privileging of particular types of experience denies access to the world for the writer subject to a dominating colonial culture" (Ashcroft et al. 88).

26. This is the solution at which both *Brown Girl* and *Bread Givers* arrive to deal with the conflicting ideologies of ethnic solidarity and individualism. Though their protagonists decide for a qualified kind of ethnic individualism, the authors raise enough questions about their protagonists' decisions so that their choices do not appear absolute. In *Brown Girl* this tendency is more pronounced than in *Bread Givers*, as the characters who stand for ethnic solidarity, particularly Silla, are explored so that one understands their motivations as well, not only those of the protagonist. While neither *Plum Bun*, *Fanny*, *Haunch*, nor *The Autobiography* are as sympathetic to the individualist point of view and do ask their protagonists to make a decision, they also explore the individualist position in painstaking detail, even if they embrace a communalist ideology. The reinterpretation of these genres along communalist lines is a result of the ideological pressure of ethnic nationalism based on a notion of ethnic solidarity that binds all members of the group.

27. Eric Sundquist argues that "At the least . . . the value of a work of literature—what defines it as literature, for that matter—derives from its contribution to articulating and sustaining the values of a given culture, whether or not that culture is national or 'racial' in scope" (Sundquist *To Wake* 18).

28. The individualist fragmentation of modern capitalist Western culture, which goes hand in hand with the collective cultural dismissal of colonized and exploited peoples, triggers an "in-group" tightening, to use Allport's term, which expresses itself ideologically as the concept of ethnic solidarity or in essentialist constructions of ethnic identity. At the same time, a more communal vision of an ethnic community may not only be a response to outside pressures but a survival of a pre-American and, as it were, pre-ethnic cultural element, that is, an element which existed before the given group became ethnic in America. Whatever the source of the values may be, they help to define the ethnic group vis-à-vis the mainstream via "symbolic boundary-construction which increases cultural vitality" (Sollors *Beyond Ethnicity* 247), and thus they have a "nation-building" function, a function which the literature that embraces those values shares.

29. See Sollors's discussion of ethnogenesis (with an emphasis on typology) in chapter 2 of *Beyond Ethnicity*.

30. "Mary Antin . . . took a position of apparent self-effacement only to proclaim proudly her sense of equal entitlement. Antin continued the portraiture of America as a new Canaan from an immigrant's point of view, while leaving no doubt that the metaphor of the promised land was especially suited to Jewish immigrants. Interestingly, both Wheatley and Antin . . . claimed the American egalitarian promise defiantly by equating themselves with George Washington" (Sollors *Beyond Ethnicity* 45).

31. George Hutchinson justifiably interprets similar passages differently, not as asserting ethnic difference but as embracing an *American* cultural

nationalism: "The [Harlem] literary renaissance was in part an attempt to augment the value of black culture within the national cultural field," but he also sees the dualism in this attempt, as he argues that the Harlem Renaissance "appealed to the symbolics of American national identity even as it strove for a reappraisal and reconnection to 'African' identity" (*Harlem* 12). My analysis focuses on textual strategies emphasizing ethnic difference and intent on creating a legitimate ethnic cultural territory, as I see these as the predominant forces behind and in the texts. I have to some extent simply started from the "Americanness" of these texts and their writers, an Americanness the texts both seek to establish to some extent but also take for granted, and against which they establish ethnic difference, in part as a reaction to segregation and exclusion.

32. This reversal of positions is of note, because "in post-colonial societies, the participants are frozen into a hierarchical relationship in which the oppressed is locked into position by the assumed moral superiority of the dominant group, a superiority which is reinforced when necessary by the use of physical force" (Ashcroft et al. 172).

33. As Kenneth Warren notes for Frances Harper's 1892 novel, "in *Iola Leroy* the plot repeatedly calls upon its light-skinned African-American characters to choose between material prosperity—embodied in a white identity—and moral duty—embodied in a black one" (111).

34. Because of its spiritual nature, it is a kind of ethnic nationalism that does not have to be rejected even if one does not wish to reside with the ethnic group or follow a specific ethnic program, as the protagonists of *Brown Girl, Brownstones* and *Bread Givers*. Spiritually, however, they do not ultimately separate from their ethnic groups—Selina even returns to the geographic "fount," after all.

35. Somewhat earlier, African American author Pauline Hopkins had come to the conclusion that "Africanity . . . can be awakened in the individual psyche, just as it can be awakened in the political dimension of national consciousness," implying as much in her novel *Of One Blood* (Sundquist *To Wake* 559, 573). In Hopkins's novel, too, artistry and spirituality are signs of ethnicity: one passing character is a singer, another a psychologist dabbling in the supernatural.

36. While this may be a strategy that romanticizes ethnicity, it is a measured response. As Eric Sundquist has said about W. E. B. Du Bois, "To say that Du Bois wrote often as an ideologue does nothing to discredit his philosophy. He wrote at the high noon of racialist theory and white supremacy, when the advocates of Teutonic, Aryan, and Anglo-Saxon superiority had combined romantic historicism with pseudoscientific quantification to eliminate the 'darker' races from the scheme of civilization. Du Bois's own romanticism about Africa was a product of his times, a necessary instrument of idealization,

and a means to combat the extension of the world's political and economic color line" (*To Wake* 551). The same can be said about the essentialism of all the novels, or at least the first four: it was an attempt to counteract virulent racism, and create a cultural space for valuing what the mainstream consistently devalued. For its time, it may well have been appropriate, and that many of the time's best thinkers adopted this strategy should make one cautious about dismissing it anachronistically.

37. I owe this insight—and many others—to Michael Kramer.

WORKS CITED

Adams, Maurianne and John Bracey. "Strangers and Neighbors: Teaching and Writing about Blacks and Jews." *The Chronicle of Higher Education* 3 November 2000: B7–10.

Adams, Timothy Dow. *Telling Lies in Modern American Autobiography*. Chapel Hill: University of North Carolina Press, 1990.

Allen, Carol. *Black Women Intellectuals: Strategies of Nation, Family, and Neighborhood in the Works of Pauline Hopkins, Jessie Fauset, and Marita Bonner*. New York: Garland, 1998.

Allport, Gordon W. "Formation of In-Groups." In *Race, Gender, and Human Identity in a Diverse Society*. Ed. Chuck Smith. Acton, MA: Tapestry Press, 1998.

Anderson, Benedict. *Imagined Communities: Reflections on the Origin and Spread of Nationalism*. London: Verso, 1983.

Antin, Mary. *The Promised Land*. Boston: Houghton Mifflin, 1912.

Appiah, Kwame Anthony. *In My Father's House: Africa in the Philosophy of Culture*. New York: Oxford University Press, 1992.

Ashcroft, Bill, Gareth Griffiths, and Helen Tiffin. *The Empire Writes Back: Theory and Practice in Post-Colonial Literatures*. London: Routledge, 1989.

Azim, Firdous. *The Colonial Rise of the Novel*. London: Routledge, 1993.

Baker, Houston A. Jr. *Blues, Ideology, and Afro-American Literature: A Vernacular Theory*. Chicago: University of Chicago Press, 1984.

———. *Singers of Daybreak: Studies in Black American Literature*. Washington: Howard University Press, 1974.

Baldwin, James et al. *Black Anti-Semitism and Jewish Racism*. New York: Richard W. Baron, 1969.

Barton, Rebecca Chalmers. *Black Voices in American Fiction*. Oakdale, NY: Dowling College Press, 1976.

Bassett, John E. *Harlem in Review: Critical Reactions to Black American Writers, 1917–1939*. Selinsgrove: Susquehanna University Press, 1992.

Basu, Biman. "'Oral Tutelage' and the Figure of Literacy: Paule Marshall's *Brown Girl, Brownstones* and Zora Neale Hurston's *Their Eyes Were Watching God*." *MELUS* 24.1 (1999): 161+. From Ebscohost (Academic Search Premier. Article 2595308) West Virginia State College Library, Institute, WV <*http://ehostvgw19.epnet.com*>.

Batker, Carol. "Literary Reformers: Crossing Class and Ethnic Boundaries in Jewish Women's Fiction of the 1920s." *MELUS* 25.1 (2000): 81+. From Ebscohost (Academic Search Premier. Article 3914249) West Virginia State College Library, Institute, WV <*http://ehostvgw19.epnet.com*>.

Baum, Charlotte, Paula Hyman, and Sonya Michel. *The Jewish Woman in America*. New York: The Dial Press, 1976.

Beddow, Michael. *The Fiction of Humanity: Studies in the Bildungsroman from Wieland to Thomas Mann*. New York: Cambridge University Press, 1983.

Bell, Bernard W. *The Afro-American Novel and Its Tradition*. Amherst: University of Massachusetts Press, 1987.

Berman, Paul, ed. *Blacks and Jews: Alliances and Arguments*. New York: Delacorte Press, 1994.

Birch, Anthony H. *Nationalism and National Integration*. London: Unwin Hyman, 1989.

Blasing, Mutlu Konuk. *The Art of Life: Studies in American Autobiographical Literature*. Austin: University of Texas Press, 1977.

Blassingame, John M. "Black Autobiographies as History and Literature." *Black Scholar* 5 (December 1973–January 1974): 2–9.

Boelhower, William. "The Brave New World of Immigrant Autobiography." MELUS 9 (1982): 5–23.

———. *Immigrant Autobiography in the United States*. Verona: Essedue, 1982.

———. "The Making of Ethnic Autobiography in the United States." In *American Autobiography: Retrospect and Prospect*. Ed. John Paul Eakin. Madison: University of Wisconsin Press, 1991. 123–140.

———. *Through a Glass Darkly: Ethnic Semiosis in American Literature*. New York: Oxford University Press, 1987.

Braendlin, Bonnie Hoover. "Bildung in Ethnic Women Writers." *Denver Quarterly* 17.4 (Winter 1983): 75–87.

Braxton, Joanne M. *Black Women Writing Autobiography: A Tradition within a Tradition*. Philadelphia: Temple University Press, 1989.

Brennan, Timothy. "The National Longing for Form." In *Nation and Narration*. Ed. Homi K. Bhaba. London: Routledge, 1990. 44–70.

Brodzki, Bella and Celeste Schenck, eds. *Life/Lines: Theorizing Women's Autobiography*. Ithaca: Cornell University Press, 1988.

Brooks, Neil. "On Becoming an Ex-Colored Man: Postmodern Irony and the Extinguishing of Certainties in *The Autobiography of an Ex-Coloured Man*." *College Literature* 22.3 (October 1995): 17+. From Infotrac (Expanded Academic ASAP) West Virginia State College Library, Institute, WV <*http://web5.infrotrac.galegroup.com*>.

Buckley, Jerome Hamilton. *Season of Youth: The Bildungsroman from Dickens to Golding*. Cambridge, MA: Harvard University Press, 1974.

Budick, Emily Miller. *Blacks and Jews in Literary Conversation*. Cambridge, UK: Cambridge University Press, 1998.

Buelens, Gert. Review of *Beyond Ethnicity: Consent and Descent in American Culture* by Werner Sollors and *Through a Glass Darkly: Ethnic Semiosis in American Literature* by William Boelhower. *Journal of American Studies* 23.2 (1989): 315–320.

Buell, Lawrence. "Autobiography in the American Renaissance." In *American Autobiography: Retrospect and Prospect*. Ed. Paul John Eakin. Madison: University of Wisconsin Press, 1991. 47–69.

Carby, Hazel V. *Reconstructing Womanhood: The Emergence of the Afro-American Woman Novelist*. New York: Oxford University Press, 1987.

Carr, Glynis. "Storytelling as Bildung in Zora Neale Hurston's *Their Eyes Were Watching God*." *CLA Journal* 31.2 (1987): 189–200.

Carson, Clayborne. "The Politics of Relations between African-Americans and Jews." In *Blacks and Jews: Alliances and Arguments*. Ed. Paul Berman. New York: Delacorte Press, 1994. 131–143.

Caton, Louis F. "Romantic Struggles: The *Bildungsroman* and Mother-Daughter Bonding in Jamaica Kincaid's *Annie John*." *MELUS* 21.3 (1996): 125–142.

Chametzky, Jules. *Our Decentralized Literature: Cultural Mediations in Selected Jewish and Southern Writers*. Amherst: University of Massachusetts Press, 1986.

Christian, Barbara. *Black Feminist Criticism: Perspectives on Black Women Writers*. New York: Pergamon Press, 1985.

———. *Black Women Novelists: The Development of a Tradition, 1892–1976*. Westport, CT: Greenwood Press, 1980.

Clarke, John Henrik. *Marcus Garvey and the Vision of Africa*. New York: Vintage, 1974.

Collier, Eugenia. "The Closing of the Circle: Movement from Division to Wholeness in Paule Marshall's Fiction." In *Black Women Writers (1950–1980): A Critical Evaluation*. Ed. Mari Evans. Garden City: Anchor Books, 1984. 295–315.

———. "The Endless Journey of an Ex-Coloured Man." *Phylon* 32.4 (1971): 365–373.

Cooke, Michael G. *Afro-American Literature in the Twentieth Century: The Achievement of Intimacy*. New Haven: Yale University Press, 1984.

———. "Modern Black Autobiography in the Tradition." In *Romanticism, Vistas, Instances, Continuities*. Eds. David Thornburn and Geoffrey Hartman. Ithaca: Cornell University Press, 1973. 255–280.

Craig, Gordon A. "Becoming Hitler." *New York Review of Books* May 29, 1997: 7–11.

———. "How Hell Worked." *New York Review of Books* April 18, 1996: 4–8.

———. Reply to letter from Marion Gräfin Dönhoff. *New York Review of Books* May 23, 1996: 52.

Crèvecoeur, J. Hector St. John de. *Letters from an American Farmer and Sketches of Eighteenth-Centruy America.* Ed. Albert E. Stone. New York: Penguin Books, 1988.

Davies, Carole Boyce. *Black Women, Writing and Identity: Migrations of the Subject.* New York: Routledge, 1994.

Davis, David Brion. "Jews and Blacks in America." *New York Review of Books* December 2, 1999: 57–63.

Davis, F. James. *Minority-Dominant Relations. A Sociological Analysis.* Arlington Heights, IL: AHM Publishing Corporation, 1978.

Davis, Lennard J. *Resisting Novels: Ideology and Fiction.* New York: Methuen, 1987.

Davis, Lenwood G. *Black-Jewish Relations in the United States, 1752–1984.* Westport, CT: Greenwood Press, 1984.

Deak, Istvan. Reply to letter from R. J. Tyndorf. *New York Review of Books* September 25, 1997: 75–76.

Dearborn, Mary V. "Anzia Yezierska and the Making of an Ethnic American Self." In *The Invention of Ethnicity.* Ed. Werner Sollors. New York: Oxford University Press, 1989. 105–123.

Denniston, Dorothy Hamer. *The Fiction of Paule Marshall: Reconstructions of History, Culture, and Gender.* Knoxville: University of Tennessee Press, 1995.

Dickerson, Vanessa D. "The Property of Being in Paule Marshall's *Brown Girl, Brownstones.*" *Obsidian II* 6.3 (Winter 1991): 1–13.

Dickson, Bruce D. Jr. *Black American Writing from the Nadir: The Evolution of a Literary Tradition 1877–1915.* Baton Rouge: Louisiana State University Press, 1989.

Dilthey, Wilhelm. *Das Erlebnis und die Dichtung. Lessing. Goethe. Novalis.* Leipzig: Hölderlin, 1922.

Diner, Hasia R. *In the Almost Promised Land: American Jews and Blacks, 1915–1935.* Baltimore: Johns Hopkins University Press, 1995.

Dittmar, Kurt. *Assimilation und Dissimilation. Erscheinungsformen der Marginalitaetsthematik bei juedisch-amerikanischen Erzaehlern (1900–1970).* Frankfurt am Main: Peter Lang, 1978.

Dönhoff, Marion Gräfin. Letter. *New York Review of Books* May 23, 1996: 52.

Du Bois, W. E. B. *The Souls of Black Folk.* New York: Bantam, 1989.

Dudley, David L. *My Father's Shadow: Intergenerational Conflict in African American Men's Autobiography.* Philadelphia: University of Pennsylvania Press, 1991.

Eakin, Paul John, ed. *American Autobiography: Retrospect and Prospect.* Madison: University of Wisconsin Press, 1991.

Ebest, Ron. "Anzia Yezierska and the Popular Periodical Debate over the Jews." *MELUS* 25.1 (2000): 105+. From Ebscohost (Academic Search Premier. Article 3914258) West Virginia State College Library, Institute, WV <*http://ehostvgw19.epnet.com*>.

Egan, Susanna. *Patterns of Experience in Autobiography.* Chapel Hill: University of North Carolina Press, 1984.

Evans, Mari, ed. *Black Women Writers (1950–1980): A Critical Evaluation.* Garden City: Anchor Press/Doubleday, 1984.

Faulkner, Howard. "James Weldon Johnson's Portrait of the Artist as Invisible Man." *Black American Literature Forum* 19.4 (Winter 1985): 147–151.

Fauset, Arthur Huff. *Black Gods of the Metropolis: Negro Religious Cults of the Urban North.* Philadelphia: University of Pennsylvania Press, 1944.

Fauset, Jessie. *Plum Bun: A Novel without a Moral.* Boston: Beacon Press, 1990.

Fenton, Steve. *Ethnicity: Racism, Class and Culture.* Lanham, MD: Rowman & Littlefield, 1999.

Ferber, Edna. *Fanny Herself.* New York: Grosset & Dunlap, 1917.

———. *A Peculiar Treasure.* New York: Literary Guild, 1939.

Ferraro, Thomas J. *Ethnic Passages: Literary Immigrants in Twentieth-Century America.* Chicago: University of Chicago Press, 1993.

Fine, David Martin. "American Jewish Fiction, 1880–1930." In *Handbook of American-Jewish Literature: An Analytical Guide to Topics, Themes, and Sources.* Ed. Lewis Fried. New York: Greenwood Press, 1988. 15–34.

Fleishman, Avrom. *Figures of Autobiography: The Language of Self-Writing in Victorian and Modern England.* Berkeley: University of California Press, 1983.

Fleming, Robert E. "Irony as a Key to Johnson's *The Autobiography of an Ex-Coloured Man.*" *American Literature* 43.1 (March 1971): 83–96.

———. *James Weldon Johnson.* Bloomington: Indiana University Press, 1987.

Foreman, P. Gabrielle. "Looking Back from Zora, or Talking out Both Sides My Mouth for Those Who Have Two Ears." *Black American Literature Forum* 24.4 (1990): 649+. From Ebscohost (Academic Search Premier. Article 9710151817) West Virginia State College Library, Institute, WV <*http://ehostvgw19.epnet.com*>.

Franklin, John Hope. *From Slavery to Freedom: A History of Negro Americans.* 4th ed. New York: Knopf, 1974.

Franklin, V. P. and Harold M. Kletnick, eds. *African Americans and Jews in the Twentieth Century: Studies in Convergence and Conflict.* Columbia: University of Missouri Press, 1998.

Friedman, Murray. *What Went Wrong? The Creation and Collapse of the Black-Jewish Alliance.* New York: Simon & Schuster, 1993.

Friedman, Susan Stanford. "Women's Autobiographical Selves: Theory and
Practice." In *The Private Self: Theory and Practice of Women's
Autobiographical Writings.* Ed. Shari Benstock. Chapel Hill: University of
North Carolina Press, 1988. 34–62.

Fuss, Diana. *Essentially Speaking: Feminism, Nature, and Difference.* New
York: Routledge, 1989.

Gates, Henry Louis Jr., "Introduction." In *The Autobiography of an
Ex-Coloured Man.* James Weldon Johnson. New York: Vintage, 1989.
v–xxiii.

———, ed. *"Race," Writing, and Difference.* Chicago: University of Chicago
Press, 1986.

———. *The Signifying Monkey: A Theory of African-American Literary
Criticism.* New York: Oxford University Press, 1988.

Gayle, Addison Jr. *The Way of the New World: The Black Novel in America.*
Garden City: Anchor Press/Doubleday, 1975.

Giddings, Paula. *When and Where I Enter: The Impact of Black Women on
Race and Sex in America.* New York: William Morrow, 1984.

Gilroy, Paul. *The Black Atlantic: Modernity and Double Consciousness.*
Cambridge, MA: Harvard University Press, 1994.

Girgus, Sam B. *The New Covenant: Jewish Writers and the American Idea.*
Chapel Hill: University of North Carolina Press, 1984.

Goellnicht, Donald C. "Passing as Autobiography: James Weldon Johnson's
The Autobiography of an Ex-Coloured Man." African American Review 30.1
(1996): 17–33.

Goffman, Ethan. "Unresolved Conversations." *Contemporary Literature*
XLII.1 (2001): 176–191.

Gohlman, Susan Ashley. *Starting Over: The Task of the Protagonist in the
Contemporary Bildungsroman.* New York: Garland, 1990.

Goldberg, David Theo, ed. *Anatomy of Racism.* Minneapolis: University of
Minnesota Press, 1990.

Greenberg, Irving. Letter. *New York Review of Books* November 2, 2000: 77.

Griffin, Farah Jasmin. *Who Set You Flowin'? The African American Migration
Narrative.* New York: Oxford University Press, 1996.

Guttmann, Allen. "The Conversion of the Jews." In *Contemporary
American-Jewish Literature: Critical Essays.* Ed. Irving Malin. Bloomington:
Indiana University Press, 1973. 39–61. (Originally published in *Wisconsin
Studies in Contemporary Literature* 6.3 [1965]: 161–176.)

———. *The Jewish Writer in America: Assimilation and the Crisis of Identity.*
New York: Oxford University Press, 1971.

Hacker, Andrew. "Jewish Racism, Black Anti-Semitism." In *Blacks and
Jews: Allainces and Arguments.* Ed. Paul Berman. New York: Delacorte
Press, 1994. 154–163.

Harap, Louis. *Creative Awakening: The Jewish Presence in Twentieth-Century American Literature, 1900–1940s*. New York: Greenwood Press, 1987.

Hardin, James. "Introduction." In *Reflection and Action: Essays on the Bildungsroman*. Ed. James Hardin. Columbia, SC: University of South Carolina Press, 1991. ix–xxvii.

Harris, Leonard, ed. *The Philosophy of Alain Locke: Harlem Renaissance and Beyond*. Philadelphia: Temple University Press, 1989.

Hathaway, Heather A. "Cultural Crossings: Migration, Generation, and Gender in Writings by Claude McKay and Paule Marshall." Diss. Harvard U., 1993. Ann Arbor: UMI, 1993.

Helms, Janet E., ed. *Black and White Racial Identity: Theory, Research, and Practice*. Westport, CT: Greenwood Press, 1990.

Heyd, Milly. *Mutual Reflections: Jews and Blacks in American Art*. New Brunswick: Rutgers University Press, 1999.

Hill Collins, Patricia. "The Social Construction of Black Feminist Thought." In *A Turbulent Voyage: Readings in African American Studies*. Ed. Floyd W. Hayes III. San Diego: Collegiate Press, 1992. 657–677.

Hirshler, Eric E. "Jews from Germany in the United States." In *Jews from Germany in the United States*. Ed. Eric E. Hirshler. New York: Farrar, Straus and Cudahy, 1955. 19–100.

Hoffman, Eva. "The Uses of Hell." *New York Review of Books* March 9, 2000: 19–23.

———. Reply to letters from Steven T. Katz and Peter Novick. *New York Review of Books* June 15, 2000: 78–79.

Holte, James. *The Ethnic I: A Sourcebook for Ethnic-American Autobiography*. New York: Greenwood Press, 1988.

———. "The Representative Voice: Autobiography and Ethnic Experience." *MELUS* 9 (1982): 25–46.

Hooks, Bell. "Keeping a Legacy of Shared Struggle." In *Blacks and Jews: Alliances and Arguments*. Ed. Paul Berman. New York: Delacorte Press, 1994. 229–238.

Howe, Irving. *World of Our Fathers*. New York: Harcourt Brace Jovanovich, 1976.

Hsiao, Ruth Yu. "Stages of Development in American Ethnic Literature: Jewish and Chinese American Literatures." Diss. Tufts University, 1986.

Hutchinson, George. *The Harlem Renaissance in Black and White*. Cambridge, MA: Harvard University Press, 1995.

———. "Mediating 'Race' and 'Nation': The Cultural Politics of *The Messenger*." *African American Review* 28.4 (Winter 1994): 531–548.

Johnson, James Weldon. *Along this Way: the Autobiography of James Weldon Johnson*. New York: Viking Press, 1935.

———. *The Autobiography of an Ex-Coloured Man*. New York: Vintage, 1989.

Jones, Gavin. "'The Sea Ain't Got No Back Door': The Problems of Black Consciousness in Paule Marshall's *Brown Girl, Brownstones*." *African American Review* 32.4 (1998): 597–606.

Jordan, Winthrop D. *The White Man's Burden: Historical Origins of Racism in the United States*. London: Oxford University Press, 1977.

Kallen, Horace. *Culture and Democracy in the United States: Studies in the Group Psychology of the American Peoples*. New York: Boni and Liveright, 1924.

———. *Judaism at Bay: Essays Towards the Adjustment of Judaism to Modernity*. New York: Arno Press, 1972.

Karp, Abraham J. *Haven and Home: A History of the Jews in America*. New York: Schocken Books, 1985.

Katz, Steven T. Letter. *New York Review of Books* June 15, 2000: 78.

Kawash, Samira. *Dislocating the Color Line: Identity, Hybridity, and Singularity in African-American Narrative*. Stanford: Stanford University Press, 1997.

Kessler Harris, Alice. "Introduction." In *Bread Givers*. Anzia Yezierska. New York: Persea Books, 1975. v–xviii.

Kinnamon, Keneth. "James Weldon Johnson." In *Afro-American Writers from the Harlem Renaissance to 1940*. Ed. Trudier Harris. *Dictionary of Literary Biography 51*. Detroit: Gale Research Company, 1987. 168–182.

Köhn, Lothar. *Entwicklungs- und Bildungsroman: Ein Forschungsbericht*. Stuttgart: J. B. Metzler, 1969.

Kubitschek, Missy Dehn. *Claiming the Heritage: African-American Women Novelists and History*. Jackson: University Press of Mississippi, 1991.

———. "Paule Marshall's Women on Quest." *Black American Literature Forum* 21.1–2 (Spring–Summer 1987): 43–60.

Kymlicka, Will and Christine Straehle. "Cosmopolitanism, Nation States, and Minority Nationalism: A Critical Overview of Recent Literature." *European Journal of Philosophy* 7.1 (1999): 65+. From Ebscohost (Academic Search Premier. Article 3252249) West Virginia State College Library, Institute, WV <*http://ehostvgw19.epnet.com*>.

Labovitz, Esther Kleinbord. *The Myth of the Heroine: The Female Bildungsroman in the Twentieth Century*. New York: Lang, 1986.

Layoun, Mary N. *Travels of a Genre: The Modern Novel and Ideology*. Princeton: Princeton University Press, 1990.

Leibowitz, Herbert. *Fabricating Lives: Explorations in American Autobiography*. New York: Knopf, 1989.

Lester, Julius. "The Lives People Live." In *Blacks and Jews: Alliances and Arguments*. Ed. Paul Berman. New York: Delacorte Press, 1994. 164–177.

Le Seur, Geta. *Ten Is the Age of Darkness: The Black Bildungsroman*. Columbia: University of Mississippi Press, 1995.

Levering Lewis, David. *W. E. B. Du Bois: Biography of a Race, 1868–1919*. New York: Henry Holt, 1993.

————. "Parallels and Divergences: Assimilationist Strategies of
Afro-American and Jewish Elites from 1910 to the Early 1930s." In
Bridges and Boundaries: African Americans and American Jews. Eds. Jack
Salzman, Adina Back, Gretchen Sullivan Sorin. New York: George
Braziller, 1992. 17–35.

Levy, Eugene. *James Weldon Johnson: Black Leader, Black Voice*. Chicago:
University of Chicago Press, 1973.

Lewis, Vashti Crutcher. "Mulatto Hegemony in the Novels of Jessie
Redmon Fauset." *CLA Journal* 35.4: 375–386.

Lewisohn, Ludwig. *The Island Within*. New York: Harper, 1928.

Lichtenstein, Diane. *Writing Their Nations: The Tradition of
Nineteenth-Century American Jewish Women Writers*. Bloomington:
Indiana University Press, 1992.

MacKethan, Lucinda H. "Black Boy and Ex-Coloured Man: Version and
Inversion of the Slave Narrator's Quest for Voice." *CLA Journal* 32.2
(December 1988): 123–147.

Marshall, Paule. *Brown Girl, Brownstones*. 1959. Old Westbury, NY:
Feminist Press, 1981.

————. "From the Poets in the Kitchen." In *Reena and Other Stories*. Paule
Marshall. New York: The Feminist Press, 1983. 3–12.

McDowell, Deborah. "Introduction." In *Plum Bun*. Jessie Fauset. Boston:
Beacon Press, 1990. ix–xxxiii.

McLendon, Jacquelyn Y. *The Politics of Color in the Fiction of Jessie Fauset
and Nella Larsen*. Charlottesville: University Press of Virginia, 1995.

Melnick, Jeffrey. *Black-Jewish Relations on Trial: Leo Frank and Jim Conley
in the New South*. Jackson: University of Mississippi Press, 2000.

————. *A Right to Sing the Blues: African Americans, Jews, and American
Popular Song*. Cambridge, MA: Harvard University Press, 1999.

Meltzer, Milton. *Taking Root: Jewish Immigrants in America*. New York:
Farrar, Straus and Giroux, 1976.

Meyer, Adam. "The Need for Cross-Ethnic Studies: A Manifesto (With
Antipasto)." *MELUS* 16.4: (Winter 1989–90). 19–39.

Michaels, Walter Benn. "Race into Culture: A Critical Genealogy of
Cultural Identity." In *Identities*. Eds. Kwame Anthony Appiah and Henry
Louis Gates Jr. Chicago: University of Chicago Press, 1995. 32–62.

Miller, Gabriel. "Introduction." In *Haunch, Paunch and Jowl*. Samuel
Ornitz. New York: Markus Wiener, 1986. ix–xxiii.

————. "Samuel Ornitz." In *Twentieth-Century American-Jewish Fiction
Writers*. Ed. Daniel Walden. *Dictionary of Literary Biography 28*. Detroit:
Gale Research Company, 1984. 207–213.

Moretti, Franco. *The Way of the World: The Bildungsroman in European
Culture*. London: Verso, 1987.

Morgan, Ellen. "Humanbecoming: Form and Focus in the Neo-Feminist Novel." In *Images of Women in Fiction: Feminist Perspectives.* Ed. Susan Koppelman Cornillon. Bowling Green: Bowling Green University Popular Press, 1972. 183–205.

Morrison, Toni. *Playing in the Dark.* New York: Vintage Books, 1993.

Mosse, George L. *Confronting the Nation: Jewish and Western Nationalism.* Hanover, NH: Brandeis University Press, 1993.

Neumann, Bernd. *Identität und Rollenzwang: Zur Theorie der Autobiographie.* Stuttgart: Athenäum Verlag, 1969.

Newton, Adam Zachary. *Facing Black and Jew: Literature as Public Space in Twentieth-Century America.* Cambridge, UK: Cambridge University Press, 1999.

Novick, Peter. Letter. *New York Review of Books* June 15, 2000: 78.

Omi, Michael and Howard Winant. *Racial Formation in the United States: From the 1960s to the 1980s.* New York: Routledge, 1990.

O'Neale, Sondra. "Race, Sex, and Self: Aspects of Bildung in Select Novels by Black American Women." *MELUS* 9.4 (1982): 25–37.

Ornitz, Samuel. *Haunch, Paunch and Jowl: An Anonymous Autobiography.* New York: Boni and Liveright, 1923.

Outlaw, Lucius. "Toward a Critical Theory of 'Race'." In *Anatomy of Racism.* Ed. David Theo Goldberg. Minneapolis: University of Minnesota Press, 1990. 58–82.

Painter, Nell Irvin. *Sojourner Truth: A Life, a Symbol.* New York: Norton, 1996.

Pascal, Roy. "The Autobiographical Novel and the Autobiography." *Essays in Criticism* 9 (1959): 134–150.

Patterson, Orlando. "Context and Choice in Ethnic Allegiance: A Theoretical Framework and Caribbean Case Study." In *Ethnicity: Theory and Experience.* Eds. Nathan Glazer and Daniel P. Moynihan. Cambridge, MA: Harvard University Press, 1975. 305–349.

Payne, Ladell. *Black Novelists and the Southern Literary Tradition.* Athens, GA: University of Georgia Press, 1981.

Pettis, Joyce. *Toward Wholeness in Paule Marshall's Fiction.* Charlottesville: University Press of Virginia, 1995.

Pfeiffer, Kathleen. "Individualism, Success and American Identity in *The Autobiography of an Ex-Coloured Man.*" *African American Review* 30.3 (1996): 403–419.

Philipson, Robert. *The Identity Question: Blacks and Jews in Europe and America.* Jackson: University Press of Mississippi, 2000.

Phillips, William M. Jr. *An Unillustrious Alliance: The African American and Jewish American Communities.* New York: Greenwood Press, 1991.

Ra'anan, Uri. "Ethnic Conflict: Toward a New Typology." In *Ethnic*

Resurgence in Modern Democratic States: A Multidisciplinary Approach to Human Resources and Conflict. Ed. Uri Ra'anan. New York: Pergamon Press, 1980. 1–29.

Radhakrishnan, R. "Culture as Common Ground: Ethnicity and Beyond." *MELUS* 14.2 (1987): 5–19.

Renan, Ernest. "What Is a Nation?" In *Nation and Narration*. Ed. Homi K. Bhaba. New York: Routledge, 1990. 8–22.

Rideout, Walter B. *The Radical Novel in the United States, 1900–1954: Some Interrelations of Literature and Society*. Cambridge, MA: Harvard University Press, 1956.

Roche, John P. "Immigration and Nationality: a Historical Overview of United States Policy." In *Ethnic Resurgence in Modern Democratic States: A Multidisciplinary Approach to Human Resources and Conflict*. Ed. Uri Ra'anan. New York: Pergamon Press, 1980. 30–76.

Rodgers, Lawrence R. "Introduction." In *Fanny Herself*. Edna Ferber. Urbana: University of Illinois Press, 2001. vii–xvii.

Rose, Toby. Letter to the author. June 1998.

Rosenblatt, Roger. "Black Autobiography: Life as the Death Weapon." *Yale Review* 65 (Summer 1976): 515–527.

———. *Black Fiction*. Cambridge, MA: Harvard University Press, 1974.

Rueschmann, Eva. "Sister Bonds: Intersections of Family and Race in Jessie Redmon Fauset's *Plum Bun* and Dorothy West's *The Living Is Easy*." In *The Significance of Sibling Relationships in Literature*. Eds. Joanna Stephens Mink and Janet Doubler Ward. Bowling Green: Bowling Green State University Popular Press, 1993. 120–131.

Said, Edward. *Culture and Imperialism*. New York: Vintage, 1994.

Sammons, Jeffrey L. "The Bildungsroman for Nonspecialists: an Attempt at a Clarification." In *Reflection and Action: Essays on the Bildungsroman*. Ed. James Hardin. Columbia, SC: University of South Carolina Press, 1991. 26–45.

Schoen, Carol B. *Anzia Yezierska*. Boston: Twayne, 1982.

Schultz, Elizabeth. "To Be Black and Blue: The Blues Genre in Black American Autobiography." *Kansas Quarterly* 7 (Summer 1975): 81–96.

Shaked, Gershon. *The Shadows Within: Essays on Modern Jewish Writers*. Philadelphia: Jewish Publication Society, 1987.

Sheehy, John. "The Mirror and the Veil: The Passing Novel and the Quest for American Racial Identity." *African American Review* 33.3 (1999): 401–415.

Sherman, Bernard. *The Invention of the Jew: Jewish-American Education Novels (1916–1964)*. New York: Thomas Yosselof, 1969.

Singh, Amritjit. *The Novels of the Harlem Renaissance: Twelve Black Writers 1923–1933*. University Park: Pennsylvania State University Press, 1976.

Skerret, Joseph T. Jr. "James Weldon Johnson." In *African American Writers.* Ed. Valerie Smith. New York: Scribner's, 1991. 219–233.

Smith, Curtis C. "Werner Sollors' *Beyond Ethnicity* and Afro-American Literature." *MELUS* 14.2 (1987): 65–71.

Smith, Sidonie. *Where I'm Bound: Patterns of Slavery and Freedom in Black American Autobiography.* Westport, CT.: Greenwood Press, 1974.

Sokoloff, Naomi B. *Imagining the Child in Modern Jewish Fiction.* Baltimore: Johns Hopkins University Press, 1992.

Sollors, Werner. *Beyond Ethnicity: Consent and Descent in American Culture.* New York: Oxford University Press, 1986.

———. "A Critique of Pure Pluralism." In *Reconstructing American Literary History.* Ed. Sacvan Bercovitch. Cambridge, MA: Harvard University Press, 1986. 250–279.

———. "Ethnicity." In *Critical Terms for Literary Study.* Eds. Frank Lentricchia and Thomas McLaughlin. Chicago: University of Chicago Press, 1990. 288–305.

———, ed. *The Invention of Ethnicity.* New York: Oxford University Press, 1989.

Spengemann, William C. and L. R. Lundquist. "Autobiography and the American Myth." *American Quarterly* 17 (1965): 501–519.

Stepto, Robert B. *From Behind the Veil.* Urbana: University of Illinois Press, 1979.

Stone, Albert E. *Autobiographical Occasions and Original Acts: Versions of American Identity from Henry Adams to Nate Shaw.* Philadelphia: University of Pennsylvania Press, 1982.

Sundquist, Eric J. *Cultural Contexts for Ralph Ellison's Invisible Man.* Boston: St. Martin's Press, 1995.

———. *The Hammers of Creation: Folk Culture in Modern African-American Fiction.* Athens, GA: Georgia University Press, 1992.

———. *To Wake the Nations: Race in the Making of American Literature.* Cambridge, MA: Harvard University Press, 1994.

Swales, Martin. *The German Bildungsroman from Wieland to Hesse.* Princeton: Princeton University Press, 1978.

Sylvander, Carolyn Wedin. *Jessie Redmon Fauset, Black American Writer.* Troy, NY: Whitston Publishing Company, 1981.

Thomas, Laurence Mordekhai. *Vessels of Evil: American Slavery and the Holocaust.* Philadelphia: Temple University Press, 1993.

Tyndorf, R. J. Letter. *New York Review of Books* September 25, 1997: 75.

Urofsky, Melvin I. *American Zionism from Herzl to the Holocaust.* Garden City: Anchor Press/Doubleday, 1976.

Vauthier, Simone. "The Interplay of Narrative Modes in James Weldon

Johnson's *The Autobiography of an Ex-Coloured Man.*" *Jahrbuch fuer Amerikastudien* 18: 173–181.

Wald, Alan. "Theorizing Cultural Difference: A Critique of the 'Ethnicity School'." *MELUS* 14.2 (1987): 21–33.

Wald, Gayle. *Crossing the Line: Racial Passing in Twentieth-Century U.S. Literature and Culture.* Durham: Duke University Press, 2000.

Warren, Kenneth W. *Black and White Strangers: Race and American Literary Realism.* Chicago: University of Chicago Press, 1993.

Washington, Joseph R. *Black Sects and Cults.* Garden City: Doubleday, 1972.

Washington, Mary Helen. "Afterword." In *Brown Girl, Brownstones.* Paule Marshall. Old Westbury, NY: The Feminist Press, 1981. 311–324.

Watson, Carole McAlpine. *Prologue: The Novels of Black American Women, 1891–1965.* Westport, CT: Greenwood Press, 1985.

West, Cornell. *Race Matters.* Boston: Beacon Press, 1993.

Wexler, Laura. "Looking at Yezierska." In *Women of the Word: Jewish Women and Jewish Writing.* Ed. Judith R. Baskin. Detroit: Wayne State University Press, 1994. 153–181.

White, Walter. *A Man Called White: The Autobiography of Walter White.* New York: Viking Press, 1948.

Whitinger, Raleigh. "Lou Andreas-Salome's Fenitschka and the Tradition of the *Bildungsroman.*" *Monatshefte* 91.4 (Winter 1999): 464–480.

Wilentz, Gay. "Cultural Mediation and the Immigrant's Daughter: Anzia Yezierska's *Bread Givers.*" *MELUS* 17.3 (1991): 33+. From Ebscohost (Academic Search Premier. Article 9601294668) West Virginia State College Library, Institute, WV <*http://ehostvgw19.epnet.com*>.

Willis, Susan. *Specifying: Black Women Writing the American Experience.* Madison: University of Wisconsin Press, 1987.

Wisse, Ruth R. *The Modern Jewish Canon: A Journey through Language and Culture.* New York: Free Press, 2000.

Wong, Sau-Ling Cynthia. "Immigrant Autobiography." In *American Autobiography: Retrospect and Prospect.* Ed. Paul John Eakin. Madison: University of Wisconsin Press, 1991. 142–170.

Wright, Julia M. "'The Order of Time': Nationalism and Literary Anthologies, 1774–1831." *Papers on Language and Literature* 97.3 (1997): 339+. From Ebscohost (Academic Search Premier. Article 9711172557) West Virginia State College Library, Institute, WV <*http://ehostvgw19. epnet.com*>.

Yezierska, Anzia. *Bread Givers.* New York: Persea Books, 1975.

Yudkin, Leon Israel. *Jewish Writing and Identity in the Twentieth Century.* London: Croom Helm, 1982.

INDEX